THE MAGDALEN CODES

Reclaiming Ancient Wisdom

Ashtara

Published by Tara Rising in 2018
P.O Box 640
Nerang, QLD 4211 Australia
www.themagdalencodes.com

Copyright © 2018 Ashtara

Prepublication Data available from the National Library of Australia.
ISBN: 978-0-9876007-2-1 (pbk)
Also available as an ebook
ebook ISBN: 978-0-9876007-3-8

All rights reserved. No part of this book may be reproduced or transmitted in any form or by any means, electronic or mechanical, without written permission from the author or publisher except for quotations embodied in critical articles or reviews.

Cover design: In2Art Designs

Book design and publishing assistance by
Publicious P/L
www.publicious.com.au

Also written by Ashtara
Gaia, Our Precious Planet
Tara, Emissary of Light
The Great Cosmic Joke
A Treasure Trove of Gems
A Crack in the Cosmic Window
Your Recipe for Empowerment through Spiritual Astrology
Volumes One, Two and Three
Esoteric Astrology, The Astrology of the Soul
I Am an Experiment, An Extraordinary Spiritual Adventure

DEDICATION

I dedicate this book to Gaia, our Earth Mother, who willingly gives unconditional love to all creatures living upon her.

GRATITUDE

I am deeply grateful to my trainers and guides on the inner planes. Mary Magdalen, the ascended Masters Djwhal Khul and Lord Kuthumi guide my life and work, as do the Council of Nine from Sirius. Two different groups of Light Beings from Antares and Arcturus trained me to broaden my perspective, and to retrieve from my memory banks ancient wisdom. Lord Maitreya, Archangel Michael and a host of other celestial Lights, supported me through challenging inter-dimensional experiences. Without the teachings, support and the training received by them this book could not have been written. They gave me a rare and precious gift to share with you.

On this earth plane, four astrologers helped this book's birthing process. Maggie Kerr, my first astrology teacher, introduced me to a different and exciting world and, through her teaching I learned to view life from a higher and broader perspective. Jeff Green introduced me to the subconscious realms through his profound book, *Pluto, The Evolutionary Journey of the Soul* and Steven Forrest, through his amazingly accurate description of Neptune in his book, *The Book of Neptune*, provided the words I needed to make sense of my meditation experiences. Barbara Hand Clow's books: *The Pleiadian Agenda, Chiron, Rainbow Bridge to the Outer Planets* and *The Alchemy of Nine Dimensions* resonate with my soul and I've devoured them as manna from heaven.

Many authors of spiritual books provided heart and soul food, especially *Anna, Grandmother of Jesus* by Claire Heartsong and the book *Anastasia*, the first in *The Ringing Cedars* series, written by Vladimir Megre. These authors enabled me to make connections in my mind, the resonance of which I felt in my body as truth. Without them, I may still be wandering in a Neptune fog, unable to make sense of my reality. Thank you so much.

Peruvian Fredy Conde and Bolivian Rosse Mary Vargas, my loving and knowledgeable South American tour guides, supported not only me, but also the different groups who journeyed with me to Peru and Bolivia. Archaeologist Eduardo Pajera provided me with remarkable esoteric information about the Bolivian sacred sites. Thank you so much for your open heartedness and care. I value and treasure your gifts. Friends Judith McDougall, Karen Christie, Pauline Alcock, Joan Johnson and Britt Woessner assisted the editing of this book, preparing the way for me to hand it to professional editor Rose Allan. Thank you Rose for your suggestions and attention to detail. It's a pleasure to work with you.

Through the love and support of my students I've developed the confidence to pursue my unusual spiritual path. You know who you are. Thank you from the bottom of my heart. I love you all.

CONTENTS

PREFACE	i
PART ONE	**1**
THE LOOM WEAVINGS	**1**
A Story of Human Consciousness Evolution	1
Chapter One	**7**
Consciousness, Astrology and Human Evolution	**7**
Questions and Answers	7
The Role Consciousness plays in Human Evolution	15
Time is a No-thing	19
Astrology, a Spiritual Path to Ascension	24
Chapter Two	**33**
Indigenous Wisdom	**33**
Heartland and the Rainbow Serpent	33
The First Australians' Creation Story	40
Separation from Love	43
Indigenous Records	46
Esoteric Research Expeditions	48
Ancient Mystery Schools	55
Chapter Three	**58**
Purposeful Spiritual Missions	**58**
Spirit, Matter, Time, Space and Astrology	58
A Three - Part Mission	61

The Mysterious Lands of Peru and Bolivia	70
Spiritual Adventures in the Mountains	76

Chapter Four — 87
Mary Magdalen, the Aquarian Age Divine Feminine — 87

Activating the Divine Feminine	87
The Magdalen Codes	94
Emotional Intelligence	97
Awakening to Truth	101

Chapter Five — 104
Remembrance of Ancient Wisdom — 104

Andean Connection to the Stars	104
Lake Titicaca and the Island of the Moon	108
A Sacred Trinity	115
Tibet	121
A Journey of Remembrance	135

PART TWO — 143
The Weavings Reveal — 143
A Cosmic System through which Human Consciousness Evolves — 143

Chapter Six — 145
Astrology and Higher Consciousness — 145

Multi-Dimensional Consciousness	145
The Law of One, The Law of Love	152
Esoteric Astrology	154
Chiron, the Centaur and Cosmic Guide	159
Uranus, the Illuminator	161

Saturn, Lord of Karma and Time	163
Neptune's Psychic Wall	164
Pluto, the Transformer	168

Chapter Seven — 170
A New Player in the Light Game — 170

Sedna	170
The Mermaid	172
Sedna, Our connection to Multi-dimensionality	174
Sedna, Goddess of Synthesis	176
Sedna, Goddess of Synthesis	189
Sedna - Andes	193
Sedna and the Magdalen Codes	195
A Lemurian Treasure	198

Chapter Eight — 204
Human Connections to the Stars — 204

The Pleiades	204
The Pleiades & the Andes Mountains of Peru and Bolivia	208
Sirius	211
Human Connection to Sirius	214
Training on Antares	218
Adventures in to Unknown	227
Sound and Sacred Geometry	230

Chapter Nine — 234
A Cosmic System Revealed — 234

The Great Bear	234
Pegasus, the White Winged Horse	241
Draco, the Dragon	245

Aquila, the Eagle	250
Arachne, Spider Woman	253
The Sacred Pathway	256
Hopi Creation Myth	258
The Sensual Woman	262
Our Galactic Heritage	265
Archangel Michael and the Obelisk	269
Orion	273
The Comet	277
The Southern Fish, Pisces Austrinus	280
Chapter Ten	**287**
A New Astrology for the Aquarian Age	**287**
Cosmic Triangles	287
Arcturus Training	290
The Living Light of Love	298
A Review	300
Ten, the Perfect Number	304
The Journey Ends	306
The Southern Cross Constellation	309

PREFACE

The ocean of emotion is familiar territory. Two mental breakdowns and a year-long period of depression were enough. There had to be another way. Through determination and persistence, I healed myself naturally.

Regular spiritual practices including meditation and yoga as well as eating healthy, mostly raw food, and doing regular physical exercise, were of paramount importance to my rehabilitation, as was the daily application of astrology to my life. I am writing this book as a healthy, and active eighty-year old.

Astrology, when studied from an esoteric, evolutionary and spiritual perspective, is an incredibly accurate and valuable tool that, when the teachings are personally applied, enables access to the subconscious and super-conscious mind. Our birth chart indicates our potential. It also provides accurate information as to the psychological lessons we have incarnated to identify and overcome. Unseen and anonymous benefactors guided my way and I became aware of, and took action upon, their spiritual guidance. Some of them are introduced in this story.

I also sought the help of alternate natural therapists, those practicing hypnotherapy, acupuncture, chiropractic, past life regression and rebirthing. Gradually, as I was able to appreciate finer psychological distinctions, my mind became sharper. I committed to helping those with similar mental health problems because I didn't want them to suffer as I had.

This book is a sequel to *I Am an Experiment, An Extraordinary Spiritual Adventure*. Described in that book is the journey I took to reclaim my identity and take responsibility for my unconscious creations in this life, and times past. Consciously, and with clear intent, I chose to build a strong foundation of emotional intelligence. Without it, I reasoned, a healthy and productive life would be out of my reach. Emotional intelligence can be learned. It can naturally improve with age however this depends on the intent and consciousness level of the individual.

During my daily meditation practice celestial and extra-terrestrial beings trained me to 'remote view'. Remote viewing is the ability to mind travel to an intentional location to view places, events, people and things. NASA trains people to do this. I was also taught to communicate telepathically and to bi-locate i.e. to use all six senses and experience full bodily sensations while operating in multi-dimensional localities. Most of my training involved navigating celestial realms and meeting, identifying and inter-acting with the highly evolved light-beings residing there. They taught me to awaken within my mind and body different frequency ranges. The training processes were fun. My trainers were incredibly loving and considerate, and the processes felt familiar and natural, as if I'd experienced them before, in another time.

Very early in the training I realised that my consciousness could travel to areas my rational mind couldn't access. My trainers asked that I record my experiences and share them at the appropriate time. That time is now.

My work is to awaken and catalyse people into the understanding and experience of broader realities and of the infinite nature of consciousness and divine love. I am dedicated to my work. The content of this book is true for me. It is for you to ascertain its truth through your intuition and heart-felt response.

In 1996 Mary Magdalen made herself known to me when I began to study evolutionary astrology. I share that experience in Part One. Through her guidance I grew to understand that all of life is a lesson in self-knowledge. The more self-knowledge we have the more we are able to joyfully move through life. In order to know ourselves we need to develop our feminine side. This process involves paying close attention to our feelings, intuition and psychic sensibilities. Truth emerges as we do so. Higher consciousness arises through self-awareness and self-knowledge.

The content of this book is based on penetrating subjective enquiry, objective observation and correlation. Learning to interpret my dreams has been, and still is, a valuable aid to my journey. 95% of dreams are symbolic and given by an internal dream teacher to aid our consciousness journey into greater light. I take note of them. I hope you decide to do the same.

A message received: 2 September 2016. Of being granted funding by an anonymous benefactor to write a book on the three levels of consciousness as the subconscious, conscious and the super-conscious realms of experience. I know these realms well having learned to carefully navigate them. It's the adventurous research I began exploring in 1987.

The message made sense of the annual journeys to Peru and Bolivia I made between 2000 and 2011. According to my local indigenous tour guides, and the esoteric books recommended, the three ancient carved stone steps, clearly evident at most of the sacred sites visited in Peru, symbolise three levels of consciousness. The bottom step, the subconscious realm, is symbolised by the serpent: the middle step, the conscious world, is symbolised by the puma. The third carved step, the super-conscious world, is symbolised by the condor, the bird that flies closest to the Sun.

This same symbolism is evident in other ancient cultures and sacred sites, although the creatures of the two upper steps differ. In ancient Egypt the three consciousness levels were depicted as a cobra (serpent), the right eye of Horus, and the vulture. To the North American Indians, the snake, mountain lion and eagle symbolise the subconscious, conscious and super-conscious mind. The serpent symbolises the power of the sacred feminine to source cause in the subconscious for all that blocks attainment of super consciousness.

Consciousness is not generated through an unconscious, robotic process. It is self-generated through intention, and the desire to change one's life for the better. The process involves becoming conscious of, and correcting, debilitating psychology. The desire to do so usually arises when life becomes difficult. Eventually the realisation occurs that 'for things to change, first I must change'. The evolution of consciousness is not analogous to the growth, or aging, of the body. It comes through struggle and challenge.

A brief definition of the three main levels of human consciousness follow:

Subconscious: (Feminine) Contains priceless soul knowledge from all incarnations that can only be accessed through feelings, body sensations and heart intelligence. The process needed to access this realm requires self-awareness.

Conscious: (Masculine) is everyday consciousness. It's the known and unknown intermingled. The personality is unaware of the soul's knowledge and wisdom, gained from experiences over many life-times. Duality abounds. Opportunities are given throughout life to access the soul's hidden treasures of truth and they usually come through life's many challenges. The challenges are connected to emotional upheaval. We have the opportunity to 'wake up' to truth when our mind is prodded by emotion. If the opportunities are taken to know self on a deeper level, the soul work for the incarnation begins. Life starts to be perceived from a higher perspective. Millions of people on our planet are now taking this path. The light is spreading quickly.

Super or Christ Consciousness: The individual has full access to, and is determined to heal, old karma that includes soul wounds. Resolution of duality occurs when this is complete. A self-aware, enlightened and love-filled individual, at-one with self and spiritual source, emerges from the ashes of the former personality. Jesus attained this state of being and said that whatever he did we could also do.

Ascension into Christ Consciousness can be attained by clearly defining and working through the problematic content of the subconscious. Dedication to working through past life causes of current life psychological issues is a step towards the development of super consciousness.

Throughout the book I share personal stories that demonstrate my experiences of the three levels of consciousness. I also write about the evolution of human consciousness and the star systems that aid humanity's developmental process. Within the stories I introduce you to a wide range of history and myth. These experiences enabled the telling of her-story.

History (his story) is the recording of specific events, usually written a long time after the events from the particular perspective of the author. The perspective depends on the level of consciousness of the author at the time of writing. Most of recorded history is written from a masculine perspective. From this recorded history so called 'facts' are derived and these 'facts' are claimed to be truth. As more facts emerge, the truth changes. What really is truth?

Two historic facts relevant to this story are:

Fact one: On October 19, 2006 SBS World News reported that *Nature* magazine had announced the findings of a 400 million-year-old fossil, complete with fin. This fin has the same components as a human arm. The fish is referred to as *gogonasis*. It never stepped on land. This fossil find throws new light on human evolution that began in the sea.

Fact two: A report in the December 2006 edition of *Scientific American* journal confirmed that a three million five-hundred-thousand-year-old skull of a human baby was discovered in Ethiopia. The child walked upright. This find pre-dates the skull called *Lucy* who was believed to be the originator of our human race.

Attempting to connect the linkages between history and her-story into a coherent whole is one of the aims of this book. Through reading it you may make connections in your minds and feel a resonance of truth in your hearts that activates remembrance of your ancient wisdom. I invite you to relate the material I am sharing to your internal experiences, as it can act as a catalyst for your spiritual evolution into higher consciousness.

Many children being born now have an advanced consciousness to that of their parents. I do hope parents of young children listen carefully to what they have to say. These children enter this world with love in their hearts and the desire to assist humanity's evolution into higher consciousness. Some are old souls conscious of their incarnational purpose and I've had the privilege of speaking with some of them. Their clarity of thought and wisdom astounds, and inspires, me.

Parts of this book is highlighted in italics because it contains a thought-provoking connecting story transmitted to me by celestial Light beings.

Like the cosmic Arachne, I weave a mystical web with the intention of connecting the many dimensional levels of human life experience by making practical sense of them. Having lived for many decades conscious of these dimensional levels, I've learned to appreciate their value. Unique experiences exploring multi-dimensional realms cannot be learned from books. Inner guidance is always present and can be invoked. To hear and feel this guidance requires mindfulness. Mindfulness is present-time self-awareness. Reception to higher frequency ranges is poor when chaos and static rule an unconscious and undisciplined mind.

The personal stories I share are likely to have you gasping for breath. The journey I offer is one from third dimensional consciousness into multi-dimensional realms. It is the path of the heart. An adventure story of mammoth proportions, I will take you into a wonderland of cosmic symbols coded with meaning and purpose. My story is also your story. Christ, super or multi-dimensional consciousness is available to all who choose the Way of the Heart.

Like a never-ending mountain stream the cosmic waters nurture and nourish the human soul with spiritual fuel. Should you choose to drink of this water, your perceptions of life will broaden according to your levels of fear and control. Unimpeded, without limitations the celestial spring waters of everlasting life will flow into all parts of the body, rejuvenating your life force. I invite you to drink of these celestial waters with me. Join me and we shall journey together.

***

PART ONE

The Loom Weavings

A Story of Human Consciousness Evolution

In order to reveal the hidden mysteries learned, experienced and taught in previous incarnations it is necessary to recap a major life event. Following a light lunch on October 2nd 2000, I felt an overpowering need to rest on my bed. Completely relaxed I meditated and experienced the most amazing internal expansion.

In my book, *I Am an Experiment, an Extraordinary Spiritual Adventure,* I wrote: *"I felt as if my energy field became so large it encompassed the entire universe. Fully conscious and alert I nestled into this expanded state of awareness, observing myself in the experience. I saw that I was one with a myriad of stars and we were a mass of vibrating energy. My energy field expanded even further until I felt I was infinite, without beginning and without end. I was a no-thing, without form, in a state where there were no boundaries and no limitations. This state of cosmic bliss expanded yet again to a place where there was no sound or motion. I experienced pure stillness and ecstasy, and knew I was one with Source.*

Time stood still as this state of bliss expanded again. Then I observed the Spiritual Hierarchy gathering around me, along with masses of other ethereal light beings. I became aware that a joyous celebration was about to take place. I was asked to stand in front of the spokesperson whereupon I was awarded a gold medal for the soul work I had done. There was much applause. I received tremendous love and respect from the assembled gathering.

From high above I saw a bright light descend, an etheric substance in the shape of a light being. Then I observed an etheric light substance ascend from my body. It was the soul/spirit essence of Barbara ascending to a higher dimensional plane of existence while simultaneously Ashtara's soul/spirit essence descended to take her place. It appeared as if they were passing each other in a cosmic elevator. I clearly felt the different energy and essence of Ashtara enter my body.

Ashtara 'walked in' to a perfectly healthy, aware and conscious human being.

I, the observer of the experience, was told that Barbara had fulfilled her incarnational purpose and had gone on to experience other realms. It had been her final incarnation on Earth and it may well be Ashtara's. She has an issue with recognition and approval that Barbara did not have and her real work could only begin when this issue has been healed through the transmutation process.

Symbolically the exchange had to take place after the Sydney Olympic games. Olympic athletes receive medals for endurance, discipline, persistence, effort and will. Barbara received her medal for demonstrating these qualities on her journey to ascension and the attainment of Christ consciousness. She left in a blaze of Olympic glory having accomplished all she set out to do, with honour, integrity and love.

And now it was Ashtara's turn."

I wanted to understand. Who was I really? I was not the same person internally so how could my external world be the same? Fortunately, I retained a practical side and had written of the experience in my journal. Months of attempting to live a normal life followed before I felt able to refer to these notes.

Shock registered when I realised the walk-in 'birth' occurred at exactly the same time as the birth of my former personality. How could this be? What cosmic order orchestrated such a precise event? I needed to make sense of this new reality. I constructed a birth chart for the ascension experience and had another shock, one that took months to get over. When placing the new chart over my original one I noticed that the Moon is positioned in Sagittarius in 12th house within minutes of my former Rising sign. What does this mean?

Esoteric astrology, a subject I've studied and worked with since 1993, posits that each incarnating personality can have the same rising sign in their birth chart for up to seven incarnations. This is often how long it takes for the lessons associated with that particular zodiacal sign to be understood and worked through. When this process completes a new set of challenges arise, via a new rising sign. The former ascendant (or rising sign) becomes the Moon in the birth chart of the next incarnating personality.

The teachings also say that, in the following incarnation, similar cosmic configurations to that of the most recent transition are chosen by the incarnating soul. It was for me. I am living proof of these esoteric teachings. My original birth chart has Neptune in Virgo posited in the 11th house. The theme and potential are an unbounded consciousness, with a spiritual future. Virgo enables practical mysticism. A mystical rectangle pattern in my birth chart aided this evolutionary progress.

Through Virgo detailed self-examination, and using the priceless tool of my birth chart, I uncovered self-sabotaging psychological patterns from countless past lives. Determined to seek cause, rather than deal with effect I knew that, when I realised truth and took responsibility for my unconscious shadow creations, the causal energy would transmute. Let's look at the process another way. When the light switch of self-awareness is turned on in the mind, and personal responsibility taken for what is revealed, the darkness dissipates. It is then forgiveness time. Confronting oneself and one's past can be terrifying, yet the reward of freedom is so great. It has to be done in some incarnation so why not in this one? This is the conscious evolutionary growth process that leads to spiritual ascension from the third dimensional plane of experience. While the shadows of ignorance remain, internal and external wars continue to rage.

Working with my 'walk-in' chart brought new psychological and physical challenges. Self-observation and self-examination enabled the realisation of its accuracy. The challenges referred to in the *Experiment* book, those of fear of rejection that led to an unconscious need for recognition and approval, a Leo/Aquarius theme, manifested through a traumatic separation from a fifty-year long relationship. I learned that, whatever we fear the most, we manifest. Aptly demonstrated in the birth chart I realised the timing for this new growth phase was a cosmic set-up. I needed freedom to explore and couldn't do so while bound to another's expectations. Shattered and heart broken, I surrendered my fear of surviving on my own to Divine Intelligence. Peace and grace descended and from that moment God became my partner. (Neptune in Aquarius in the 12th house conjunct asteroid goddess Juno, the goddess of marriage). The horoscope never lies.

From a little blue and white country cottage I continued to explore my inner mechanics. My love for Mother Earth and God/Goddess sustained and nurtured me. I knew that any trauma connected to separation from love creates a barrier around the heart so I did my best to keep my heart open.

Accepting that this new life phase was for the greater good, I began a new evolutionary journey into conscious spiritual growth. I knew this journey would be different. I was willing to face the psychological challenges and determined to seek cause of them rather than to band aid effects.

***

Chapter One

Consciousness, Astrology and Human Evolution

Questions and Answers

We evolve, or devolve, according to our levels of consciousness. Each of us vibrates at individual frequencies depending upon our level of consciousness, the amount of love within our hearts and the amount of light within our soul. Consciousness is self-awareness and self-knowledge. The greater the self-awareness and self-knowledge, the greater is the inner light and the higher is the consciousness vibration.

I willingly stepped on board the consciousness train in 1987 and it's been an amazing ride. There were only a few of us then, now there are millions. The numbers continue to increase.

Why am I a 'Walk-In?' Why did Ashtara walk in to a healthy sixty-three-year old female body? What was her agenda? I kept on asking this question until I received an answer. It came through a highly respected, now deceased, psychotherapist, Wendy Munro, who transmitted the insights of an evolved celestial being. It took me many years to understand the seemingly coded words, and their significance, because my mind would immediately spin into a Neptune fog whenever I tried to do so. Perhaps you will understand in a much shorter time? I share it in the hope you may understand your journey on a deeper level.

The Transmission:

Ashtara was called from afar her name given many thousands of years ago. It contains certain vibratory codes that elucidate and bring clarity to others. It stirs ancient soul memories that activate remembrance of truth. Ashtara lives a parallel life in synchronicity, was incarnate at the time of Jesus and a shared life with him. She has three different energetic fields. The lineage of her physical body is masculine while her emotional body is feminine. When these bodies were mastered in previous times the spiritualized Christ energy entered.

Through her masculine Ra aspect, she mastered the dying process and took the knowledge to Egypt. She has, within her cellular memory, the principles of metamorphoses. She provides the energy, the light waves, to enable others to experience the same. In Lemuria, she developed crystal cities and achieved significant levels of initiation but was obstructed when that ancient land collapsed. Reaching that same level this lifetime she realised there was still more to be mastered. A galactic vibration to assist her to move through 3D limitations was needed, so an exchange took place. She is a galactic aspect of her former personality aligned with her Higher Self.

Ashtara was in the Atlantean temples initiating and facilitating the ascension process. Her masculine Ra aspect mastered it and took it to Egypt. She knows the alchemical process and her body chemicals have been sensitized to the sub-atomic level where her light body cells became activated.

Removing the veils of thousands of years of density obscuring the light based on beliefs, decisions and emotions is part of her journey. Ashtara is an energetic vibration that allows her to be a living example of the transformation and transmutation process. She has come to master light on this Earth plane and to enlighten others. Having an Atlantean consciousness she offers a gateway, an opening, to access greater light. She knows cosmic organizational structures and was once known as one of the Tall Ones who worked with symbolic designs. Identifying with certain planets and stars she studied astrology in the Atlantean temples of Light. She has a deep identification with the Masters of the East and carries within her soul memory historic records. A record keeper and a chronicler of events she has the Book of Life available to her should she choose to open it.

Ashtara carries the energy of the Rainbow Serpent and the Winged Plumed serpent and these qualities enable her to have wings and fly often to visit lands she knew in previous times. When in Peru she aligned with extra-terrestrial energy. A pioneer from Sirius she helped create a City of Light at Machu Picchu where opportunities were provided to enlighten others. Re-capping and reclaiming formerly mastered spiritual initiations has been part of her journey this time around enabling her to catch up to formerly attained vibratory levels. This process enables her to ground the energy this life because, in former times, her physical body could not anchor the higher vibrations of her spiritualized self.

She was allowed access to master teachers in previous times and has been able to do the same this time. Sai Baba was one of these teachers. He was an avatar who consciously moved from one body form to another and she has the spiritual challenge to do the same.

She connects with others who journeyed with her in previous times both in form and not in form. She travelled into places of unknown frequencies within the greater universe. Astrology has been a vehicle. She understands that every planet is a living evolving consciousness and we all have the ability to connect to the consciousness of these great beings and integrate their characteristics and qualities. Her high level of sensitivity enables her to feel their movement in her brain and she's becoming aware that her perception of astrology is changing as she becomes more spiritually empowered.

Ashtara provides stepping-stones and tools to personal enlightenment through transmutation of form into spirit and reveals to others how they can reclaim the light that shines within them. Her journey is to be very different from previous cycles and many adjustments will be needed."

It took me years to re-stabilise on this Earth plane following the walk-in experience, and it was a strange and wondrous process. I needed to constantly and carefully observe others as they carried out simple everyday tasks so I could do the same. The capable individual I had once been was no more. I needed to re-learn basic everyday skills and chose a country life in relative isolation in which to do so. Because of being bitten frequently by ants and other bugs I quickly realised it was the energy of my suppressed anger and frustration that attracted them. Responsibly letting off steam became a weekly practice until balance was restored.

Many spiritual lessons were learned. Developing greater self-awareness was needed so I could identify, seek cause of and correct, my self-sabotaging behavioural patterns. One pattern was my fear-based control. My impatience was another. It was only when my lower vibrational psychology was realised and transformed that the veil of forgetfulness began to lift. There were many adjustments needed, especially to my mind and body. I realised how the dense energy of unresolved emotional dross lodges in different parts of the body according to an individual's astrological blueprint. While suffering extreme physical pain I learned to access, and to transform some of my psychological patterning. I chose not to take painkillers. My body responded positively according to the degree of self-awareness and self-love I embodied.

It felt strange being contained within a physical body. Yoga was my "truth" arena. When unable to do a particular posture, I knew there was resistance stored in the immovable body part so I worked psychologically, astrologically, spiritually and metaphysically on the area to free up the blockages. Sometimes I called upon spiritual healers to help me become aware of, and to overcome psychological density. This transformation of consciousness process continues to this day. Rebellious, I often faltered. Going on strike, I separated for years from regular spiritual practices. This rebellious behaviour was arrogance based. Eventually I returned to regular spiritual practices, and immediately benefitted. My mind began to clear and my body lightened as a result.

Spiritual growth into higher consciousness occurs through identifying and alchemising personal dense psychology; embodying divine love and acting on our soul's guidance. This process is the key to our species survival.

When I realised that my soul had a specific agenda and purpose for incarnation that took precedence over my personality's agenda, I surrendered to it. Surrendering to the soul's unknown agenda needs to be deeply heart felt to be genuine and sincere. Trust and faith are involved. Prior to incarnation our soul chooses the most appropriate psychological and physical components to aid the imminent incarnational journey. Resistance to the soul's agenda leads to life difficulties. Often fear-based control is underneath the resistance. I learned it was wise to become aware of, and follow, my internal prompts.

Along the journey I developed a far-reaching perspective of our universe, and how we, as an evolving intelligent species, will eventually return to merge once again with the One Source.

We are in the process of becoming galactic, or multi-dimensional, humans. Currently, we are experiencing a transition phase from thousands of years of creating dense psychological matter through many destructive past-life experiences, hurt and pain. The trauma and pain of these experiences are contained within our subconscious. These can be accessed, provided there is the willingness to do so. Accessing them requires self-observation. By paying close attention to the moment we feel an emotional reaction occur, we can ascertain the psychological cause of our behaviour. Our feelings are our main indicators. When we stop repeating the same old self-sabotaging pattern, our life changes for the better. When self-aware we have the choice to change our thinking, and to act differently.

Should we choose to change, and learn to consciously respond, rather than re-act robot-like to emotional situations, we begin to progress. Dense psychology can be likened to a condensed magnetic ball of dark energy. With each negative thought, and its associated dark emotion, the energetic mass of psychic toxicity grows. Eventually, it begins eating into the organs of the body, causing disease.

When inner psychological and spiritual growth work is advanced, a light body or aura appears around our physical body. Sensitive people and clairvoyants can see it. It can be photographed. This light body, of a finer frequency to that of the physical body, responds to heart-felt divine love. When the frequency of divine love is accessed and maintained, higher dimensional light beings are attracted to our light and love. They assist us in attaining our soul's evolutionary purpose. Psychological challenges are always involved. The spiritual path to higher consciousness requires a different approach to that of normal societal beliefs and expectations. When personal subjective desires fade, our light body brightens, our level of divine love is high and our focus becomes that of service to the greater good of humanity, and to our planet.

Through many light filled meditative experiences I learned that our solar system and beyond is surrounded by a spiritual management system comprised of highly evolved light beings. Known as the Great White Brotherhood (white meaning light) they exist in a higher dimensional realm. We refer to them as angels, archangels, and ascended masters. Their purpose is to act as spiritual guides for the human evolutionary process into super, or multi-dimensional consciousness. These loving and light-filled angelic beings transmit their energies through appropriate inter-dimensional portals into our third dimensional world (3D). Archangel Michael can be likened to the Chief Executive Officer of the spiritual beings involved in this great work.

We can each assist our evolutionary process by committing to doing the inner work necessary to transmute our shadow psychology into divine love and light. By so doing we accelerate the collective human evolutionary journey into higher consciousness. Archangel Michael guides the life energies down through the different dimensions to Earth. Archangels Michael and

Gabriel are two celestial overseers who coordinate with the Sirians - light beings from higher dimensional realms who work under the auspices of the Galactic Federation. They are involved in bringing to receptive, self-aware humans the energies of Christ, or multi-dimensional consciousness.

The light of higher consciousness that comes through self-awareness transmutes darkness to produce an even greater light, comprised of divine love. The frequency wave of divine love is transforming our world raising it towards the Supreme Creative Force.

Many years ago, while researching the constellation Ophiuchus, the Serpent Holder, I was given a message:

"Great Spirit gifted her sons and daughters with individuality and purpose. You have the ancient mysteries stored within your soul and it is your mission to reveal the truth of your sacred wisdom to a troubled and dying species. A new race is birthing, one aligned to truth, wisdom and love and it is for you to retrieve and release your sacred serpent wisdom at the dawning of this new Age. Until then you will be forgotten. Guard and protect your wisdom well. Keep it close to your heart until guided to share."

My guidance to share was granted on 14 October 2013. This book is the result.

***

The Role Consciousness Plays in Human Evolution

The evolution of consciousness is an Ageless Wisdom science. According to *Esoteric Psychology 1*, written by Alice A. Bailey, this evolutionary process begins when the personality becomes aware of its soul essence. When the personality is self-aware enough to progressively identify with its spiritual source, it has the opportunity to gradually become at-one with it. This unifying process comes through consciously identifying, accepting and integrating the soul's agenda into daily life, and living it. The evolutionary process into higher consciousness involves mastery of the four elements, our emotions and our mind. This process is gradually becoming accepted in our modern world. Consciousness is an Ageless Wisdom science that goes beyond what is currently known.

Spiritual Masters throughout the ages have known and practiced this science and now quantum physics and quantum mechanics are proving its validity. The language is different but the understanding is the same. Each one of us creates and affects the reality we see and experience, and we can become conscious of how we do this.

Imagine our capabilities if we were to use our brain to its fullest extent? Currently we use about 15% of it. What will activate the sleeping part? Consciousness is the answer. By becoming fully conscious human beings, an evolutionary process developed through self-awareness, our brain expands to embrace a higher perspective to life. Through this conscious process we can learn to see different realities with our eyes closed, as well as with our open eyes. We do need to be willing to open our hearts and minds to see reality clearly though, otherwise we perceive it through an illusionary haze.

Our brain is like a computer, a personal device that stores information. Old software, unconsciously inserted in previous times, rules our thoughts and associated emotions and actions. We live our lives according to the old stories. But they don't work anymore. New software needs to be installed. I suggest to my students they intentionally spend quiet meditative time imagining they are deleting old toxic psychological software. And then, when each toxic file has been deleted, to begin the process of downloading new software into their brain. I recommend they carefully select the highest, most loving, noble and pure contents. This symbolic gesture, when practiced with concentration, sincerity of feeling and intent, especially at a new Moon, can ignite the soul into activity.

What is your soul's truth? Only you can discover it. Truth needs to be experienced to be known. As a starting point why not ask yourself the questions: 'Who is responsible for my feelings? Who is responsible for my thoughts and actions? Am I willing to take responsibility for them? Who and what chooses the reality I experience?' Your answers will decide your future.

Geneticists have proved that our genes contain memory and are coded strips of DNA. But what is it that turns our memory on or off? Within each memory is an experience. The experience may be painful or joyful. The thoughts and decisions made at the time of the experience, in whatever lifetime, are stored in an etheric memory bank. When the energies of a transiting planet connect with that specific memory, depicted as a placement in the individual's birth chart, energetic 'sparks' awaken the sleeping consciousness. The "ON" switch activates the psychological theme or issue contained within the unconscious memory. Unconscious thoughts and feelings re-play. The physical circumstances differ each time until full conscious self-awareness of the causal theme occurs. Until then, when someone presses our emotional buttons, we react, much like a robot or puppet.

Memory can be activated through our senses by food, smell, voice, word or sound. Sacred sites and other special places also activate soul memories. I experienced this activation process while exploring sacred sites high in the Andes mountains. The necessity to breath more slowly and deeply enabled me to experience many 'wake-up' calls. What was I awakening to? A remembrance of truth. Through the debilitating psychic influence of cloudy soul memories, I frequently experienced pain and psychic attacks when visiting certain areas. Through these experiences, I learned to understand my mind and how it works. I learned that shadow thoughts and emotions are dense psychological energy that coagulate to form mass. The mass attracts like and gathers more density. Eventually it becomes a disease that eats into the body.

Because of the universal Law of Attraction, we naturally attract situations and people to help us become conscious of the shadows we carry. When we become conscious of our disabling thoughts and emotions we have a choice. We can continue playing the same old psychological games and experience the same results in life, or we can choose to change. When we choose to change, we learn to alchemize our dense shadows into light. Our bodies and minds demonstrate the change. We do not need to experience ill health and the normally accepted aging effects.

Our DNA is alive. Consciousness and soul memories inhabit its internal space. Consciousness weaves itself into a variety of geometric shapes. As we evolve, human consciousness is slowly changing from a square shape into a diamond shape. Some psychically tuned medical intuitives can see these consciousness shapes in an individual's blood. Years ago, a medical intuitive saw diamond shapes in my blood and wondered what it meant. At the time I didn't understand so wasn't able to enlighten her. I'm sharing this information to assist others who have seen the same shapes.

We are unique and wondrous human beings and contained within our soul's memory is a vast and accessible storehouse of information. From the beginning of human development, the knowledge of our consciousness evolution has been told through stories, passed down orally from generation to generation. The stories became our myths and legends. I discovered that many cultures have the same themes in their stories. When the veil between dimensions is thin, as it is now, we have the opportunity to decode the stories and reveal truth.

***

Time is a No-thing

For many years celestial and extra-terrestrial spiritual guides taught me to navigate my inner space, develop sixth sense skills such as remote viewing, mental telepathy and the ability to traverse higher dimensional realms of consciousness. These are skills I had mastered in previous lives. It was relatively easy because my memories of having experienced them before arose in my conscious mind as I was guided to re-use them. I know the cosmos, space travel and the many dimensions of consciousness. I wrote of many of these experiences in my book, *I Am an Experiment, an Extraordinary Spiritual Adventure*. One of my celestial guides is Lord Kuthumi, an Ascended Master. I'll refer to Him as K. from here on. He taught me so much. Following are two of his teachings. I share them in the hope they will assist in opening your mind and raise your consciousness.

When humans incarnate into form upon the 3D earth plane a change occurs to their consciousness. 3D denseness envelops the energy field, which in turn reaches into those denser energy patterns of a specific nature that the soul has chosen to work with during the life. The hard aspects in the birth chart depict this dense patterning. There are many clues to this dense patterning carried in the energy field from previous existences. It is simply blocked energy. The goal of the soul is to clear the dense patterning in order to create a greater lightness of being, so it chooses an earthly sojourn to work towards its goal.

All is energy, vibrating at different frequencies.

A lighter frequency results from becoming conscious of, and fully understanding and integrating, the information contained within the blockages and then using the energy constructively. Once integrated, the cellular memory re-adjusts and energy can then flow freely. Illumination has occurred. The 'lights are on' in the consciousness. It is simple.

We on the finer vibratory planes of existence do not encounter the density of energy that humans do. We offer our assistance yet we need to be asked. Our role is to provide a higher frequency to souls who ask. When a higher frequency develops within the human then a higher frequency is attracted. Circumstances change as the new level is accessed.

Love is the highest frequency. When operating from this place only high frequency is attracted. It is so.

His second teaching relates to time.

Time is a no-thing. Cycles are the influencing factor. The cycles of seeding, rooting, flowering, harvesting and decay. Every planet and every human have a cycle. A time to retreat into the womb and a time to start anew. A time to sow and a time to reap.

K. helped me to experience being a no-thing: without feeling, thought, or action. Nothing, timeless and mindless. Stillness. Observing a tiny spark of energy, of consciousness, enter the no-thing space I realised it would create change. It would stir the no-thing into action. But where did this spark come from? A little later I noticed a second spark and knew it would also create change. But where did it come from? Questions and more questions!

There is always plenty of time, said K. You have the ability go forward, or back in time. Ashtara, once an ascended master, 'walked-in' to a human body to attain that same state again. It would be beneficial if you choose to practice intentional mind travel, as it would help you understand your role. Ashtara's path is different to that of her former self. She's being trained in a way you cannot imagine so there's no point spending energy on such imaginings.

K. asked me to follow his impulses that arise in my heart as warm feelings, and those that enter my mind in quiet and still moments. He knows my workload and will take it into account. All my needs will be taken care of if I allow the process. I agreed. Easy to say – not to do. I'm much better at it than I used to be! K. said that if we allow ourselves to receive cosmic impulses and act upon them at the time of receiving, life flows effortlessly. Our higher self knows our workload and priorities. All we, the personality self, need do is to get out of the way and act upon our higher guidance. Then there is no tension in the body or mind. Trust is developed, which brings about emotional security. This allows Spirit to work through us. By practicing this state of being abundance follows.

All evolutionary progress takes place in cycles of time. The cycles can be broken down into phases, and the Moon's phases can be used as the model. K suggested I spend time understanding and integrating this process. He recommended I draw the Moon's eight phases on a large sheet of paper so I could integrate his teachings as I did so. He also suggested I connect these phases, and their meanings, to my journey through life to aid my understanding. Kuthumi said we were both in training, at different frequency levels and my travels are part of a cycle. I'm to allow time to pass, and the cycle will work out. K again asked me to work with cycles of time, especially the planetary cycles. He said the future is a result of the past and present, and asked me to be constantly aware.

He showed me a spiral with each ring of the spiral forming a circle. *When a cycle completes a new one begins. All energy works in spirals, from the smallest particle to 3D denseness of matter. When a soul chooses to leave Source, the process of devolution into denser vibratory levels occurs.*

Particles of energy begin to descend down the spiral. This is what occurred in humanity's evolutionary process. Humans devolved into darkness, which is the ignorance of light. Light is analogous with consciousness. All humans are at varying stages of evolution and at different levels in the spiralling cycles of time. Eventually all will move into higher consciousness, according to the cycles of time.

He then showed me a holographic sphere, explaining that all I'm learning about cycles of time can be applied to a hologram. I'll be able to view the hologram with its many layers from the top to see how it all fits together and am to teach this concept when I understand it. My current role, he said, is to help raise human consciousness.

Sometime during the study of cycles and phases of time I realised my process of learning was much like a prisoner in a dark cell, desperately wanting to become free and move into the light. The prisoner digs a tunnel, works in the dark, keeps on digging until finally he or she sees a glimmer of light at the end. Then daylight dawns, and full illumination into the light is obtained. Intercepted signs in a birth chart operate this way. When unfamiliar psychological issues emerge from my subconscious I keep on digging into the dark until I see the light. I dug into the themes of recognition and approval, feeling them as lower vibrational waves in my mind that sought outlets in my body. I knew recognition and approval from external sources could never be experienced until I developed genuine recognition and approval of myself. To do so I needed to know myself.

Psychological and physical purification is needed to attain transfiguration and ascension. It is a journey every soul takes. How long, or how many lifetimes, it takes is up to each individual. Transfiguration requires synthesis between body, mind, soul and spirit. This process arises from using our spiritual will to be the best we can be, to lovingly and willingly serve our fellow human beings and Mother Earth, and to realise and fulfil our incarnational purpose. Divine love is the pathway.

All life is a hologram and is how the universe was created. It can be viewed from above, below, and from the sides. In the beginning was the word, a tone, that created a perfectly formed and programmed hologram. Every human cell contains within it the knowledge of everything the evolving soul has ever experienced. Each soul decides, prior to incarnation on Earth, the parts of the great hologram it wants to experience to further its journey to the light. This life is experienced by all other parts of the hologram simultaneously.

***

Astrology – A Spiritual Path to Ascension

The return journey to the One Source, known by many names such as God, Goddess and Great Spirit, is one every soul takes. How long it takes is a decision made by each evolving soul. Our 3D earth plane is where conscious evolutionary acceleration takes place and this is why so many souls seek incarnation here. We each have the choice to commit to our evolutionary journey into higher consciousness or not. The journey requires discipline, and the willingness to open our hearts to experience divine love. These processes enable the embodiment of greater light. More and more people are making this choice rather than living out endless incarnations replaying the same old self-sabotaging games. Which path do you choose?

Devoted to spiritual growth and conscious evolution I learned, through study of esoteric astrology, that evolved light beings watch over and guide the evolution of humanity. Some of their members guided me into the study of astrology and the spiritual growth journey I've taken. They are as real to me as physical humans. One of their roles in the Creator's cosmic management system is to assist the consciousness evolution of humanity by downloading the frequencies of love, wisdom and spiritualised power to individuals willingly opening their hearts and minds to receive.

We are experiencing a new astrological Age, the Age of Aquarius. It has a different vibration to that of the previous Age of Pisces. Connecting to the biblically prophesied 'a new heaven and a new earth' it requires dissolution of sabotaging Piscean Age expression.

Through self-questioning and self-examination, I learned to penetrate the veils of illusion that comprise the Piscean astral realm of experience. Through Pisces, Neptune and the twelfth house in an individual's birth chart, this foggy realm of ghosts from the past creates a veil of amnesia that prevents access to multi-dimensional realms of consciousness, the super-conscious mind. It's from this foggy realm that mental health problems arise. Addictions also fall under the Pisces, Neptune and twelfth house themes. Addictions lead to lack of mental clarity and confuse the mind even more. The birth chart can reveal cause of the psychological weakness behind the addictive nature. Judging the problem, or the sufferer, as wrong doesn't heal. It only adds more negativity, creating more dense matter.

Genuine compassion, forgiveness and love are the healing tools. Deeper understanding of underlying causes can lead to the decision to take responsibility for personal mental states and actions. The cause of health problems is contained within the subconscious realm of the mind. Stressful external events can trigger subconscious psychology and memories.

Through serious intent and willingness, we can transmute our density and 'die' to our lower personality self. Resurrecting into our light body we can fly into higher realms of consciousness. We can now become enlightened human beings in one lifetime.

When self-realisations occur and related positive corrective action is taken, we begin to awaken to higher dimensional levels of reality because of the shift occurring in our brain. The right brain expands enabling further self-realisations. Working with your birth chart can accelerate your conscious evolutionary growth. Humanity is moving from a three-dimensional level of consciousness to fourth, fifth and even higher levels. The willingness to change and make this move, is the first step. To those willing, welcome aboard the consciousness train. You will learn to value, and truly appreciate, the ride.

For far too long we have left Spirit out of our lives. Connecting to the internal spiritual flame in our hearts enables feelings of divine love. This is the motivating force behind our evolutionary process.

The Aquarius Age has been prophesied as a 'Golden Age of Peace' whereby individuals with the sincere desire to ascend into higher consciousness, and who are willing to do the inner work needed, will be provided with opportunities to do so. These opportunities are usually internally and externally challenging. Many human souls will attain the spiritually enlightened Christ Consciousness state of being and become prophets and masters during The Age of Aquarius. They will ascend, joining the ranks of the Great White Brotherhood.

Through experience of the astrological time cycles, I realise human consciousness evolution is divinely orchestrated and timed by a cosmic clock. I learned to allow this clock to guide me. Control and force doesn't work. Whenever I attempted to control, accidents happened and I suffered physical damage, mostly to my limbs. Committing to assisting those with mental health problems I persisted with my inner and outer research. Taking responsibility for my creations through my habits, attitudes, thoughts, emotions and actions, I learned to feel within my heart the frequency of divine love. This practice enables the light of higher consciousness to infuse the mind. Daily prayers of sincere gratitude also assist. One of my thanksgiving prayers is for the wondrous gift of life; my challenging life teachers, my amazingly intricate body and mind, and for Mother Earth for all she provides to aid my journey. This sincere daily prayer creates warm feeling sensations in my heart that aids the integration of divine love. I'm also incredibly grateful to live in this wonderful country of Australia and to have the opportunity to grow spiritually.

The application of these practices takes me on adventures into higher dimensional realities, and I thoroughly enjoy the ride. I teach astrology as a spiritual path to ascension because it enables students to become self-aware so they can accelerate their consciousness evolution. I cannot solve another's mental health problems. However, by practicing the healing concepts presented in this book those with mental health problems can instigate self-healing.

The Magdalen Codes is the name I've given to a soul lineage of consciousness found deep within the subconscious minds of many people on our planet. It is accessible through memory, sensitivity, intuition, inner experience and feeling. By tuning into a different and finer frequency on the wave bands of energetic universal flow, now proven by scientists to exist, we can access this knowledge. We are our own record keepers.

Cosmic forces govern and aid our consciousness development. It is as if there is a giant plan for human development created by an amazing light being. We have free will to choose how we play our game of life but many people are unconscious of this choice. This is gradually changing as more people seek to transform their shadow psychology.

The old way of being no longer fulfils or enriches life. When it's time for psychological and spiritual growth, challenging situations arise in our life. They provide an opportunity for us to learn about ourselves. This inner journey requires the development of self-awareness and the willingness to take personal responsibility for all we think, feel and create. This inner revolution occurs according to cosmic timing. It's dependent upon the specific relationship of celestial bodies to each other, and the effect of their energetic force field on individuals, and the collective consciousness. Ageless Wisdom, involving esoteric astrology, identifies and defines this cosmic system and provides information as to how best to manage it.

Some esoteric principles govern my understanding and are:

- We humans are, in essence, divine.
- We are each a fragment of the Universal Mind, the Mind of God.
- We have a lower and higher nature.
- Our higher nature is that of spirit.

When realisation and acceptance of our higher nature (Higher Self) occurs, life changes. We can no longer operate unconsciously, robotically replaying the same old psychological games. We learn to function as a soul. When we realise that the most precious jewel of our existence resides as a flame of divine love burning in our heart, we choose to daily tend this flame. We do this through regular meditation, prayers of thanksgiving and also through sacred ritual or ceremony.

- The goal of self-realisation is to become conscious of the soul because it is the medium through which spirit works.
- When consciously operating as a soul powerful spiritual insights and instant broader perceptions occur regularly, as does instant manifestation of thoughts.

- Spirituality is not based on religious matters. Spiritual is the internal light of spirit that drives an individual forward towards higher consciousness through growth and development.
- There is One Source of Light that permeates all of creation, known by many names.

The Age of Aquarius is frequently referred to as The Age of Light. Light contains information in the form of consciousness and knowledge. Through the detailed application of astrological knowledge to oneself, higher consciousness and wisdom develops. We are then able to view life from a higher and broader perspective. We have all the tools we need to evolve consciously into higher frequencies of light. This state of being enables longevity and perfect health. Currently, we are experiencing an unstoppable knowledge/consciousness explosion. It offers an opportunity for a giant leap forward in human consciousness evolution. To evolve spiritually requires we learn to:

- Know the personality self
- Know the Self (the Higher Self)
- Know we are all connected as One

Only by developing self-knowledge is it possible to know the One, to know Great Spirit as Self. Through loving thoughts and actions of good will, and without regard for outcomes or results, the path of the spiritual warrior unfolds. The Great Plan gradually reveals as each courageous, positive, and light-filled forward step into the unknown is taken.

Self-knowledge advances by developing an understanding of our elemental nature, and the four bodies through which they express. The four elements are the fire of spirit; the air of our mental body; the water of our emotional body and the earth of our physical body. They are known through experience. There are many levels to these four bodies. The levels form an energy field around the physical body. Disease begins from the spiritual, works through to the mental and emotional bodies and lodges in the physical. One of the greatest causes of human disease is our perceived separation from Spirit, from God/Goddess, the Source of all Light. It's a perceived separation from divine love. When the heart is thus afflicted heart problems occur. By changing the perception, life is enhanced.

The five senses bring physical plane knowledge. Psychic sensitivity brings knowledge of the astral plane. The mind brings intellectual perception. On a finer frequency band, intuition, a higher level of soul expression that connects to the Higher Self, enables the revelation of divine purpose.

The Higher Self leads us to individuality, through the development of intuition. It is then the abstract mind awakens to its purpose for incarnation.

The soul is the medium through which spirit works. As we become more self-aware and conscious of our soul's agenda, and work with it, we become internally lighter. Our body demonstrates this lightness of spirit. The soul's nature is love and the will-to-good. When internal light manifests the individual appears to glow. The human spirit manifests as the will to live, to be, to act, pursue and evolve consciously. The essential qualities of the soul are what make each person so unique and different. Everyone has a unique psychology, with individual moods, desires, inhibitions, feelings and characteristics that set up the vibratory activity of the body.

The physical body, comprised of atoms and cells, has a life of its own, an individual consciousness. The soul resides in the denseness of a physical body throughout many incarnations. Soul memories are contained within every cell of our bodies. These memories can be activated as feelings and impressions when visiting places formerly known by the soul. For instance, my soul experienced memorable incarnations in South America and Tibet. These memories were reactivated this lifetime when I visited some of sacred sites of Peru and Bolivia. I write of some of these experiences to demonstrate this principle.

The lower concrete mind is the reasoning principle. The soul mind carries the intelligence of lessons well learned from previous incarnations. Often these well-learned lessons, based on experiences, can be unconscious this time around. They emerge into our daily life as natural gifts and talents. Think about a gifted musician: How does someone naturally play the piano, flute or any other musical instrument, without any training? Because it was learned and practiced with love and devotion in a previous incarnation.

Why not reflect on your gifts and talents? You do have them.

If unaware of them you may like to ask a close and trusted friend, or family member, to assist you to see them.

The higher or abstract mind is the custodian of ideas. It 'magically' conveys these ideas to a receptive and calm lower mind. Maybe you receive bright ideas when under the shower, or when relaxed and walking in nature? These are the times when the lower mind can connect to the soul. The gap between the lower mind and the soul needs to be bridged before intuitive realisations of truth can be experienced and understood. Some people feel truth realisations in the body as 'goose-bumps'. It's wise to take notice.

Throughout our journey to super, or Christ consciousness, we learn many lessons in discernment so we can grasp finer distinctions. This requires we pay close attention to not only our thoughts but also our feelings and body sensations. Discrimination also needs to be developed. When heart intelligence is learned, intuition grows. The mind can be developed to become an agent of the soul. This requires we learn to consciously manage and employ our mind into soul service.

Future civilisations will be based on the infallible sensitivity of intuition that comes from direct knowledge arising from within self. Direct knowing is gnosis. An idea that comes from the intuitive level is a true idea. The cultivation of sensitivity to telepathic impressions is one of the most potent agencies in developing intuition.

A tidal wave of light is sweeping our planet, embracing all it touches. Sensitive people feel it. It can be scientifically measured. How can we embrace this light to access soul records and our truth? By choosing to enter the abyss of darkness and stillness, the void from which memories stir and awaken. This is the place of the sacred feminine.

***

Chapter Two

Indigenous Wisdom

Heartland and the Rainbow Serpent

The biblical evolution story correlates to myth and legend. Genesis: chapter six.

And it came to pass, when men began to multiply on the face of the earth, and daughters were born unto them that the sons of God saw the daughters of men, that they were fair; and they took them wives of all they chose. And the Lord said, my spirit shall not always strive with man for that he is also flesh.

There is telling information in this quote. There are hundreds of bible interpretations, all written from the consciousness perspective of the author. This particular passage referring to the sons of God can be likened to the indigenous myths of the great white giants who roamed the earth, teaching ancient wisdom to the local inhabitants. The giants, semi-etheric beings who came from the stars, were perceived as white because their spiritualized light glowed from within. In the ancient Sumerian records, and in the bible, these gods were called the Nephilim. In ancient Peruvian myth, the main deity was a white giant called Wiracocha. I encountered two others in the Andes Mountains, Lord and Lady Meru.

According to Mayan myth their god was Quetzacoatal, the Plumbed Serpent. The indigenous Australians refer to their creation being birthed through the Rainbow Serpent.

Once upon a time when two great beings of light walked upon this planet storm surges were commonplace. Torrents of water would unpredictably drench the land and dissipate as quietly as they had come. Seas would churn. The planet was lush and green. These two great beings of light had a task. They were aware of their purpose for being and were intent on carrying out their designated role.

Their purpose involved the seeding of the spark of divine consciousness into the minds of a species already existing. Their technique for carrying out their task was quite simple. It was based on energy currents and frequencies. With no apparatus other than their own mind and body they were able to infuse selectively chosen individuals with this transfusion. The seeds of consciousness were planted into the minds of the new born who were most receptive. Their receptivity was determined by the degree of light they carried. The human experiment began.

For aeons of time the seed germinated. The species developed greater skills as a consequence of their seeding. At the appropriate time for an advancement to the seeding another similar procedure took place. An acceleration of consciousness took place. This was done with purpose and intent. It was an experiment, and closely monitored. And, so it is today. The experiment has been deemed successful yet there are adjustments that need to be made. It is time for a more advanced consciousness to flower. The germinating time is complete. The flowering is at hand. Many will resist this step. It is comfortable to rest in the fertile seed. It requires a determined effort to reach for the light.

In a far distant land surrounded by water a species thrived for thousands of years. They lived in harmony with the land and regarded the land as feminine in gender. They honoured her for her many gifts. From her they received food, shelter and beauty. They also honoured the bright light in the sky that provided light and warmth.

These people nurtured the seed of divine consciousness and the seed grew into a beautiful flower that, in turn, returned itself to the soil to seed again. And so, the seed of divine consciousness flourished.

At a given time weeds invaded this garden. Another species chose to claim this land as their own. The weed spread and gradually covered the landmass. The ancient reverence and nurturance of the divine consciousness seed ceased. The weed also had a seed of consciousness deep within but refused to nurture it. It was intent on domination and control.

In some areas, this divine seed broke away from its host choosing to develop on its own. It needed freedom to pursue its own path and sought the light of the sun and a place to nurture its seed. It reconnected to the beauty and abundance of the land. Many such pockets of light developed in this distant land and the people and land began to flower. The seeds of divine consciousness spread and the weed reduced its influence. Its hold was still strong but the roots from the divine seeds began to thrive and grow in equal strength. There was room for both.

Visualise a group of three hundred dedicated spiritual seekers sitting in silence, deep in meditation. I was one of them. During this meditation, at an inaugural Australian spiritual conference in Sydney in the year 2000, we were guided to travel to the great red rock mountain, Uluru, in the centre of Australia. Uluru is a unique global sacred site. This was where the next conference was to take place. During this meditation, my inner teacher asked I enter inside the Uluru mountain to be close as possible to Mother Earth's core crystal. Here I encountered an old aboriginal man who handed me a book of Gaia's records. He telepathically asked I keep them safe until such time as I was guided to share the contents. He said I would know when that time was right. It is now.

When nearing the completion of the three-day Uluru conference the following year, and while taking a break at a coffee shop, an aboriginal woman approached me. Tina, a complete stranger, was the local 'wise woman'. Her message involved the sacred circle dance Paneurythmy. The reason I travelled to Uluru was to teach, at the conference, this circle dance to approximately 250 people. In return for her message I gave her a copy of my book, *Tara, Emissary of Light*. Glancing at the cover she registered shock. Recovering, she told me she had been shown the same cover image in a vision, two days previously.

During the afternoon of the last day of the conference I was given a second, even more powerful message. Tina had directed the tribe's senior representative, Uncle Bobby Randall, to take me to the Heartland, some kilometres from Uluru. Uluru, in the centre of Australia, is a huge red rock monolith and considered Australia's most important sacred site. I agreed to accompany him the following day. Collecting me early in the morning he drove along the main road for some time until suddenly veering off the road into bushland. Driving along a bumpy bush track he slowed to show me the shed where his mother had lived and been born. Instinctively and spontaneously I asked him to stop the truck, feeling the need to perform a thanksgiving ceremony at the shed. Following the ceremony Uncle Bobby drove on slowly over the unmade track giving me time to connect to the land. Out of the corner of my eye I noticed, some distance ahead, a high rocky ridge. Driving on further for maybe five minutes Uncle Bobby suddenly stopped. He said I was to climb this same rocky ridge to attend to spiritual women's business. I had no idea what he meant. He suggested his wife, Hazel, accompany me. Saying he would come back when the time was right we watched him drive away into the distance. We didn't see any other sign of habitation or human life.

Hazel and I began to climb. Close to the top of the ridge I felt intense pulsating energy activating my heart so I began breathing deeply into it. The energy gathered force, as did my breath. I began to feel emotional as unconscious memories awakened, flooding my body. When the powerful energy reached my throat deep penetrating sounds emerged that became heartfelt sobs. Soul memories consumed me. My conscious mind could not comprehend. I was telepathically guided to lie down on the narrow strip of red soil at the top of the ridge, with my face to the ground. My entire body began to heave and writhe. The primal sounds became deeper and more intense as the waves of overpowering internal energy gathered force. Stronger and more powerful sounds erupted through my throat. Inner guidance directed me to place the red soil over my hands, face, and any other exposed parts of my body. The instant I rubbed the red soil on my face I felt a penetrating heart-felt and ancient soul connection to this land, and to Gaia, Mother Earth.

More primal sounds erupted as I connected to her. Feeling myself as the rainbow serpent I began to writhe, twist and slither along the ground. I moved, face and body down, hands grasping the soil, sobbing deeper with even more profound sounds. Time ceased to exist. Then, I felt myself giving birth. As the rainbow serpent, I experienced birthing many human souls into Mother Earth's warm embrace. I knew then that the First Australians had not walked across the Bering straits, nor did they come to Australia from other countries. They were birthed here, into this land. Time seemed to stand still. Energetically and emotionally spent I was unable to move, still immersed in the reality of the powerful experience.

Eventually I sensed Hazel sitting behind me, patiently and silently supportive.

Much later she rested her hands on my shoulders and helped me to sit up, asking if I could manage to scramble down the steep slope with her help. She could see Bobby's truck returning. Unsteady on my feet but with Hazel supporting me, we climbed slowly and cautiously down the embankment. Spent, stunned and completely depleted of energy, I was unable to speak. It was the most powerful experience I have ever had. Uncle Bobby picked us up and drove back to Uluru. When he dropped me at my hotel I sat, still stunned, on a chair in the courtyard garden, covered with red dirt, where I remained for hours.

Sometime after midday Hazel returned asking if I wanted to talk about the experience. I shared, saying that one of the deepest emotions I felt was loss. The loss suffered by humanity of the wisdom and knowledge of the primal archetypal force behind creation, the Mother Goddess. Hazel told me the Rainbow Serpent goddess, considered sacred, is so steeped in mystery, secrecy and magic she is not spoken about. She is the ultimate Creator, the feminine aspect of God. I felt blessed, and also humbled to have had the experience of being her, birthing humanity. I went to bed very early that night.

Next morning, I felt compelled to walk around the base of Uluru. While still dark I caught the sunrise bus from my hotel. Stepping off the bus at my destination I observed a small bird trying to get my attention. I allowed it to lead as I walked slowly around the great red rock mountain. I stopped whenever the little bird did, and immediately experienced past life memories, most of them as an aboriginal record keeper. At each stop the memories deepened. Some were unpleasant and dark. Unconsciously, through negative thoughts, emotions and deeds, I'd created karma. Karma is the Universal Law of Cause and Effect. Whatever we cause, in a previous life or this one, has an effect. Because the clear memories emerged into my conscious mind on this walk, I committed to working through the associated psychological issues still replaying in my current life. Why postpone the inevitable?

Stopping beside a water hole I noticed a coiled water snake lying in the mud. Telepathically conversing, I acknowledged its soul and purpose for being, and immediately felt its energy enter my base chakra entwining with the etheric energy of an existing land snake. One memorable night a year before this current experience, snake energy entered my base chakra with a distinct 'hissss'. That is another story. The energy of these two resident entwined serpents, representing the kundalini force, rose into my heart. Telepathically I was told that the rainbow serpent likes to lie at the bottom of water holes to aid the conception process. This Uluru conception place is sacred to the First Australians because it connects them to this part of the land.

***

The First Australians' Creation Story

According to some First Australians, Biami is their word for Prime Creator or God. Their understanding of the creation story and human spiritual evolution is, in essence, the same as the esoteric and spiritual teachings of our western world. I include my understanding of their perspective because it may help readers grasp the concepts presented in this book.

They say that Biami spends his days dreaming everything that exists. There is one Creation and everything that exists, or has existed, is part of this One. Biami is the essence of love and carries inside Himself birthing seeds, sprinkling them into a space called the Dreamtime. He is the essence of Oneness. Everything you see in the sky is Biami. Everything on land is Biami. His essence is in everything. We are born into many, many lives to experience different parts of his essence yet some people still do not embrace him as their internal spirit and a vital connection to their soul.

Creation began in Australia when Biami reached into Himself and took his own essence to breathe life into the land. This became the first feminine essence. He fell in love with His created land spirit and fertilised her seed with light. Their first-born was a giant rainbow-coloured serpent. Creation continued. Stars and planets were born. The sky changed with all the little sky lights sparkling brightly. The seed of creation had been fertilised and many seeds sprang from it. Biami gave us the breath of life eternal. He will always be, because we are of Him. We are also of the Earth, and the stars that came from His seed.

We came from the Earth and she acts as our mother, feeding us until the day we die.

When we destroy our Earth, we destroy our very existence. We have an obligation, as Biami's creation, to our children. This obligation involves demonstrating to them that we are a part of Biami, whether we grow up in Australia or elsewhere. And whether we are a Christian, Muslim, Buddhist or come from a non-religious family. Everything and everyone on our planet is part of Biami's creation. Even if our unconscious games are enormous we owe it to our children to teach them that we are part of the tapestry of creation and if one thread breaks, the fabric weakens. If our children understand this they will develop spiritual strength. Knowing they are connected in oneness to the Creator they will not want to do evil deeds nor will they become lost in a spiritual wasteland.

The First Australians speak of the Age of Light differently to the western world yet the meaning is the same. They speak of Dreaming Tracks comprised of the Creator's Light. These are spirit lines and are not to be confused with song lines. The spirit lines are referred to in our western world as ley lines that criss-cross our Earth and the cosmos. In some places around the earth the Dreaming Tracks have turned into negative vibrations because humans have done bad things there. The people dishonoured pure light, love and compassion because of resentment, greed, arrogance and ignorance. Negative vibrations attract other negative vibrations and wars are fought in those places.

The wise elders speak of how the Dreaming Track of Mother Earth is moving into higher spiritual consciousness. For the past five thousand years, humans have been on the path of developing physical knowledge. Now is the time for developing spiritual knowledge. We are being given the opportunity to absorb Biami's essence. To do so we need to have the intent and willingness to develop spiritually. We will be tested on this path as to our commitment to truth, honesty and integrity and as to whether our values are based on loving compassion, or otherwise.

Many indigenous tribes around the world have this story as the basis of their spiritual beliefs. It is similar to the creation story told in the Christian bible. It's also similar to the stories I heard in North and South America, and those I've read in *The Ringing Cedar* series from Russia. The stories contain the essence of truth.

(Reference: *Under the Quandong Tree*, Minmia)

***

Separation from Love

A perceived separation from love, from Deity, is one of the main causes of human discord.

In the beginning Deity (pure consciousness) was in bliss. A question entered this all-encompassing mind 'Who am I when not in this state of bliss?' This question acted much like a pebble does when thrown into the waters of a still, calm lake. Ripples emerge from the disturbance and become concentric widening circles.

'To know who I am I'll create a family of souls in my likeness (ie consciousness) and give them free will to create as they please. I'll also create a system of cosmic bodies that include galaxies, stars and planets, each with their own over-lighting presences and individual souls. To each of my creations I will give a unique vibratory tone'. I imagine this to be much like the individual instruments in a symphony orchestra. If one instrument is out of tune the entire orchestra – and any listening audience, feels it. It creates irritation and discord.

'I'll create a dimensional system of descending frequencies as a playground for my creations. Most of my family will eventually remember their experiences in these many playgrounds.' These experiences are stored in each soul's 'akashic records' and can be accessed when each soul has evolved to a certain level of consciousness and has developed the desire to remember and know.

'Everything I create is interconnected – each creation is a different aspect of My Being. I am always connected to my creations'.

On the evening of the day a great peace overcame the Lord of Host. Stillness reigned. From this peace a great sigh echoed across the heavens. Source called forth the formation of the celestial beings to assist the Great Work. Source rested. The celestial beings awakened.

Our small planet in the outer reaches of the Milky Way galaxy is a playground for souls to experience density, which is a 3D experience. It's a place where we can accelerate our remembrance journey into higher consciousness. Many celestial and star beings chose not to separate from Deity so have not experienced the dense 3D dimension of planet Earth.

Others chose to be adventuring pioneers desiring to experience all they could on their journey into the unknown. After spending lifetimes experiencing life in other dimensions many of these souls descended to Earth. Some of these pioneers still remembered their origins and maintained a conscious connection to Source while experiencing life on Earth. They assist those who have developed the perception of separation.

At this time in human evolutionary development many of these pioneers are feeling the call to begin the return journey home to Source. Ascension from 3D consciousness is the first step. There are so many other consciousness dimensions to access and experience. We can access some of them while in a human body.

Esoteric Astrology is a consciousness system designed to assist souls ascend.

The first step on this journey to is 'Know Thyself'. This means knowing the personality – and the psychological games played. This is exoteric astrology. Then comes the 'why'. 'Why do I play these games? What memory is it attached to? What's the meaning and purpose of life? Why am I feeling so bad? What's the cause? I need to know.' This is esoteric astrology.

The soul stirs. It is awakening. Feelings are its guide to truth. We feel emotions and we feel body sensations. We can feel the energy of discord in our body and minds.

Astrology is a system created to aid humans raise their consciousness, so we can know ourselves, understand and have empathy for others, and to know Deity. The energy of Source, of God/Goddess is in every part of us, in every cell and in every particle. No matter how hard we might try, we cannot be disconnected from Source.

Our solar system and the stars that inform this system have a different consciousness to humans. They play an important role in our human evolutionary development. Through our system of chakras, we receive and transmit cosmic energy, according to our levels of consciousness. Full consciousness comes through self-awareness and self-knowledge.

***

Indigenous Records

You will have heard of Gondwana land if you've explored the National Parks of Australia around Uluru because there are many written commemorative plaques containing stories of its origin. Way back in the distant past it was the first name for the region of Australia. Then it was a much larger landmass than it is now. The Pacific Islands, including Hawaii and New Zealand, were part of it.

I learned more about Gondwana when exploring the heart of Australia in 2006 with a small group of friends, including my Peruvian tour guide, Fredy. We were told there is obvious geological evidence of rock formation at Ormiston Gorge that dates back to 800 million years ago, during the Cambrian Age. 300 million years ago the oldest river in the world, the Finke, was formed and 200 million years ago Australia was joined with South America, Tibet and India, forming Gondwana land. Gondwana land was apparently originally located near to South Africa. Mega fauna in the form of huge animals unrelated to dinosaurs roamed this land. Much later dinosaurs lived upon Gondwana land and eventually became extinct around 65 million years ago.

In early Australian history, the kangaroo was used to show the way to water-holes. The First Australians have myths and stories about following the large steps made by kangaroo to access life giving water. Australia is a dry continent, especially in its centre. Water holes are few and distances between them long. Relying on the animals to lead them to food, or provide them with food and water, was natural. This was how they survived in such harsh terrain. Humans and animals lived side by side each relying on the other to sustain life. Animals and birds provide indicators to sustain life. Times have changed. Respect for Nature and its many blessings is no longer experienced by the masses. This will change.

The First Australians tell stories of living on the land for at least fifty thousand years. They, and the Q'ero indigenous people from high in the Andes, lived their lives uncontaminated by other races until fairly recently in human history. Europeans only colonized Australia a little over two hundred years ago. The indigenous stories contain coded truth of human evolution. The Q'ero came down from their Andean mountaintop homes (approximately five thousand metres above sea level) to share knowledge as recently as the year 2000.

In planet Earth's distant past there were a series of ancient islands in the Pacific Ocean referred to in story and myth as Lemuria, or Mu. Gondwana broke up into the islands known as Lemuria millions of years ago. Lemuria was primarily a goddess-based culture with spirituality as its focus. In these early times, beings from a variety of star systems visited our beautiful planet, revelling in her beauty. Some of them decided to settle here in order to anchor their evolved consciousness and act as a bridge between humans and star beings. A visionary long-term plan was activated. After the passing of a certain cosmic cycle it was deemed appropriate for us to be genetically seeded with the wisdom and knowledge of the evolved star beings. Some of these light beings came from the star system of Sirius. Several contingents of God-like giant angelic beings known as the *Watchers* also descended to planet Earth. Their mission was to establish large ceremonial complexes such as pyramids, or cities of light, that were to be used as frequency beacons.

***

Esoteric Research Expeditions

In the year 2000 I accepted an invitation to travel to South America and experienced a remarkable memory awakening at the ancient sacred site of Machu Picchu in Peru. Just before my journey I received a telepathic message to find an alcove in which to meditate in the sacred City of Light. The vision depicted it as rectangular and carved out of stone. With only one hour to spare before catching the bus down the mountain from Machu Picchu I followed intuitive guidance to the appropriate alcove. Squeezing through the narrow entrance and walking into the cave's depths I saw an alcove situated beside an altar. A tiny beam of light guided the way. Thanksgiving flowers and seeds had already been placed on the altar in honour of Pacchamama, the Andean name for Mother Earth. The alcove was exactly as I'd been shown in my meditation. Sitting down with my back against the ancient, carved and smooth, stone wall I began to meditate.

Relaxing my body and stilling my mind I was shown an image – of myself as a star being from Sirius arriving at this same location with a group of pioneering Sirian spiritual scientists. We had a job to do. To create and build a Light City – a Mystery School. We were to build it at this exact location because the co-ordinates were perfect for the task. Our task was to teach some of those living here to embrace natural law so their consciousness could evolve into greater light. My current task, I was told, was to remember my heritage.

The scene changed. I was shown a long line of tiny Andean women dressed in their bright national costumes preparing to file past me, their hands joined over their heart in prayer and reverence. Their leader stepped forward, bowing, saying she had a request. She asked if I would consider returning to these mountains annually bringing with me groups of people to dance the sacred circle dance, Paneurythmy, at specific sacred sites. She said that I would know and feel the specific places in my mind and body. At these ancient knowledge-holding sites I was to re-activate the light codes of ancient wisdom stored within the frequencies of the land. And, at the same time, I was to activate my personal cellular memory and the memories of those who chose to travel with me. This request warmed my heart. I had travelled to the high Rila Mountains in Bulgaria in 1996 to learn Paneurythmy and had practiced it with many groups since then so I accepted the commission.

For nine consecutive years, I took groups to dance at sacred sites in the Andes mountains of Peru and Bolivia. Following sunrise on the winter solstice 2001 a group of men and women danced for the first time in front of the Temple of Mother Earth, at Machu Picchu in Peru, one of the great wonders of the world. In our western world we refer to the spirit being of Mother Earth as Gaia. To the indigenous Peruvians she is known as Pacchamama. We dedicated the dance to her. As soon the dance completed, Pacchamama came into our circle, thanking and blessing us. It was a profound experience for all twelve dancers. Following this heart-opening experience, we each needed to spend integration time alone.

Having the rest of the day to explore the site I felt the need to re-visit the stone alcove where I had meditated the previous year. Another powerful experience followed. Emerging from the Cave of the Condor and feeling the need to ground the high frequency energy buzzing through me I sat on the grass under the only tree. As soon as I did, my hands became highly charged with electrical currents. Telepathically, I was asked to place them, palms down, upon the earth. Doing so I immediately saw, through my inner vision, a part of a huge crystal blocking the entrance to an underground Light City close to where I was sitting. Through the spiritual force moving through my body and hands, the crystal cracked, as if a lightning bolt hit and spilt it asunder. 'Pacchamama doesn't come to many people', I was told. The splitting of the protective crystal enabled the inner earth beings access to the outer world where their knowledge could be shared. And, it also enabled those visiting to open their minds and hearts to receive memory downloads.

From the seven sacred lakes in the Rila Mountains of Bulgaria I took Paneurythmy to many Andean sacred sites in Peru and along the shores of Lake Titicaca in Bolivia. The unified loving energy generated among the dancers was consciously transmitted to the lake. This dance of the angels connected the two countries at ancient sacred places. Copacabana, a small fishing village on the shores of Lake Titicaca, was where the group began dancing in Bolivia.

I conducted many magical ceremonies with the different groups around this lake and on the Islands of The Sun and Moon. The ceremonies brought tears to our eyes and joy to our hearts. We offered prayers of gratitude and blessings to the Apus, (spirits of the mountains), the lake and to Pacchamama and Father Sun (Titi Inti). The Sun always shone brightly reflecting diamond lights dancing on the water. It was as if we lived a fairy tale. Every adventure brought self-realisations for each of the participants. An adventure mystery school of major evolutionary advancement, the teachings were not only for me, but also for those who accompanied me.

The acceleration of consciousness journey began the moment the doors closed on the departing plane. It's a long trip from Australia to South America. I often imagined my guides rubbing their hands with great glee. "Now she's captive for a long time and can't be distracted – what are we to feed her?" Soul food was what I received. Download followed download and my pen was busy writing notes in my journals. On each arrival into South America, whether at Lima, the capital of Peru, or La Paz in Bolivia, I received clear spiritual guidance, often through dreams or meditation. Boundless energy enabled me to sure-footedly climb the high mountains, even though they are steep and rugged. Feeling a great affinity to the local indigenous people I intuitively understood them, even though they spoke a foreign language. There were so many sacred sites to visit, and soul memories to be activated.

Lake Titicaca is the highest and largest lake in the world that can be navigated. It is so large it appears as an inland sea. It has habitable islands. Taquile island is situated on the Peruvian part of the lake. On the first journey across the larger part of the lake one of the group spontaneously opened her mouth to intone an ancient Inka priestly blessing. Immediately I felt excruciating pain, as if I was being cut open around my waist. Years before I'd had an exceedingly painful experience triggered by a specific sound. That sound activated a past life memory. Realising this was another memory activation, I asked a fellow traveller to help.

Together we saw how, in a past time at this same spot, I was about to release important secret information connected to a crystal city situated under the lake. To silence me I had been forcibly tied with a heavy rope around my waist anchored by a large donut shaped rock and then tossed overboard. I was re-experiencing the excruciating pain of drowning while my body felt it was being sliced open at the waist. The memory pain lessened considerably as a result of this detailed awareness, condensing to a small area above my navel.

Tour guide Henry told us that Jaques Costeau, the famous French diver, had tried unsuccessfully to locate a crystal city under the lake around this area. Henry said the lake was deep at this particular spot, around 232 metres, however parts of it are immeasurable because of canyons under the lake. Satellite pictures show them as dark spots. Reaching Taquile Island we walked about halfway up the hundreds of steep rocky steps and my pain intensified again. As we reached the central square courtyard and church, I experienced so much pain I collapsed and fainted. The woman who had previously intoned on the boat performed a vibrational healing over my body. This spiritual healing practice released the dense energy from my memory cell including the part she had originally played in the ancient drama. Awakening, I looked up. Above me, on the top parapet of the old church, were two large stone carved phallic symbols. Laughing, I drew the group's attention to them. All pain had gone.

Sitting beside me on our return boat trip tour guide Henry showed me a diagram of how the Peruvian sacred symbol, the Andean Cross, depicts twelve constellations of stars as well as the solstices and equinoxes. He pointed to the ley line positioned diagonally across the Andean Cross diagram that connected the sacred sites. It also connects to the Milky Way galaxy.

A few years after this incident, and with a different group, we were taken by boat to a clearly visible underwater temple in a different area of the lake. The lake is so huge there could be many others. The local indigenous people say that there are however they can only be discovered by those who live in the Light. While viewing this underwater temple, I was given another mission – that of bringing to Lake Titicaca the following year a particular crystal sourced from near Uluru, the sacred heart of Australia. The crystal was to come from a mine operated by the First Australians. My guidance was to hold this crystal close to my heart at all times, from the time of being given it, to the time I found the owner. Its new owner would be a man.

The following year, in my Australian home town and a few days before my departure to South America, a girl friend asked me to go with her to purchase some crystals at a wholesale crystal store. The store owner gave me a milky quartz crystal, exactly as described above, saying I was to take it with me on my next journey to the Andes. How did he know?

I carried it close to my heart for three weeks, as I'd been asked to do. I trusted I would know who to give it to when the time was right. I also carried in my pocket a similar 'sister' crystal, given at the same time. The owner of the store had been given the telepathic message to give me the specific crystals as soon as I entered his store.

The day before returning to Australia I met the man I knew intuitively was the new owner, an archaeologist. He was expecting the crystal and knew exactly where it needed to be placed. He works with, and is guided by, the spiritual Masters. At 12.00 noon, on the day of the following March equinox, he, and a team of three trusted Bolivian grandmothers, rowed their small boat to the underwater temple I had previously visited, to perform a sacred ceremony. He reverently placed the crystal in an offering parcel of flowers and leaves, wrapped it with larger leaves, tied it and then placed it in the entrance of the underwater temple between two inter-dimensional doorways. The crystal symbolically and energetically connected the two most ancient continents through the waters of Lake Titicaca. It also has another function, to activate a golden sun disc.

***

Ancient Mystery Schools

During pre-historic times, in the high Peruvian Andes Mountains, a temple City of Light was built to train humans into higher states of consciousness and the understanding of star lore. Semi-etheric light beings began teaching esoteric star lore to those who were seen to embody light. This evolutionary state of being could be determined by the degree of light radiance emanating from an individual's energy field, their light body. Our level of light increases as consciousness awakens and develops. Over time many spiritual initiations took place in this temple city. These initiations led to spiritual ascension. Many indigenous myths, legends and sacred texts tell of white giants, or gods, who walked the Earth, teaching and sharing their wisdom and higher powers.

Mystery Schools were conducted in many different parts of planet Earth during Lemurian and Atlantean times. Students on the path to spiritual ascension participated in varying and diverse training procedures. Initiates were chosen to attend these schools of higher learning and were only admitted when they demonstrated their willingness to move beyond their comfort zone of thought, emotionally re-active behaviours and dysfunctional attitudes. Spiritual Masters from higher dimensional realms would assist the training of these initiates and would make their presence felt, usually through meditation.

These civilisations died out because of human density. We become dense when we allow negative thoughts to take over our lives. When the material life became more important to the masses than their spiritual life civilisations destroy themselves.

I'll continue to add the transmissions I received that illustrate the points made in this book. These transmissions occur when I'm in a relaxed, open and receptive state of meditation. I feel them coming through. They enter my conscious mind through my right brain and I feel expansion occurring in that part as if my brain is being stretched.

Once upon a time on another planet to our own much deliberation was taking place. The experiment on Gaia was working yet often time the divine spark of consciousness remained buried in the heavy soil of the human mind. Layer upon layer of dense matter covered the seed and the seed struggled to fulfil its destiny.

Water was needed to wash away the excess of heavy soil. Preparation was made and the plan executed. A deluge swept the planet. Those who survived had to climb higher. Much soil was washed away. The seeds now had room to grow. Aeons passed. Many seeds flowered beautifully but there were also many that faltered, shrivelled and crumbled through lack of nurturing. A seed needs attention, nourishment and love otherwise it will wither and die. The seed of consciousness is no exception. A seed cannot flower on barren land. A seed cannot break through a hard layer of soil. It must have water.

The knowledge taught and practiced by the ancient civilisations is being awakened in the hearts and minds of today's spiritual seekers. Arising through heart-felt resonance it reflects information taught at the sacred Mystery School of Machu Picchu, high in the Andean Mountains. At that place and time, the energies were so refined that access by Master teachers operating on higher dimensional levels of consciousness was easy. The Spiritual Masters contact us when they see we have reached a certain vibratory level of light. Light = consciousness. Machu

Picchu was the first female Mystery School on the planet and much of the knowledge learned is being made known to those with ears to hear, eyes to see and an open heart to feel.

In ancient days, the science of energy (consciousness) was considered to be one of the most important of the sciences. An ancient form of astrology was the subject used to understand, define and qualify specific energies emanating from various sections of our Universe. Esoteric Astrology, the psychology of the soul, is the study of these energies and how they impinge upon all living things. We can understand them by learning to feel their subtle flow within our body. As a finely tuned instrument, our body is designed to specifically work in harmony with the cosmic forces that permeate it on a daily basis. Once our solar system energies are understood and mastered, we can use their energies consciously and constructively. It is then that finer and subtler energies from outside our solar system become apparent. At this spiritual growth stage, the initiate is ready to move up the evolutionary spiral to a higher dimension of self-awareness. This is how evolution into higher consciousness takes place.

***

Chapter Three

Purposeful Spiritual Missions

Spirit, Matter, Time, Space and Astrology

From the beginning of time the ancients studied the stars. Why was their wisdom relegated to a wasteland in our modern world? Ancient esoteric truths and the great wisdom of cultures before the 'historic period' appear to have little influence in modern educational curriculums. Surely there is a relationship between the cosmos and humans? Source/Great Spirit infuses all of matter; time as we think of it is a fabrication, and space exists everywhere and is in everything including our minds and bodies. Cosmic cycles govern the timing of life events.

The basis for science is to observe and find correlations between one phenomenon and another. This is also the fundamental premise of astrology, that the movements in the heavens are energetically connected to events on Earth and to each living creature. Time cycles exist. The variable is how each human reacts to them. This entirely depends on human psychology and the consciousness level of the individual. As the consciousness light increases in human minds and hearts, those leaders who do their best to keep us in the dark become concerned. Can they carry out their power and control agendas without thoughtless human robots?

Like actors in a world of matter we create, direct and act in our own life story. We play the same games over countless lifetimes until we become conscious of our self-destructive psychology. We then have a choice. To keep on replaying the same game or change it. We don't need to do it the hard way and keep on experiencing the same problematic results. We can free ourselves. One way to do so is to learn to view our external world as a mirror because it provides continual feedback. We create our lives from our current levels of consciousness. Another way is to learn astrology and to apply the teachings to your daily life.

Are you willing to go beyond the narrow confines of current conditioning and open your heart and mind to a broader perspective of human evolution and your purpose for being on this planet? As psychologist Carl Jung once said, 'Astrology is deeper than psychology and is the basis of medicine'.

How amazing is the Full Moon, gliding through the night sky in all her beauty and splendour? How come so many people are affected emotionally by it? How come hospital psyche and emergency wards, and the police, prepare for more casualties at these times? Our ancestors watched the night sky the way we watch television. What could be more natural than to spend time in nature at sunrise or sunset observing the magnificence interplay between light and dark?

The ancients observed that the seasons of the year followed the movements of the Sun and Moon. Realising that time was cyclic they learned to predict the return of each season. This knowledge enabled them to navigate the seas, and at a later date in human development, to grow food. They were able to determine the solstices and equinoxes and ascertain the best timing for specific earthly events.

Recent and current cosmic alignments indicate a time of accelerated change. It is time for humans to permanently raise their consciousness and develop a higher and wider perspective to life. The invisible is becoming visible. Logic and intellect, attributes of the left-brain, can meet and engage with right brain intuition, abstract concepts, and psychic abilities. The right spatial brain 'sees' further and understands vast concepts and, when the logical intellect can make sense of what's seen and understood, integration occurs. Each attribute is as important as the other. Activation of subconscious memories connected to important soul history occur when the body and mind are completely relaxed, the right brain is engaged, and intent and desire to understand are strong.

***

A Three-Part Mission

May 2013: I was given an internal directive in the form of a mission. It was divided into three parts.

- *Expose the rape of the feminine by extra-terrestrials.*
- *Expose the cause of the killing of brotherly love.*
- *Resurrect an ancient archetype from the soul of humanity.*

My inner guidance asked me to access the information from within my subconscious and disseminate it. Apparently writing about it will bring a shift in mass human consciousness. Hence the reason for exploring it now. Where to start? Until the time of this present writing, I did nothing. My resistance was great.

The first part of the mission: *Expose the rape of the feminine by extra-terrestrials.*

What immediately comes to mind is the first play I decided to produce. Many years ago, while living in remote mining towns, I used to act in, and direct plays for the local theatre groups. If there wasn't a theatre group I created one. The first play I produced was *The Rape of the Belt* by author Benn W. Levy. It was about a battle between two Greek heroes and the warrior-woman tribe of Amazonian women. The men hoped to claim the Amazonian Queen's prized possession, her belt. I understand the 'belt' was a chastity belt. From memory, the women won. Why did I choose this play? What ancient memory connected to the decision?

I've mentioned giants in this story. Our world is dualistic. Up – down; light – dark; hot – cold; above – below; etc. There are light and dark humans. I've encountered many light giants. There must have been dark ones. It's a part of our spiritual growth process to release judgements and bring into balance our opposing poles.

Imagine yourself as a female human at the time of the gods, the 'not of this Earth' giants written about in the bible and in other ancient texts. They were probably between 15 and 30 feet tall. You were the height you are now, or even smaller. Imagine if the 'dark' giants wanted to steal your chastity. They wanted to get something for themselves. How comfortable would you be? Would you have been able to resist? Would it have hurt? Wouldn't it feel like a small child does when raped by an older man? Parts of your body and mind could be damaged for life.

I have memories of creating the opposite scenario, off-planet. Strong woman wants to get something for self from a male leader and, abusing her sexuality and wisdom of the stars, takes what is not rightfully hers. His death followed at a precise moment of cosmic timing. Whoops – not a good move! The Universal Law of Karma, of cause and effect, is relentless. As the originator and perpetrator of the causal deed, I suffered lifetimes of sexual abuse. Whatever we cause, in whatever incarnation, we attract similar themed psychological energy until we become self-aware enough to balance our internal scales. Commitment, forgiveness and compassion play a major part in the remembrance and healing process. Then the shadows begin to lift. Accepting the truth and taking responsibility for our part in the causal deed, is necessary. It takes courage, intent and willingness to face one's own demons.

On a lighter note, I want to take you to a different giant. This time it's a statue, one that mesmerised and awakened cellular memories in me. I was privileged to see an incredibly special, relatively unharmed by age, statue of Paccamama, an Andean representation of Mother Earth.

This colossal statue, discovered in 1932, stands alone, in a room of her own, in the small museum at Tiahuanaco, an ancient sacred pyramid site high in the Andes Mountains of Bolivia. Authors and researchers H. S. Bellamy and P. Allan date this statue, and other Tiahuanaco monuments, to approximately 22, 500 – 25,500 years ago. This was before the planetary ice melted and the Age of Leo began. The authors say the idol is a calendar. They present their cosmological findings in a book *The Great Idol of Tiauanaco*.

When I walked into the darkened room of the small archaeological museum with the only light highlighting the giant statue, I was spellbound. I felt the stirring of ancient memories and emotion as if I'd seen her before. The authors say there could have been three main periods of human civilisation.

The first civilisation: Tiahuanaco, beginning with an unknown date and having the capacity for art, memory, creativity, mathematics and cosmology. Certainly not primitive cavemen. Could this have been Lemuria?

The second civilisation: Atlantis. Destroyed approximately 12,500 years ago before the great flood.

The third civilisation: Our own era: Earliest known development in Egypt and Sumeria 6,000 – 7,000 years ago. I ask the question – "What about the first Australians? They developed on an isolated island continent that no one knew about more than 60, 000 years ago. Are they remnants of the Lemurian civilisation?"

This colossal statue, and the Tiahuanaco pyramid, were created and built on the shores of Lake Titicaca in Bolivia. Tiahuanaco is now situated a few hours' drive from Lake Titicaca and archaeologists uncovered an advanced irrigation system underneath the pyramid ruins. This pyramid was built similarly to the Egyptian ones. Like the important Egyptian pyramids, stone walls were erected thousands of years ago to block the sacred chambers so the esoteric knowledge stored within could be made available when the time was right. A tunnel underneath the pyramid ruins has its opening aligned to the Southern Cross constellation of stars. The four corners of the pyramid are oriented to other constellations. The giant statue of Paccamama was found intact under the ruins of the existing serpent temple within the pyramid complex. The Andeans used to mummify their dead, as did the Egyptians. The first mummy discovered was two-metres tall. My mind immediately flashed to an article that appeared in the *Australian* newspaper decades ago, showing detailed colour photos of mummy discoveries in Mongolia. These mummies are about two metres tall.

Over time Lake Titicaca reduced considerably and the area between the lake and the pyramid is now barren and dry.

The past is over. When memories come to the light of consciousness see them for what they are: They've come into your consciousness for a purpose. That purpose involves your evolutionary journey into greater light. Work through the psychological themes associated with the memories and learn to view them objectively, from a compassionate observer perspective. This takes dedicated practice but is so worthwhile. You will know when the issue is completely healed because you no longer have any emotional reaction to it. The darkness has lifted and the light of higher consciousness fills its space. Life continues, and we create it through the decisions we make, and actions we take every moment of every day. It's wise to become self-aware otherwise we fight darkness with darkness (ie jealousy, rage, revenge, blame, arrogance, criticisms etc.). Our dark psychology attracts dark situations.

Doesn't it make sense to become conscious of what's hidden in our subconscious realms? How to do this? Serious intent is the first step. Commitment to self-healing is the next. Meditation helps. Past-life regression and psychotherapy works and will help. Mindfulness is necessary. This requires present-time self-awareness. In the 'now' space keep observing internally and, when experiencing discord, ask questions such as: 'Why did I attract this?' and, 'What do I need to learn about myself so I no longer attract darkness?' and 'How is my heart feeling as this situation is happening?' and, 'How is my body responding in this situation?' Your honest answers reveal truth and provide opportunities for growth.

Determination to resolve past issues is needed in order to attain balance. You can help yourself by developing the qualities of gratitude, forgiveness, compassion and divine love, and practice these qualities daily. They reside in everyone and, when accessed and experienced, change our vibration to a higher one.

Lord Kuthumi helped me uncover a psychological pattern that kept me bound in chains. It was connected to a low level of self-worth and self-value, the result of the abuse experience mentioned above. He also suggested I get over the issue I had about other people de-valuing my work. He said that millions of people de-value his work but that millions value it. He values it because all he does is carry the flame of God/Goddess in his heart and it's this flame that reaches millions. He suggested I use whatever technique I need to move beyond this issue.

The second part of the mission: *Expose the cause of the killing of brotherly love.*

The ancient Egyptian story of Osiris and Isis record they were sister and brother. They had two other siblings: Nephthys and Set. These two also married each other. Osiris and Isis ruled the kingdom wisely but jealous Set, Osiris's brother, wanted to take it over. To get this power he killed his brother, placed him a box and floated him down the Nile River. Isis was distraught and she and Nephthys reclaimed the body. Set found out and stole the body, cutting it into fourteen pieces. Distraught, the two women found only thirteen body parts. They couldn't find the male member, the phallus. They carefully put the other pieces back together using not only their own healing powers but also those of Thoth, the 'father' of ancient Egyptian mystery school teachings. Isis fabricated a new phallus. Isis and Osiris mated and Horus was born.

This story has been told for many thousands of years and probably originated from Atlantis. Many Atlanteans travelled to Egypt before their country was destroyed. Some created the ancient Egyptian Mystery schools. Apparently, Thoth (Hermes/Mercury) was one of the pioneering adventurers.

Many years ago, when visiting a male student friend, I received an unexpected message from Thoth. I'd not encountered him before but he was my friend's spiritual guide. His message, that didn't make sense until recently, was 'You are about to expose a hidden truth and you have my blessings. It is time'.

The biblical story of Cain and Abel and of how one brother killed the other to gain power demonstrates how this same power-over theme has been perpetuated through the Ages of time. Just view the daily news for similar themed stories. How much longer will we continue to perpetuate power abuse? How long will we continue to play the dark games of hatred, jealousy, revenge – and others? Until we become conscious of our inner motivations and see clearly how repetition of our psychological shadows perpetuates from life to life. When we clearly see we can consciously transmute the shadows into light. Then we will stop playing childish games, and there will no longer be wars.

In times to come humans will remember these times as the dark ages, a time when the light of consciousness was dull. Changes are to take place upon the planet that will bring about greater light. A major illness is usually needed for humans to wake up to the truth of their being and so it is on a world-wide scale. Some humans eagerly seek higher consciousness and they are the Way Showers. They tell of another way to view life. They see and understand from a higher perspective. They are old souls whose memories of former cataclysms are close to their level of consciousness. They remember and are willing to do whatever it takes to share their knowledge. It is wise to listen to them.

The earth will be cleansed of human pollution.

At the time of writing there are many who are at different phases of their awakening process. Many veils between dimensions are opening. There is hope in their hearts as they consciously choose to move towards the light. This takes willingness, dedication, self-awareness and self-knowledge. There are many tools to obtain this level of consciousness and astrology is one. Numerology and the tarot can also assist the awakening process. Astrology is an ancient system purposefully designed as a major awakening tool. It is now used in this way by millions of people. It is also abused and used as a tool for manipulation and control. Where there is light there is darkness. It has always been so.

When the darkness overtakes the light imbalances occur. These imbalances create pollution in the etheric as well as the physical realms. When the scales weigh heavily on the dark side nature steps in. It is a natural consequence of human imbalance. The extent of the cataclysms depends entirely on human consciousness levels. The density and darkness of human thoughts, emotions and deeds creates etheric pollution. This pollution can be seen and felt by sensitive empaths and some clairvoyants. Humans are emotional creatures. Dense and negative emotions cloud the mind and confusion reigns. Clarity disappears. Degeneration takes over. It need not be so.

When human energy fields are filled with dense negativity, beings from the lower astral plane feed from it. There are many people who need this food to sustain them. Like vampires, they suck other's energy. This feeding programme weakens the energy field of the humans involved and they become more negative. It is a vicious cycle that can only be corrected through self-awareness. There needs to be the desire to change before change can occur. The people who allow themselves to be vampired devolve rapidly. It is not long before they are on the human scrap-heap. It is their evolutionary process. However, help is always at hand should they be willing to reach out for it and choose to change their perceptions.

It takes practice, effort and time to attain higher levels of consciousness. Earth is the training ground for this process. Anyone can change their perceptions, and perceptions create experience. Thought is energy. Energy follows thought. What we think and feel is what we create. Choosing to think, feel and act upon higher purpose through love creates loving experiences.

The third part of the mission: *Resurrect an ancient archetype from the soul of humanity.*

There are two flickers of light I'm intuiting connected to this theme. Maybe the divine feminine, in the guise of Mary Magdalen, is the archetype I've been asked to resurrect. Connected to her is the embodiment by humanity of Christ, or super-consciousness. And/or – maybe it's the new astrology system I've been shown and am about to share? Trusting the answer will reveal itself, I continue to write.

***

The Mysterious Lands of Peru and Bolivia

Totally at home in the high mountains of Peru and Bolivia I feel as if my soul belongs there. My energy levels rise to greater heights and I have more courage, confidence and daring than anywhere else in the world. What is it about this area that engenders this expansiveness? Each trip I made uncovered more ancient memories of knowledge and information about our human evolutionary past and I realise that, unwittingly, I'd become a spiritual archaeologist – a job I'm passionate about.

Bolivia used to be part of Peru until about two hundred years ago. The Andean Peruvian culture is ancient. The founders used sacred sites as spiritual initiation centres, as was the case in ancient Egypt, and substantial resources were used in their construction. These centres were considered necessary because they connected people to divinity. In the Sacred Valley, situated between Cusco city and Machu Picchu in Peru, sacred geometry was used to build structures that demonstrated a direct connection to the celestial realms and to the people's mythical and spiritual reality.

The Andean sacred sites were used as timepieces to track solstices and equinoxes, the movements of the planets, stars and constellations. The solstices and equinoxes were necessary and practical time indicators, used to determine crop planting and harvesting times. On a spiritual level these special sites were used to open energy portals to higher planes of consciousness, and, as such, were regarded as sacred. These consciousness gateways were deliberately closed when the god-men realised the dark ages were coming. How did they know? Through their study and understanding of the stars.

They also knew that the Age of Aquarius – often referred to as The Age of Light, was the time when coded individuals would be activated to reopen these gateways.

Throughout the astrological Ages, the seemingly invisible majestic 'city of light', Machu Picchu, remained untouched by invaders until 1911 when an American explorer Hiram Bingham, rediscovered it. This awesome and magnificent site, situated in high isolation between the Sacred Valley and the ancient Inca capitol of Cusco, was built long before the Inca civilisation. It contains information of ancient history. From my experience it was specifically chosen, because of its particular geographical and vibratory location, as a place where the teachings of star lore, esoteric wisdom, consciousness and spirituality could be handed down. There were cities upon cities and temples upon temples built at this site. The landscape and design indicate the builders had an advanced knowledge of sacred geometry and utilised the natural geography of the land to build this and other pyramids.

A small group of people called Q'ero live in isolation in the high mountains of Peru. Many hundreds of years ago they moved to higher mountain areas so they could maintain their spiritual practices and remain psychologically and spiritually untainted by the invasion of Spanish foreigners to their lands. They see the world as a living energy field, with everything connected, as did the ancient wise ones. They live and operate their daily lives in multiple dimensional realities. Since the year 2000 some of them chose to descend from the mountains to share their knowledge. A select few westerners have been fortunate to learn from, and be blessed by, them. I was one, on my first trip to the sacred sites of Peru.

Our Cusco tour guide had never seen Q'ero people before so was overwhelmed when he encountered a group, dressed in their national costume, at the first sacred site we visited. They were apparently waiting for us so they could perform a ceremony. As we arrived the Q'ero leader approached our group and asked that one of us join them in a ceremony. I was the lucky one. I can't remember the ceremony details, nor could I understand the language, but I do remember their leader working above my crown chakra, speaking or chanting as he did so. They gave me a hand-made bracelet and belt, woven from natural local fibres.

The Andean prophecies say that, with the return of this new Age, a new beginning involving a stepping beyond 3D time is to take place. According to their understanding this new Age is characterised by the emergence of the sacred feminine. All people on Earth will be influenced to progressively recognise, develop and bring into balance the feminine aspects within their psyche, through divine love and heart-felt feelings. As this occurs, higher consciousness emerges from behind the veils of the past.

Many things occurring on Earth now are beyond human understanding. Our planet is undergoing massive energetic change, and so too is humanity. A huge leap in human consciousness evolution is taking place. Archaeologists are continually re-writing history as more ancient sacred sites and relics are discovered and uncovered. These finds force us to re-think our evolution and history and awaken us to a new, broader and more conscious understanding of reality. A huge spiritual awakening is taking place and the wave of higher consciousness is becoming stronger. The old souls who hold the ancient codes of wisdom are again opening the consciousness gateways to other dimensions. The prophesy of the ancients is manifesting.

In my journey to uncover the ancient mysteries of the ancient Peruvian culture, I discovered that an evolved civilisation had lived there long before the Great Flood. This civilisation had knowledge of astronomy, astrology, mathematics and the science of consciousness. They also had expertise in organisation, order, community, agriculture, drainage, road and city building and the art of weaving. Many of the ancient hieroglyphs depict giant beings with wings. Like angels. There was a strong focus on the building of sacred sites over interconnected ley lines and underneath specific constellations of stars. Some select Cities of Light were built so that children could be trained in the science of energy and the development of higher, or multi-dimensional consciousness.

In many of the creation stories of indigenous people around the world there are indicators that great white gods walked our planet, teaching and sharing their wisdom. These messengers had the role of encouraging the development of higher consciousness within the local people and are often depicted as coming from other star systems. Some esoteric texts suggest that the Pleiades, Sirius and Orion were three such systems that sent divine messengers to Earth. My memories and life experiences confirm it.

According to ancient texts, including the writings of last century, light beings lived approximately 200,000 – 250,000 years ago in a Garden of Eden, or a continent called Lemuria, sometimes referred to as Mu, or the Mother Land. This continent was geographically placed in the Pacific Ocean, with one side near where South America is now. As previously mentioned some remnants of this great continent are Hawaii, the Pacific Islands and New Zealand.

The existence of this great continent is confirmed by:

- Naacal tablets, books and writings.
- Inscriptions found in India, China, Burma, Tibet and Cambodia.
- Evidence from ancient Maya, symbols and legends from the Yucatan, and from stone tablets in other parts of Mexico.

These ancient people had profound knowledge of cosmic forces and were spiritually and psychically tuned to higher frequencies. Their consciousness was highly developed. They had an understanding of other dimensions of time and space and the ability to experience direct contact with higher intelligence. They were telepathic, with a collective perception. Colonisation of other lands began some 70,000 years before Lemuria sank into the Pacific Ocean.

The philosophy of these ancient people was based on natural law and the love of nature, as is most indigenous cultures. They believed nature to be the best teacher. It does not lie. They also had the understanding that we humans can only govern earthly forces when we have learned to master and consciously utilise our internal divine force. They also understood that all energetic forces are vibratory and these vibrations form waves in the atmosphere, and that humans are capable of producing higher vibrations than any other earthly force. Nowadays, many spiritual seekers are learning to raise their vibrations by thinking, feeling and demonstrating loving thoughts, and by being in a state of love, grace, gratitude and equilibrium. When this happens our spiritual, mental, emotional and physical bodies create union and harmony. The ancients understood these principles and applied them to their daily lives.

Many of the sacred sites around the world were built on ley lines. These are electro-magnetic convergence points that can be likened to Earth's 'acupuncture' points. These points were known in the ancient world and were accurately mapped and built upon. There was a planned network of astronomical and geometrical lines that criss-crossed the entire planet. Some of these sites are simply vast blocks of stone that function as massive astronomical instruments. Our ancient predecessors had remarkable understanding, advanced consciousness and incredible powers. They knew that at the time of cosmic energy alignments, such as the solstices and equinoxes, there is an increase in energetic potency. Many spiritually minded people understand that harmonic resonance can occur within an individual when one is tuned to the sacred site frequency. Some researchers think that the bevy of sacred sites around the world act as 'tuning forks', giving off signals to those in celestial spheres.

The sacred sites incorporate coded information, which can be felt when one is operating at the same frequency. When we are 'tuned up' with spiritualised love and light, resonance occurs and knowledge (light) is then released from the ancient sites – and integrated into the mind and body of the individual. It may not be conscious at the time. Ancient sacred sites are libraries of coded information. We need to be in a higher state of consciousness to receive, and eventually understand, the information. The sacred circle dance Paneurythmy, when danced in a group, is a vehicle for 'tuning' the participants to a higher frequency so that coded information can be released. It is also a vehicle for consciously sending group love and light to Mother Earth.

***

Spiritual Adventures in the Mountains

On my third visit to the Andean Mountains I asked my tour guide, Fredy, to find an ancient sacred site known as the Aramu Muru Gateway. I had been told it was situated in Peru near the small village of Chiquita, not far from the Bolivian border. Fredy searched and also asked other tour guides and taxi drivers if they had heard of it. No one had, at least not by that name.

I asked him to close his eyes and meditate so he could remember its location. This was a stretch, but he trusted my guidance. He closed his eyes and entered a meditative state with the intention of invoking a memory. Immediately he saw the gateway in three different time frames. The first as a newly constructed magnificent temple built into a natural rocky formation on the shores of Lake Titicaca. His second vision was of the same temple structure submerged under the water of Lake Titicaca and the third as it is now – worn, and some distance from Lake Titicaca in an isolated farming area. In his first vision he saw other dimensional star beings being musically guided to enter our 3D world through the gateway. Never before had he had such a vision. But he now knew where the sacred site was situated – in a farmer's potato patch. His vision depicted three different astrological Ages of time.

I took the group to this ancient ceremonial place to dance the sacred circle dance, Paneurythmy. Before our dance Fredy performed a cleansing smoking ceremony, similar to that of the North American Indians and original Australians. While he was doing so I prepared the dance circle. The others found flattish rocks, or used their backpacks, to sit on the recently manually dug soil. At four thousand metres above sea level there are plenty of rocks but few trees and grass.

While preparing for the dance my internal guidance warned I was not to go up to the gateway if I felt the slightest fear. As we danced we felt a strong connection to the land and to the giant crystal some of us saw psychically under the earth. We felt as if we were dancing as one, in harmony with the rhythm of the music, the cosmos and the earth. We created such a circle of love and light that fear could not possibly penetrate.

At the completion of the dance we decided to individually walk up the rise to the gateway, a large rock formation with a specifically carved closed 'door' containing a small round circle at approximately third eye level. The site was built into a large and high rocky hill. We wanted to experience the energy independently. When it was my turn I began a slow, calm and fearless walk up the embankment. As I was doing so I was telepathically directed: 'Take off your sunglasses – I want to see you more clearly'. I'd become used to unexpected telepathic messages from my spiritual guides, so did so. I placed my sunglasses on the earth close to the rise of the site's embankment, taking a mental note of the location.

Standing directly in front of the huge stone gateway that could take people through into other dimension of time and space, I placed my forehead against the circle in the central 'eye' position of the heavy stone, carved doorway. Completely relaxed I blanked my mind. Time seemed to stand still. I, (my consciousness) immediately passed through the large stone edifice to be greeted in a different dimension on the other side by a strong and regal figure. He introduced himself as Lord Meru. I'd never heard of him. This was a new experience, one of many to take place on these wonderful exploration journeys. I had been working with spiritual guides for a long time. Some were celestial ascended masters while others were highly evolved star beings. This was something different. Here I was in a potato patch in an isolated farming area of the Andean highlands being greeted by a strong and commanding presence from another dimension. Lord Meru revealed himself behind an ancient stone inter-dimensional gateway. I saw and experienced him as clearly as I would any other human being in the third dimension.

Lord Meru seemed incredibly delighted to see me. He asked that I stand beside him as his equal counterpart, saying he had missed me and it was time to again take my rightful place beside him. Pragmatic me replied, saying I couldn't stay for long. He asked me to return to meet with him again. I agreed. When I stepped down from the embankment to pick up my sunglasses they had disappeared. No one had passed by. We all searched but they had completely disappeared. From that point on I stopped wearing sunglasses.

During a later meditation Lady Meru made herself known to me and asked me to return with a group the following year to dance the sacred circle dance Paneurythmy on the Island of the Moon situated on the Bolivian side of Lake Titicaca. The mystery deepened.

On my return to Australia I began to research Andean esoteric spirituality in order to make sense of the above memorable experience. I discovered that two of the most highly evolved light beings in early Lemuria were Lord and Lady Meru. They later moved to the high mountains of Peru and Bolivia establishing esoteric Mystery Schools in the areas now known as the Island of the Sun and Island of the Moon, located on Lake Titicaca. The feminine Ray, a beam of cosmic high frequency fine light, enters our planet at Lake Titicaca.

Many of the spiritual Masters were trained in these Mystery Schools. Lady Meru presided over the Island of the Moon as the High Priestess and trained her many female initiates in the mysteries of star lore and energy currents. This enabled her students to develop cosmic or multi-dimensional consciousness. The star lore taught was an ancient form of astrology. She assisted the women develop their natural talents of intuition, receptivity, feeling, sensitivity and grace. She also encouraged love of, and respect for, nature's beauty, symmetry and harmony. Through the strong love connection developed between Heaven and Earth, initiates were able to open their minds to higher consciousness. The knowledge of this training is held within the soul memory of many people incarnate upon our planet now. It is this soul memory I refer to as *The Magdalen Codes*.

The Andean Masters of Wisdom searched for divine light through astronomical alignments in their attempt to connect to Divine Source. Sun worshippers, they believed the Sun was the cosmic representation of the Great Creator's infinite light.

Represented at the Peruvian sacred sites by three steps, the three human consciousness levels symbolise the three worlds in which we live on Earth, the subconscious, conscious and super conscious realms. The indigenous Quechua Peruvians say we humans inhabit the every-day conscious world whereas the super conscious world is inhabited by beings of great light. We move up the consciousness ladder because we cannot un-learn what we realise as truth. My boat experience of drowning is an example of the process. The ancient sacred site builders knew the esoteric secrets.

An invisible Christ Consciousness grid around our planet, created by the Masters of Wisdom late last century, re-activates some of the sacred sites into their former role as knowledge storage chambers.

For the first five years of my annual visits to Peru and Bolivia, when at the airport departing the Andes, I became so overcome with immense sadness, I cried. I felt such an incredibly deep soul connection to the land and people and, even though I knew I would return with a different group the following year, it was difficult to leave. One year, when we reached Lima, the capitol of Peru, I was exhausted and slept through a 7.9 magnitude earthquake centred in the sea not far away. Everyone in our hotel was safe. Some group members felt the tremors. One was having a bath and said the waves splashed onto the floor.

I began the journeys to the Peruvian Andes under clear spiritual guidance. Part of the purpose was to uncover previous life knowledge. I always looked forward to future tours because of the unknown mysteries that might be revealed. Ancient memories did unveil each year, enabling an accelerated development of my consciousness. 'Expect the unexpected' became my motto.

Following my return home from one trip, Kuthumi explained I had previously been initiated into the Egyptian mysteries as a High Priestess. This had also been my role at Machu Picchu. He said that this time around I would experience initiations differently and it was important to share them. It was through experiencing situations and sacred sites that memories would emerge and I would remember ancient knowledge. Smiling, he said I was a walking encyclopaedia from which others would benefit. I apparently differ from my counterparts because they channel knowledgeable entities. I don't need another to do so.

K. also took me into a green and lush countryside to show me a breathtakingly beautiful sunrise, saying it was a symbol that would lead me to my destiny. He asked me to remember this vision. A sunrise symbolises a new beginning, the dawning of a new life. He also said he would come to me in the future in varying guises, and to be aware. As I was completing this book in late 2017 I realised my website had the image of a sunrise on the home page. I was determined it had to be there but I hadn't remembered Kuthumi's message. Or thought I hadn't. It must have gone into my subconscious mind, resurrecting at the appropriate time.

Subsequent annual trips to the mountains of Peru and Bolivia revealed much ancient knowledge. The Spiritual Masters were with us all the way. I am grateful to my travelling companions who trusted me enough to adventure into unknown realms on varying planes of existence. We each learned and remembered so much.

Human conscious evolutionary development occurred in specific leaps, as if an external force guided the process. This external influence seems to have come from extra-terrestrial intelligence. Who were the luminous beings who first inhabited Lemuria and where did they come from? Who were the god-men spoken about in the bible and in indigenous legend? Some say they came from the Elohim, the celestial creator gods. These god-men, as world-teachers, seeded humans with the light of consciousness when the cosmic timing was appropriate. Other stories indicate they came from star systems more 'luminous' or 'lighter' than planet Earth.

The ancients knew our planet has organs just as we humans do. It has vital energetic centres, polarities, positive and negative charges, meridians and life cycles. Our planet has electromagnetic centres situated at precise regions of the globe. The Himalayan mountain range is the electrical centre, being masculine in radiation, whereas the Andes are magnetic and feminine. According to Peruvian text the earth's pole, or centre of feminine magnetic irradiation, manifests through the etheric doors of the sacred lake, Titicaca, high in the Andes Mountains of Peru and Bolivia.

The god-men built sacred sites around the world to reflect different constellations of stars. Having an advanced understanding of cosmic energy, they knew how these currents could be harnessed and used in their everyday lives. They understood that every thought causes a movement in the brain and travels at a speed faster than light. Forces connecting to the brain are cosmic forces and all forces are vibratory, traveling in energy waves faster than the speed of light. When two brains are of similar vibration mental telepathy can be experienced. The ancients knew this advanced science and used it to access higher states of consciousness.

The sacred city of Machu Picchu, situated in the centre of four mountains, represents the balance between the sacred masculine and feminine, as well as the balance between the physical and divine. This sacred citadel was a special residential school for the most sacred 'Virgins of the Sun' who were in training to serve Pachamama, the Mother Goddess.

The word 'virgin' held a totally different connotation to today's usage. In ancient times a virgin, dedicated to her spiritual life, was regarded as special because of her ability to undergo extensive spiritual training in order to become a pure, clear channel for cosmic and divine forces. Machu Picchu was an elite esoteric spiritual training school and was built in an isolated place so the inhabitants could remain internally pure and clear.

The young Inca priestesses were the last of an ancient lineage that stretched back to Lemurian times. They were the keepers of the old ways and were taught to practice and maintain the memories of ancient star lore. Trained in the correct use of their receptive vehicle, the body, they were taught to tune in to their inner senses to develop intuition and psychic perceptions. They learned the art of mental telepathy and of listening to the voice of spirit within. They learned to be in harmony with nature, holding all aspects of both the spiritual and the physical world in balance. They learned to pay attention to, and to master, their mind chatter. They also learned to master their emotional bodies. They were taught cosmic sciences and the science of consciousness.

At the end of the Inca era, after the demolition of that culture by the Spanish, the Machu Picchu seers once again sealed the portals to cosmic consciousness. Its energy field and spiritual forces awaited the return of the 'Children of the Light', those people who embody specific codes of higher consciousness in their cellular memory. Through these light codes that I refer to as *The Magdalen Codes*, the gateways to ancient knowledge could be re-accessed.

There is a link between the Inca and Maya culture and both, I believe, were derived from Lemuria, as there appears to be a common base of belief and spiritual practices. There is evidence to prove that the incredible astronomical instrument, the Machu Picchu *intihuatana*, a vertical sun dial monument carved out of an enormous rock, known as the hitching post of the Sun, dates back to before the Incas.

Many things are happening on Gaia beyond current human understanding. Our planet is undergoing massive change, as are the people upon her. Wherever there is resistance to the light the changes are greater. A leap in the evolution of consciousness is, and will continue, to take place. Peru and Bolivia are earthquake prone areas, and earthquakes often uncover ancient sites and records buried for aeons of time. Archaeologists are continually re-writing history as more sites are discovered but some refuse to release their new knowledge because of fear of the consequences of doing so. Imagine what could happen to the tourist trade or high-level educators in some countries if new archaeologically proven information was uncovered that discounted former history?

The Children of Light are returning to assist the process of raising the consciousness of humanity. We do this by consciously working on ourselves to raise our own frequency through psychological self-examination and correction. By becoming self-aware through clearing our dense emotional and mental dross that inhibits spiritual growth we begin to consciously live our lives in joy, peace, balance and love. As our inner light becomes stronger we magnetise brighter light. When we enter sacred sites in a state of peace and grace resonance occurs. Ancient codes awaken. Information, in the form of light, enters our consciousness system and we experience perceptual breakthroughs. Memories are triggered as ancient cellular codes break through existing consciousness levels. An energetic wave of understanding takes place and this vibration fills an internal vacuum. We carry this higher vibratory energy and those we meet experience it. We pass it on. This is the way we assist planetary awakening.

Humanity is cosmically programmed to make a giant leap into a higher level of consciousness. As a collective, we still operate at a third dimensional level. To attain the next, or fourth dimensional level of consciousness, mental and emotional density needs be identified, accepted and responsibility taken for it. Then it needs to be loved to death until it has been erased and there is no longer emotion attached. You will know this has been achieved when you no longer emotionally react to external stimuli.

This level of consciousness corresponds to the astral plane, the illusionary realm of Neptune. There are many sub-levels within this realm. Those operating life through lower psychic levels will have difficulties in navigating their inner oceanic tides, especially people with a majority of water signs in their birth charts. It can and must be done, for the greater good of humanity and our planet. The mind needs to become clear of psychic debris and psychological pollution.

The fifth dimensional level of consciousness involves developing a great love of, and for, 'all our relations', appreciating and fully understanding that we are all connected, and are one. When a certain number of humans attain this frequency level, a critical mass occurs along with another perceptual shift. The sixth level of consciousness brings about a luminous quality to our bodies – we look and feel light. We shine, glow and radiate love and light.

Andean prophecies say that a being of light at this sixth dimensional level will emerge, capable of balancing world power. This is when the Golden Age will really begin. However, they say it is a potential, rather than a certainty.

The gateways to other dimensions have been opened and there is an opportunity to explore the human potential and access higher states of consciousness. We can begin to access the parts of our mind that have been asleep for aeons of time. However, much cleansing of our lower nature needs to be consciously done before higher frequencies of light can be experienced. Dense patterns of thought and emotion need to be recognised and transmuted. To be able to access higher frequency light we need to once again unite with the divine feminine aspect of ourselves: our intuition, psychic senses, mental stillness, allowance and receptivity. These *Magdalen Codes* are packages of consciousness, living in every human regardless of gender. Developing an attitude of gratitude and appreciation of and for 'all our relations' assists our evolutionary journey to higher consciousness.

References for this chapter:

Return of the Children of the Light, Judith Bluestone Polich.

The Children of Mu, James Churchward.

When Time Began, Book V of Earth Chronicles, Zecharia Sitchen.

The Lost Tomb of Viracoca, Maurice Cotterell.

Inka Initiation Path -The Awakening of the Puma, James Arevalo Merejildo Mallku.

***

Chapter Four

Mary Magdalen – The Aquarian Age Divine Feminine

Awakening the Divine Feminine

Beautiful, spiritually devoted, determined, dedicated and strong are words I'll use to describe the Mary Magdalen I know well. How did I get to know her?

Five years after I began intense study and application of astrology to my life I decided to delve deeper into the mysteries of my soul. Having purchased a series of video lessons on Evolutionary Astrology I prepared to play them in my living room. When I did so I did not see the male teacher on the TV screen nor hear his words. Instead I saw a beautiful woman with long hair occupying the entire screen. How could this be? I rubbed my eyes and pinched myself, not believing what I saw. She wouldn't go away. It was the middle of the day and I was eager to learn, feeling relaxed, calm, clear minded and peaceful. I pinched myself again. She was still there. I decided to stop the video and play it again the following day. I did so, with the same result. The third day, realising there was something the beautiful woman wanted to teach me, I relaxed my body, closed my eyes and focused on blanking my mind. Having trained myself to do this process through years of regular meditation and yoga practices I found it easy.

Mary Magdalen telepathically identified herself and I experienced reliving part of her life. I saw myself with thick ankles, strong legs, feet in brown sandals with the hem of my heavily woven reddish/brown dress brushing against my ankles, walking strongly, proudly and determinedly along the shores of Lake Galilee. The sand rubbing between my toes irritated but I disregarded the sensation because I had a spiritual mission to accomplish. I had been trained for this task earlier in my life, and prior to incarnation. I felt the strength of it resonate deeply within every fibre of my being. Fully aware of the role I was to play with Yeshua: to awaken his divine masculine and assist his transfiguration to the light, I was determined to succeed. I was to do this by remembering my soul's knowledge and wisdom and by utilising my Egyptian esoteric Mystery School training.

I felt stunned after I came out of the meditation. My logical mind couldn't compute. I decided to write of the experience in my journal and then allow more information to reveal itself at the appropriate time. I decided not to continue studying the course, knowing I was to be trained the feminine way, the way of experience and feeling.

The Magdalen Way is the pathway to spiritual ascension that leads to conscious immortality. It is embarked upon through the embodiment of divine light and love. The Way of all spiritual Masters - the forms vary according to each individual. Humanity is heading in this direction through evolution of consciousness. The journey requires integration and union between body, mind and spirit.

The foundational teaching of Yeshua (Jesus) and Mary Magdalen, his counterpart, was the gnostic Way. "Know

Thyself to Know God". Gnosis is self-knowledge gained through self-awareness of inner and outer life experiences. It does not adhere to any religion or doctrine. It is the individual's own pathway to God/Goddess/All That Is and is uncovered internally.

Mary and Joseph, the parents of the baby Jesus, walked the land with reverence and appreciation of the wonder and beauty of nature, and all of life. They taught their children to also love and appreciate nature's gifts. This training formed a firm foundation for Jesus' ministry. It is not so difficult for parents to teach their children in like manner.

The esoteric mystery teachings of Egypt were brought to that country from Atlantis many thousands of years ago. The Atlantean civilisation combined astrology, cosmology, and astronomy as part of their foundational teachings. They believed that what was above in the heavens was also below within each human. According to the Christian bible, approximately two thousand years ago the Magi, the three wise astrologers from the East, travelled from afar to be present at the birth of Jesus. They followed the encoded information beamed from the stars to discover the place of Jesus' birth so they could activate his energy field with specialised light-encoded information. Only a few hundred years ago, when modern science developed, astrology was separated from astronomy because it was regarded as magical and mystical, rather than scientific.

Astrology today is used in many different ways, according to the consciousness level of the practitioner. For me it is a tool to spiritual ascension through evolution of consciousness. I use it similarly to the way Mary Magdalen was taught when she travelled to Egypt to learn in the Mystery Schools still functioning there at that time - as a healing tool to aid the transformation and advancement of consciousness. This process not only aids the individual but also those in their circle of influence. As each individual evolves to a higher level of consciousness - a higher frequency of light and divine love - the embodied energy naturally raises the energy of those around them, activating them into greater light. Consciousness is light encoded information. Mary, well trained in the Egyptian Mystery School as a high priestess of Isis, was dedicated to teaching Jesus's evolved perspective. To the ancient Egyptians, Isis was the revered divine goddess.

Yeshua and Mary publically demonstrated a synthesis between masculine and feminine energies and perspectives. Accepting and supporting each other's path they devoted their lives to being divine love and light. They planted their seeds of consciousness into the souls of those open to learning. This was deliberately done in order for others to experience a harvest of flowers when the time was right. For two thousand-years these seed codes remained in the fertile subconscious soil of the human mind. The twenty-first century is the time for mass activation and harvesting of the seeds. The higher consciousness flowers are unfolding one by one and will eventually manifest as the prophesised Golden Age of Peace.

During AD 325 Emperor Constantine convened the Council of Nicaea where it was decided the specific texts to be adopted by the Church of Rome and those that would be suppressed in the Christian bible. Any bishops who disagreed with Constantine's choices were exiled on the spot. The suppression worked for nearly two thousand years.

The Nag Hammadi manuscripts found near Phou, Egypt in 1945 revealed some of the suppressed perspectives and have become known as the Gnostic gospels. Gnosticism is the belief that spiritual development and salvation are achieved through inner knowing. *The Gospel of Thomas* and the *Gospel of Mary Magdalene* are considered Gnostic texts. The question is: 'How old are the original writings of the Gnostic texts including the two gospels mentioned above'? Some say they go back to 50AD (CE). This means they pre-date the canonical texts found in the bible that were decreed acceptable by Constantine.

Mary Magdalen was the first person to see Jesus in his light body after he had passed his most important esoteric initiation on Earth. He transcended his lower personality self, as had been his soul's intention. Jesus asked Mary not to cling to him and to let go of her emotional attachment to him so he could be free to move on to higher planes of conscious experience. Mary, because of her evolved state of being, was given the task to 'Go to my brethren and tell them I ascend to my Father, and to your Father, and my God and your God'. Once Mary Magdalen had accomplished her mission Jesus gave her another, that of teaching and sharing her advanced consciousness, cosmological wisdom and knowledge. At this point of her evolution Mary becomes the 'apostle of apostles', a teacher of Jesus' spiritual truths and understandings.

Why her? Because she was an evolved soul whose earthly task was to elevate Jesus to the point whereby he could ascend into a higher dimensional state of being, super human consciousness. He chose to do this to demonstrate that this level of evolutionary advancement could be accomplished by anyone in one lifetime. He permitted crucifixion to demonstrate his decision.

Mary could 'see' into the deepest depths of her being and into the heights of her multi-dimensional mind. It is through inner tuition, gnosis and remembrance of Mary, who I view as the Aquarian Age divine feminine archetype, that this book is written. The path she chose was The Way, the initiation path of the sacred marriage: a marriage between the inner divine feminine and masculine. The path of the spiritual disciple requires dedication to the light of higher consciousness, inner preparation, introspection and inner transformation. Alchemy. The *Way of the Heart* is the path of all initiates on the journey to self-realisation, enlightenment and ascension. It is the path many now choose to follow.

Jesus experienced multi-dimensional levels of consciousness and became Christ when he clearly demonstrated the conscious alchemical process through his crucifixion and subsequent ascension and resurrection into his light body. Mary Magdalen was instrumental in his developmental process.

Mary's task was to share Jesus' teachings wherever she could. Accepting her destiny, she began teaching the Codes of Light in the South of France. She also taught in Glastonbury and other parts of England. Her earlier training as a priestess of Isis formed the foundation for her life's work. Following the crucifixion Mary lived in these areas with her daughter, who carried on the work after she passed. Nature was her church.

Why were her teachings relegated to the garbage disposal unit for two thousand years? Maybe it was because they provide the way to liberate ourselves from duality; from our inner demons residing in our subconscious, that create stress, disharmony and disease? Maybe it was because they enable feminine empowerment that can't be controlled by religious or political dictates? Maybe it was because Mary's teachings show the way to freedom through transfiguration and super-consciousness? Heart and soul unification enables the process of transfiguration into greater light.

Mary had access to sacred knowledge. This she found within. Having an innate understanding of higher truths, accessed through openness and trust in her intuition, Mary also demonstrated visionary and prophetic right brain abilities. This is the power of the divine feminine. Today humanity is experiencing an unstoppable knowledge/consciousness explosion. A tidal wave of light is sweeping our planet embracing all it touches. How can we embrace this light to access our soul records and personal truth? By choosing to enter the abyss of darkness and stillness, the void from which memories stir and awaken, the home of the divine feminine.

***

The Magdalen Codes

The Magdalen Codes is a stream of consciousness seeds dormant in humanity for aeons of time. It is time for their resurrection. Mary Magdalen, the feminine counterpart to Jesus, carried these codes and left their legacy in the cellular memory of some individuals alive today. These seed codes can be accessed through the feminine stream of consciousness. This is the reflective, open hearted, still, receptive and allowing part of our nature that is so often suppressed and disregarded in our busy western world.

Following my initial experience of her, I spent years researching the life and times of Mary Magdalen. There was very little information available until 2000, when there was an explosion of material.

Mary Magdalen was an evolved and conscious human, embodying and transmitting the sacred feminine codes of light. In the Gnostic Christian tradition, she is referred to as St. Mary Magdalene. They revere her as the Holy Bride of Christ and one in whom the wisdom of the Great Goddess of Wisdom, Sophia is embodied.

During her incarnation on Earth she was sent to study with a secret sisterhood of initiates, training as a Priestess of Isis in Egypt. Isis, sourced from Sirius, was regarded as the great goddess of the ancient Egyptian pantheon. Osiris was her partner and Horus their divine child. Mary learned sacred alchemical practices and was trained to activate and manage her serpent sexual and creative power, the force of kundalini energy.

Both Mary Magdalen and Yeshua had an important role to play in the great cosmic plan for humanity's evolutionary development into higher consciousness. Mary was Yeshua's feminine and equal counterpart.

Both carried high frequency Codes of Light through their different energy streams and soul lineages. During his life Yeshua earned the right to embody the Christ/Maitreya Codes by passing many spiritual initiations. Mary, of a different yet advanced consciousness, incarnated embodying different consciousness codes and a strong spiritual flame. Before Yeshua's crucifixion Mary conceived a child. That special child carried the light codes of the united and balanced divine masculine and feminine. These light codes were anchored into earth. After the crucifixion Yeshua, in his light body, travelled to many sacred places on the earth, meeting people and planting his Christ consciousness seeds for future generations to access and nurture to harvest.

Two thousand years later these seeds are sprouting.

Following the crucifixion, Mary's life was in danger and Joseph of Arimathea, a wealthy and trusted disciple and Uncle of Yeshua, became Mary's guardian and protector. Her women friends were her trusted companions. She had to leave her homeland to find refuge in a foreign country. In mid 2009, I was given the directive to be in Israel on 1 January 2010 to follow the escape route of Mary Magdalen. It was to be a journey of remembrance. That story follows later.

Through inner experience I learned to understand more of Mary Magdalen. All of us carry a huge storehouse of knowledge within our cellular memory. Each of us is unique and the knowledge we store in our cells can be based on experiences in other realities.

My memory of the time and life of Mary Magdalen was activated while studying a course in evolutionary astrology. Other important information related to her was accessed in the area around Lake Titicaca, situated high in the mountains of Peru and Bolivia. It is here my soul's memories are closest to the surface of my consciousness.

A huge lake can hold many memories and it is around Lake Titicaca, that a large team of archaeologists began unearthing information dating back to at least 30,000 BC. But are they permitted to continue? The information I uncovered, along with my astrological understanding, correlates with current scientific findings.

Understanding that our personality is a one-time composite of soul fragments, and that souls have memory, I chose to constantly delve deeply into my subconscious. Activating memory consciously involves recognising and disengaging from mental shoulds and cant's; stilling the mind, and paying attention to the **cause** of emotions, feelings and body sensations. Blaming others for our feelings, thoughts and experiences is immature. It only creates a defensive, or attacking, reaction from the one blamed. Others can activate our already existing habits, emotions and attitudes and it's their job to do so. It's the way we humans advance in self-awareness. We also develop emotional intelligence through the process.

***

Emotional Intelligence

In 2015 a selection of Harvard Business Review articles was published under the heading of *Emotional Intelligence*. In that book Daniel Goldman wrote the article 'What makes a Leader'. His objective was to determine which personal capabilities drove outstanding performances within top business organisations and to what degree they did so. He concluded it was emotional intelligence, through a group of five skills that enable the best leaders to maximise their own and their followers' performance.

Self-awareness was at the top of the skills list. In second place was self-regulation. The others were motivation, empathy and social skills. He says that we can strengthen these abilities through persistence, practice and feed-back from colleagues or coaches.

Emotional intelligence arises from tuning into, and identifying with our feelings, natural impulses and drives in order to develop self-awareness. With regular practice this activates the neurotransmitters of the brain's limbic system, a right-brain function. The left side of the brain governs logic, analytical and technical skills.

It's so important to honour, respect and love our body, the temple of our soul. The body contains a vast reservoir of emotions and soul memories, connected to the element of water. Our emotions act as water in our bodies and store memories. Once a memory is activated and emotions from it re-experienced, a wash of self-awareness, an "Ah-ha" moment, emerges into consciousness when we realise why we've continually perpetuated the same psychological issue or theme over and over again. This self-realising process enables the development of higher consciousness.

Another element, fire, activates the kundalini and our Magdalen Codes, light encoded filaments. These tiny fibres are filled with information. Kundalini fire moving through the body gives us the opportunity to own our memories and to take responsibility for the choices we made, and still make.

Memories reside in the subconscious, in the darkness of ignorance. All of us are here to look into the dark, because only in the dark will we find the light. As mentioned, psychological darkness vibrates at a lower frequency, acts like a toxic virus and is real. Because the dark is dense it holds us captive to more earthly incarnations. We cannot reach a high level of light until we delve deeply into our memories to experience the revealed "Ah Ha" moments of truth. More and more people are now willing to do this.

I liken the bottom layer of the subconscious realm to a muddy pond. The seeds of divine, or super consciousness, are stored deep within the mud. When an individual feels emotional and is unable to identify the emotions felt, and heal the cause of them, the pond develops pollution. Pollution gathers mass and a slimy film covers the pond. The lotus flower is a symbol for spiritual truth seekers because it begins its life in the mud and struggles to the light before it flowers in all its glory.

Keeping our hearts open enables internal exploration of truth so that realisations occur without pain. Much healing takes place when greater light is embodied. We write the prescription for our health, according to our emotional reactions. When we learn to respond, rather than re-act, to emotionally charged situations through love and self-awareness, our body reflects the internal chemical transformation. Not only do we benefit but also others benefit from our embodied light. We experience re-organisation on a subatomic level when our light encoded filaments reconnect.

Emotions connect to the element of water and the body consists of approximately 80% water. Dr Masaru Emoto demonstrated that, when the shadow thoughts and emotions from a person observing water were transmitted into the water, the water, when frozen, became murky and developed strange ugly patterns. He also demonstrated the opposite. When positive emotions of genuine love and kindness were similarly treated, the frozen patterns were orderly and beautiful. This demonstration proves that, when our internal emotional 'water' is dirty, filled with shadow thoughts, our body does not function well. For example, when we become frustrated and angry the rising energy from these overheated emotions has to go somewhere. If immediate positive action is not taken, the suppressed energy goes to the liver, head or face where it creates an energetic blockage that quickly develops into headaches, migraines or red, angry skin rashes and infections. When a scattered mind is overrun with emotions accidents happen. It's the way emotional energy works. E-motions are energy in motion. People experience emotions in different ways according to specific placements in their birth charts. Some people have more of the water element in their natal chart than others.

Emotional intelligence can be learned. The study and application of astrology to daily life greatly assists the learning process. Each of the zodiacal signs relates to a different part of the body and that part develops pain, illness or disease when negative emotions are continually and unconsciously expressed or suppressed.

The dense energy package gathers mass and attracts similar psychological energy until we become self-aware.

Emotions like guilt and fear (Capricorn) weaken our bones whereas arrogance, pride, desire for self-aggrandisement (Leo) and separation from love (Aquarius) weaken our heart. These emotions vibrate at a low level. The emotions of unconditional love (Leo) and divine compassion (Pisces) operate at a high vibratory level.

David R. Hawkins MD, PhD in his book *Power vs Force* calibrated emotions on a scale from 0 to 1000. He refers it to a Map of Consciousness. The enlightened conscious human with a God-view of self and life, is rated between 700 –1000; a person completely at peace with self is rated at 600; an individual filled with, and demonstrating, human love is 500; and an individual who lives with fear, guilt, grief, apathy and shame operates their life below 100. Criticism, blame and judgements are very low on the list. We can follow the light of higher consciousness or remain stuck in the darkness of ignorance about ourselves and the way we use our mind and emotions. It's a personal choice. Following the pathway of light is not easy, yet eventually, we all will do so because other ways don't work.

***

Awakening to Truth

How does a human wake-up to the truth of their personal situation? Usually through a catastrophe such as ill health, a marriage break-up, or death of a loved one. As it is for one so it is for the collective. It need not be so. There are many aware and awake people who are doing their best to alert the sleeping. Often, they are a quiet voice among many. They know what is ahead and do their best to warn those asleep. Their hope for a better world propels them forward. Human pollution begins in the human mind. Parental and societal influences strengthen negative irresponsibility and behaviour. A time bomb is ticking away.

Within the heart and soul of every human on Earth is the memory of former cataclysms. For some these memories are close to the surface of their consciousness. For others, they are buried deep. Awakening these memories and stirring the pond of murky water is a thankless task yet it is the passion of those awake to assist their sleeping brothers and sisters. They are aware they will receive ridicule and derision however their passion for cleanliness on all levels of existence is very strong. They cannot and will not be stopped. In the past they have been killed for their level of consciousness. They know there will always be another opportunity. Life goes on. Energy never dies but it can transform into another form.

This message could be written in the form of a novel so it is more digestible. Novels arouse and can act as catalysts. They can awaken readers. A direct approach may not be as palatable. The direct approach is needed now.

Many opportunities for the creation of a cleaner world arise and are being practiced by some. Money and influence does talk. However, it is often those with little money or influence who understand the dire situation humans have created through greed and power abuse. These innovative and courageous people need support to spread their message. They are the Way Showers. Many of them act to clean up the pollution in the external world. Some are working to awaken and accelerate consciousness. Both steps are necessary.

For permanent change to occur the sleeping ones must awaken to the reality of their creations. Illness and disease are wake-up calls. Thought and emotion carry a vibration. They are energy in motion. Imagine the thoughts you think and emotions you feel as smoke. The negative ones are like foul-smelling, heavy and dense smoke. Smoke travels, polluting the atmosphere surrounding the person close to them. It affects them. They become polluted and pass it on. This dark smoke is real and can be seen and felt. External pollution is the direct result of internal pollution. If each human chose to clean-up their inner pollution external pollution clean-up would naturally follow. The Earth will rejoice.

Change is imminent and many signs given, available for all to see. Nature offers warning signals. Many are taking heed of the signals and adjusting their lives accordingly. Many others have been writing about these changes for years. Their articles and books are read yet little action is taken. It is time to act. Preparation time is over. The ocean currents are changing as the seas are warming. The birds are confused as their normal migratory routes are now unclear. It is time for action.

From the beginning of consciousness development, the knowledge of our human evolution has been told through stories, handed down orally from generation to generation. Fascinated by human origins I travelled the world to discover truth.

Most ancient cultures on Earth have similar stories and many contain the same themes. Where did the beliefs come from? Myths and legends of the astrological gods and goddesses contain aspects of truth. The archetypal energies of these immortals reside in our psyche and can be accessed when the veil between dimensions is thin. That time is now.

As you read this story be mindful of your bodily sensations. Take note of the specific section you are reading when you feel an emotional reaction, or your body heating, gurgling, twitching or paining. Stop reading to pause, question and reflect. Your body's cells contain memory and what you are reading is causing a memory to awaken. Your body will attempt to get your attention so your mind can spotlight the content veiled within the words. During that pause truth can emerge. Your body is the barometer of your soul. It's wise to pay it close attention so you can learn understand its many messages.

We have free will to choose how we play our game of life. Our consciousness evolution occurs according to cosmic timing. Astrology defines this cosmic timing system providing clear information on how to work with it. Through detailed application of astrological knowledge to oneself, self-realisations can occur regularly. Higher consciousness and wisdom develops. We are then able to view life from a higher and broader perspective.

***

Chapter Five

Remembrance of Ancient Wisdom

Andean Connection to the Stars

Some modern astronomers have researched the Andean sacred sites and come up with interesting findings. Archaeo-astronomical evidence indicates that the ancient people who built many of the sacred sites had a great deal of knowledge of the stars and built their sites in direct connection to specific constellations. One astronomer, Rolf Muller, concluded that the structures from pre-Inca times stretched over two astrological Ages as the Age of Taurus and Aries, from approximately 7,8000 years ago. Each astrological Age is approximately 2,600 years.

Researcher and scholar, Zecharia Sitchin, links the Sumerian civilisation to one of the pre-Inca civilisations. His research also suggests that the ancient Andean civilisation had knowledge of the twelve-house zodiacal system and that the city of Cusco was built into twelve wards, each one associated with a zodiac house.

Apparently, one relic remains of a golden sun disc, about five and a half inches in diameter, discovered in Cusco, the ancient spiritual capitol of Peru. It is now lodged in the Museum of the American Indian in New York.

There are many stories about solar discs. Some say they were constructed from a special gold not found on Earth that gave them seemingly "magical" qualities. Emanating a high frequency, they enabled those within their presence to raise their consciousness. A copy of one is hanging in a church in Cusco. On one of my inner adventures spiritual guides informed me that I have knowledge of the true solar disc, and of how to activate it, so that the Sirians can come through into 3D again. This is another reason I was once killed on Lake Titicaca. Some of my fellow travellers to the sacred sites of Peru experienced for themselves how derivations of the Sirian solar disc were used as transportation devises into other dimensional realms.

On my first visit to the ancient sacred site of Pisaq, situated in the Sacred Valley of the Peruvian Andes mountains, I found myself at the intihuatana, a specifically carved monument, at exactly twelve noon. At this stone monument, an ancient sundial precisely measuring the solstices and equinoxes, I became physically riveted to the spot, unable to move or think for at least ten minutes. Even though I felt stunned, the cells in my body were highly activated and 'sparking'. My soul was remembering times past when I had lived here. My conscious mind couldn't compute. In what capacity, and at what time was I a resident here? Eventually some of my consciousness returned and, becoming mobile, I hobbled to a nearby low wall and sat down still unable to speak or think. What was going on? The time was obviously a previous life because on previous occasions I'd experienced similar sensations that led to the unveiling of mysteries.

And then I remembered. I was one who knew the stars. The capacity to move the planets and stars in my mind using twelve special stones, not of this earth, was a talent I used. As the resident astrologer/astronomer, I was charged with holding the energies of the cosmos at a certain frequency so the young women attending this special school of light would be able to focus fully on their spiritual ascension training. These young women were the Mamacona, specially selected virgins who carried a great deal of light, visible in their energy field. Their task was to train their body temple to such a high level of light and love they could easily traverse other dimensions. Their work involved building a highway of light to enable the transference of information from the species on earth to the light beings in higher dimensions.

After extracting myself from the sundial memories I decided to walk the rest of the site. Suddenly, feeling weakened again I looked around for a flat rock to sit on. Immediately I did so tears of joyful memory flowed. I was sitting in my former workroom. Reunion. Instant recollections. I needed to sit on that rock for some time to anchor my newfound understanding. In the following five years, no matter the route we took, or what time our group left the hotel, we always arrived at the Pisaq intihuatana at noon. This was cosmic orchestration at its best.

I later learned that the revered and sacred solar disc is one of twelve foundational stones which maintain equilibrium in the geomantic, gravitational and bio-magnetic fields of our planet. These twelve stones are the resonant activators of the etheric, formative shield of the Earth.

So many memories were uncovered on my amazing adventures to the Andean sacred sites and much information unveiled. Research revealed that the ancient trail of Wiraccocha, the Andean deity, is angled at precisely forty-five degrees to the cardinal points, and this angle of orientation determined not only the layout of Machu Picchu but also the location of other major Andean ancient sites. Wiraccocha's trail began at Lake Titicaca and it's there we're heading next. Andean wisdom teaches that Copacabana, a small fishing village on the Bolivian shores of Lake Titicaca, is the birthplace of the seed of consciousness on our planet. The ancient stone monuments and artefacts provide clues to the direction consciousness moved across the planet. Maybe it moved to Australia from the Andes?

***

Lake Titicaca and the Island of the Moon

When I first stepped onto the Island of the Moon on the Bolivian side of Lake Titicaca ancient soul memories flooded my body. Overpowering sobs of joy emerged from deep within me. Instinctively, I fell to the earth and kissed it, feeling an overpowering reconnection to this island. Words emanating from my soul erupted from my mouth, 'I've come home – I've come home'.

Time seemed to stand still. Maybe five minutes passed. With tears streaming down my face and feeling an imperative urge to facilitate a sacred earth honouring ceremony, I gathered the group around me into a circle. Feeling I needed flowers for the ceremony, I asked my tour guide if I could use hers. She had picked them on the mainland. I have no idea what I did or said because I was operating on memory and feeling. I felt such gratitude and love and was bursting with the joy of coming home. The women around me were crying and laughing, feeling my joy.

Following the ceremony, we prepared to dance on the Island of the Moon for the first time. With the sun warming our bodies and a light breeze blowing around us we observed a group of eagles flying over our circle, welcoming us. A double rainbow around the Sun also demonstrated Nature's pleasure.

During the dance I experienced memories of being the high priestess here, in charge of training spiritual initiates. I had administered loving discipline. The willingness to accept personal responsibility for thoughts, emotions and deeds was a pre-requisite for the young women seeking to join the training school. Also, during the dance, revelatory experiences explaining my soul's lineage and the history of ancient light beings emerged into my conscious mind.

There are two mountains beyond the entrance to the Moon Island referred to as the male and female dragon mountains. The 'Dragon Lines' (or ley lines) cross at Lake Titicaca on the Island of the Moon. Both Lord and Lady Meru embody the energies of the Winged Serpent, the Plumed Serpent and the Dragon Energy. Apparently the most advanced beings to have ever inhabited Earth were serpent born white winged giants, referred to as dragons. Mary Magdalen was a Master of the Dragon Wisdom. Aspects of the souls of this lineage have incarnated into human bodies to demonstrate the ascension process. This process is a training about how to consciously transfigure the physical body into a light body without the death process. This transfiguration is the final earthly initiation.

As I understand it, Mary Magdalen's soul is of Lady Meru's lineage, and Jesus is of Lord Meru. In the beginning of their earthly sojourn Lord and Lady Meru came to Earth through the Sirian portal. Both were involved in creating, building and running esoteric mystery schools. Lady Meru created the esoteric mystery school on the Island of the Moon, and Lord Meru did the same on the Island of the Sun. Semi-etheric giants and twin flames, they embody the masculine/feminine balance of divine union. Aspects of their soul only incarnate at the beginning of each new astrological Age. Mary Madgalen and Yeshua incarnated at the beginning of the Age of Pisces.

Archaeologists and shamans, connected to the ancient Andean spirituality, have uncovered evidence that the nearby Island of the Sun was used by male initiates dedicated to their spiritual path and the esoteric mysteries. The men understood the cosmic system and practiced visualisation, bringing the creative force of the Sun into their hearts. This regular spiritual practice was a training procedure to open the human heart chakra enabling the experience of cosmic love. In ancient times, probably Lemurian, many of the spiritual Masters were trained at this temple. I was told that Jesus, in an early incarnation, was one. The nearby Island of the Moon was the female initiate training centre and I believe an aspect of Mary Magdalen's soul trained there.

The young women under the care of Lady Meru were instructed not to mix with the male initiates. Once a month, at the time of the full Moon, male initiates from the Temple of the Sun were invited to the Moon Island to watch the women dance. The dance practiced was similar to that of Paneurythmy. My groups danced there each year until the original vibratory frequency of love and light reactivated.

Andean spirituality is based on the wisdom of the stars. The Chakana, the constellation of the Southern Cross, is their most sacred symbol, as it is for Australia.

According to esotericists, Elizabeth Clare Prophet and Mark L. Prophet, in their book *The Masters and their Retreats*, Lord and Lady Meru are enlightened cosmic beings who embody the Christ energy of love and immense light. Their role is to educate people to the full use of their mind, heart and soul thus advancing Christ consciousness upon Earth. They were responsible for the training of Jesus, Mother Mary, Mary Magdalen and others.

Lord and Lady Meru's education program prepared the way for the golden age. They apparently chose the high Andean mountains of Peru to do their important spiritual work because of the isolation, elevation and pure air. Over astrological Ages of time the consciousness of the formally enlightened people deteriorated. Because of the light of the civilisation which initially lived in this area, karmic law decrees it is where Lord and Lady Meru are to maintain their spiritual focus.

Lake Titicaca, a region relatively unspoiled by human density of thought and emotion, was chosen by the spiritual Masters as a centre of light. Those people, tuned to the finer frequency of divine love, are able to access the higher dimensional light beings residing there. They are taught by the Masters during meditation; through memory recall and during their sleeping state.

More inner and outer research followed my initial visit to the Island of the Moon. I enjoy connecting dots in my mind to make sense of reality. And my reality was becoming really interesting. Where was it leading? I knew astrology played a major part but how did it all fit together?

One book that helped me connect a few jigsaw pieces was *The Return of the Serpents of Wisdom* by Mark Amaru Pinkham. His research shows that the founders of the early civilizations in Egypt, India, China, Peru, Mesopotamia, Britain, and the Americas were colonising spiritual masters associated with the serpent energy. These 'Serpents of Wisdom' oversaw the construction of magnificent civilisations that included mystery schools.

I believe Mary Magdalen was a highly-trained priestess in the lineage of Lady Meru. Lady Meru's name was Amaru Mara and Mara means Mary. Also, Amaru, or

Aramu, means serpent. Mary embodied serpent power, the super conscious power to access, and successfully manage, the subconscious realms of the human mind. This power is attributed to the sacred feminine.

Around the area of the Island of the Moon and the small fishing village of Copacabana, by the shore of the sacred lake, Titicaca in Bolivia, the Magdalen energy can be felt strongly. A wooden statue of a black Madonna is placed in a specially designed small chapel within the local cathedral. Under this cathedral is an ancient temple. Found in the cemetery area a long time ago was a blue crystal, carved into the shape of a woman. In 1580 a local Aymara man received a vision to build a statue of a black Madonna. To the local indigenous Aymara people, Copacabana has a strong feminine energy. I certainly felt it. The black Madonna symbolises an evolved female who willingly traverses the darkest, most dense Pluto realms within her psyche to uncover the truth of existence. She emerges from this experience alchemically transformed. The light content within her spiritual body increases according to the depth of soul truth accessed. The light radiates high frequency energy for all to feel and see. Her consciousness expands enabling the embodiment of higher frequencies of light and divine love.

At a later time, Lord Meru gave me information about the Aramu Muru gateway. He said it was a gateway into higher dimensions of consciousness. Built when humans were not as psychologically dense as now, visitors came to Earth from other star systems to learn and study. They could easily come and go through this, and other, interdimensional gateways. Special harmonic sounds, created through a type of trumpet, assisted their entry into, and out of, the third dimensional world. The gateway was strategically built to guard esoteric knowledge and this knowledge is to be uncovered again. Many places around the site contain consciousness keys and codes. These needed re-connecting so the ancient knowledge and wisdom can be accessed and shared. Continuing, Lord Meru told me that the gateway acts as a library of esoteric information and was built at this specific location on our planet as a conductor of knowledge. Geographically it is the highest and most pure point where higher consciousness frequencies can be disseminated to the entire planet.

A few years later, during an international indigenous peace gathering at a small and remote village in the high mountains of Bolivia, I was invited to speak to a group of approximately 100 women. The men were working on a nearby mountain helping the local villages construct a new church. Fortunately, an English/Spanish speaking indigenous female tour guide offered to interpret for me. National TV cameras and reporters filmed the weekend activities.

When presenting at a spiritual gathering I do not think about what I say. I open my heart and mouth and words pour out. The spoken words of love seemed to enrapture the audience and, as I spoke, a huge condor descended close to the gathering and circled around me, three times. The audience gasped, realising the symbolism of the words. Nature was giving them a sign, speaking to them according to their beliefs. Preparing to walk down from the natural rocky speaking platform I was stopped by the organiser. The audience wanted more. But no more words came. In its place a playful child emerged, wanting to sing. Inspired by the condor I led the non-English speaking group into singing a few rounds of an Australian bush ballad about a bird –

Kookaburra sits on the old gum tree,
Merry, merry king of the bush is he
Laugh Kookaburra, laugh kookaburra
Gay your life must be.

It was hilarious. Everyone was laughing, hugging and joyful. The condor provided an opportunity for female participants to experience unity, love, joy and laughter at a gathering of over 300 global Spanish speaking indigenous elders, representing forty different countries.

***

A Sacred Trinity

The site of Moray in the Andes Mountains of Peru brought up another past life memory. Often, when these occur, I feel nausea in my stomach, as if the psychic substance containing the memory agitates, awakens and begins to spill its content into my body. I feel weak, unable to move or think until the 'upload' is complete. Then my conscious mind intuits truth. This recently excavated site was of two large open-air circular and tiered auditoriums, occupying two separate areas of land. According to the local tour guide the largest excavated site was used as an agricultural meeting place for trade, public meetings and ceremonies. I didn't count the number of terraces because it held little interest even though it was becoming a tourist destination. However, the smaller one attracted me because it felt familiar.

The larger site contained strong masculine energy and the smaller, feminine. Fredy, my tour guide, and I scrambled down into the smaller one's centre. Built as seven tiered terraces that made up a circular amphitheatre it was overgrown with weeds. As we descended I became aware of an energy infusion. This usually comes in through my crown chakra. When we reached the bottom my inner guidance telepathically asked that we walk around the centre altar twice in an anti-clockwise direction and then in a clockwise direction, as I'd been guided to do at other global sacred sites. While doing so I thanked the spirits of the site and Pachamama for the opportunity to reconnect to this ancient sacred place and for being able to conduct a sacred thanksgiving ritual. We then proceeded to climb up and out of the amphitheatre. We didn't get far. A huge psychic wave of nausea/memory engulfed and I needed to sit on the grassy, tiered terrace at the second lowest level. For maybe half an hour I sat there, breathing deeply and slowly. I knew I'd been there before. Fredy had tears in his eyes, feeling deep emotions arise from his unconscious soul memories.

Finally, scrambling to the top and observing the two circular tiered spaces from above, I knew they were originally created as ceremonial sites to symbolically honour the divine masculine and feminine. But something was missing and we needed to find it. There had to be a third, much smaller site, symbolising the union between the divine masculine and feminine and the child birthed from that union. A sacred trinity. Searching, we eventually found it. Small. Hidden. Completely overgrown. Forgotten and unused. Untouched by humans for a long time.

Later, feeling the need to re-visit the ancient temples of the Sun and Moon in a large open field on the hills surrounding Cusco, we did so the following day. These two ancient temples are carved into the existing rocks, as are most of the sacred sites in Peru. On each side, and around the outside of this Moon temple, is a huge carved serpent. The tail is on the outside of the cave and the head inside. Inside the Moon temple is a large flat rock platform, above which is a natural circular hole, an open space. Every Full Moon the luminous soft light shines through this hole and brightens the entire platform. One of my spiritual guides, Sai Baba, asked me to walk inside the cave and offer a blessing. Having performed many spiritual ceremonies in this temple on previous visits I ascended to the platform and stood under the natural light, acting as a conduit between heaven and earth. I blessed and thanked the two sacred serpents who guarded this special area, the ancient ancestors who had built the temple, and Pachamama for the opportunity of walking on her land at this special place. I was then told that an ancient pre-historic 'dragon' guarded this sacred space. With my inner vision I saw its head, and Fredy saw its body.

Visiting the Sun temple through the adjoining passage I was reminded of an experience I'd had when leading a group to another similar spiritual initiation space, in a lava tunnel under the Big Island of Hawaii.

When we re-emerged into the daylight I knew there had to be a third temple, one we hadn't discovered before. And there was. The temple of the child, the progeny of the union between the divine masculine and feminine. A Christ child. Another trinity. The ancient Andeans created temples of worship relative to their spiritual beliefs using specific rock formations and land contours that best suited their purpose. They obviously understood the concept of trinity, as did the ancient Egyptians.

Much was learned and remembered on the annual visits to these high mountains. Every day I was trained by invisible guides. Past-life memories emerged from my subconscious, to be understood, accepted and the knowledge re-claimed. This knowledge involved cosmic design and the different states and stages of consciousness. It connected to, and opened up, unconscious previous life knowledge stored in my memory cells based on Ageless Wisdom. I was gifted with the perfect people to accompany me and the journeys were exciting adventures into unknown territories of my body, mind and soul. My soul rejoiced as it remembered former homes.

Few tourists visited the areas explored when my journeys began so the sacred sites we visited were relatively unpolluted. We were free to dance, meditate and perform ceremonies wherever we felt the need. Not so now.

Our tour guides practiced heart-opening thanksgiving ceremonies at every sacred site visited. Guided ceremonies, re-connecting the ancient lands of Lemuria to Peru and Bolivia, were also regular events. Our esoteric expedition groups also sponsored three different impoverished primary schools, two in Peru and one in Bolivia. One in Peru was so isolated it was without power even though a power pole was relatively close. It's extremely cold in the high Andes in winter. Four thousand metres above sea level snow falls regularly. There are few trees. We were able to get power connected and to supply the staff, and the one hundred and twenty children, with two second hand computers, heaters, pens, note books, necessary study material, toilets, cupboards, mats and desks. Windows, roofing and doors were repaired so the cold couldn't penetrate the classroom. Fredy motivated, organised and supervised the children's parents to carry out the repair work. One of my most precious memories of that Peruvian school is of teaching the one hundred and twenty children to dance the hokey-pokey outside in their large playground. We had so much fun. All the parents and staff were watching, enjoying the children's laughter. In the Bolivian school sponsored, the teacher didn't have a desk, chair, mat or cupboard. My beautiful Bolivian tour guide, Rosse Mary, organised the purchase of these items. We also made sure the children had all the necessary study material they needed and we had repairs done to the building to keep the cold out.

Once upon a time in the land of dreams, time stood still. In this idyllic playground, the beings upon planet earth sang and danced to their heart's content. It truly was a Garden of Eden. Nature was at her most splendid. Much gratitude for her gifts was shared and joy experienced by all. This is the natural state of human existence. Humanity and nature lived in tune with each other. No attempt was made to harness nature, nor to control and dominate. Nature responded in kind.

When the seed of consciousness was planted into the human mind the situation gradually changed. Man found he could use his will to dominate and control. This gave him a sense of power and feelings of superiority. It is not such a great distance from joy to domination. The intoxication of domination took control of the human species and a false joy developed. All humans carry this memory. True joy arises in the heart as a result of appreciation and love of nature. False joy derives from the game of power over another. True joy is life sustaining and life enhancing. False joy becomes an addiction, an unhealthy one. False joy creates time restraints and the feeling of lack. The implanted seed of consciousness was now sprouting. Weeds formed, based on man's desire for domination and power. The playground became polluted. The weeds spread like a cancer to cover the planet.

A return to pure joy is imminent. How this is accomplished is the question. Gaia is unwilling to suffer strangulation and disease. She is taking responsibility for her health. However, she is not a hard taskmaster. Opportunities will be given to humans to see the light and change their ways.

Over time humans adapted to their new seed. Many used it wisely, aware they had been given a precious gift, while others allowed their gift to atrophy. From time to time throughout the course of human evolution, cataclysms and apparent catastrophes took place. Nature always corrects imbalances. She responds to the human energetic emissions upon her. Where there is love, kindness, caring and appreciation of beauty she responds in kind. Love responds with love. What is given is received. To give is to receive. Humans and animals can live in harmony. All life is precious and all life has a function. For humans that function is to grow in conscious awareness, always reaching for the light. Seeds need light to survive. The blockage of light through human psychological pollution prevents the growth of the plant. It cannot survive in this environment. When the cause of the pollution has been identified and appropriate action taken to effect positive change, the growing plant can again reach for the light.

***

Tibet

Following a Heart of Australia tour, specially created so Peruvian Fredy could experience a re-connection to this ancient land, I travelled with a girl friend to Tibet knowing it would also be a journey of remembrance. On a stopover at Bangkok airport I noticed a store selling Tibetan books. The one that attracted me was a book about Tibet's Dali Llamas. Flipping through the pages I experienced huge rushes of heat enter my crown and descend internally through my body into my heart. This often happens when I'm about to awaken a soul memory, an ancient truth. I liken it to a 'pay attention' message.

I read that the thirteenth Dalai Lama was a re-incarnation of the fifth who had passed away aged sixty-nine around 1619 AD. After a protracted era of civil wars establishing diplomatic relations with China and other regional countries, the fifth Dalai Lama unified all of Tibet. Wielding both spiritual and temporal power, he was a prolific writer, exceptional scholar and a practitioner of the high path to liberation. This path involved gnosis and was referred to as the Great Perfection. He wrote an autobiography expressing his deepest feelings and independent interpretations. He also wrote of empowerment and how it liberates because it plants the seeds of self-realisation within the body, speech and mind. The 13th Dalai Lama allowed and embraced other religions, was a scholar, knew Sanskrit well and had to escape from Tibet because of invasion. He knew he was a re-incarnation of the fifth Dalai Lama. He passed away in 1933.

When travelling from Bangkok to Kathmandu in Nepal I reflected on the information, knowing it was somehow important to me. But how? Kathmandu was our place of departure to Tibet and we needed to find a travel agency to make appropriate travel arrangements. Although we had not pre-booked accommodation, we easily found an adequate hotel. First impressions of Kathmandu were that it was over populated, dusty, hot, with not many paved roads and seemingly a great deal of poverty. As in nearby India, hawkers and beggars lined the streets. Finding an excellent travel agency, Tibetan Travels and Tours, we spoke with the Tibetan director. Learning we could not enter Tibet unless we were with a group, he arranged for us to travel with a young couple from Italy on their first overseas trip. They could not speak English. We were to meet them in Lhasa, the capital of Tibet.

A day tour to Naragot, a beautiful and peaceful country paradise, was arranged for the following day. We decided that, should we ever return to Kathmandu, we would stay there. The following day we visited a school for children of Tibetan refugees built in Kathmandu by Lama Venerable Jampa Phuntsok. He had escaped from Tibet at the same time as the current Dalai Lama. The Srongtsen School was created in a small tent and now occupies a large area. The school provides education from kindergarten to high school for over 700 children. My friend Karen and I were escorted around the school and enjoyed visiting the kitchen where a cooked lunch is provided every day to all students. The huge cooking pots were the largest I'd ever seen, and there were many. My senses rejoiced at the delicious aroma of the curry being cooked. The Tibetan children in one kindergarten class sang us a Tibetan welcome song, and it was such a joyous, heart-warming experience. Foreign benefactors provided the funds to build the school and many, including famous film stars, support its maintenance. Lama Venerable Jampa Phuntsok provides a clean, inviting and organised environment for the Tibetan children to learn and grow, and the school is a testament to his dedication.

The plane trip from Kathmandu to Lhasa took about an hour. Quickly ascending to the Himalayan mountain range with Mount Everest in view, I became enraptured by the view of the tiny stream, the Brahmaputra River, originating from Mt Kailash, the most sacred mountain in Tibet. Living close to an Australian beach it seemed strange to see such a vast quantity of white sand either side of the small stream so high up in the mountains.

Lhasa was a pleasant surprise. The Chinese have done a wonderful job of building the modern and clean airport. I must admit I had difficulty with the hole in the floor 'squatting' toilets. I wasn't sure which way to face – the door or the back wall! The new, wide and well-constructed roads from the airport to the city, with very little traffic, were a pleasure to travel on for the hour it took to drive to Lhasa city. I was impressed by the seemingly hundreds of thousands of poplar and weeping willow trees planted on each side the road. New housing estates were also being built along the route. We noticed an impressive new hospital as well as new military buildings and schools.

A large number of irrigated and organised green crops of barley, wheat and sorghum grew each side of the road and a huge golden statue of a yak greeted our arrival into Lhasa. The air was clean and rose gardens were everywhere. The impressive white Potala palace, perched high on a hill overlooking the city, activated soul memories. I'd been there before but when? City streets were wide, clean and organised.

During meditation the next day, the 21 June solstice, my guides asked I prepare for spiritual work at two places. The first, at the highest pass closest to Mt. Everest and the second wherever I happened to be on the upcoming Gemini New Moon. There's always a bigger picture behind my adventures in foreign lands, revealed once I arrive. Having been guided before I left Australia to bring a special stone from one of the sacred sites in Peru and a stone I'd collected at Uluru, the sacred heart of Australia, the purpose for doing so became clear. These three ancient lands needed to be reconnected energetically through ceremony as they once had been physically. Consciousness is stored in the land, in crystals and stone. Ancient artefacts were stored in jars, caves and temples.

The Potala Palace is home to priceless ancient manuscripts stored, under lock and key, in glass cabinets. It also holds many ornate large gold-plated Buddha statues. The ornate tombs of various Dalai Lamas are encrusted with precious and semi-precious gemstones and the influence of Hinduism is apparent. I was interested in the few photos of former Dalai Lamas, and one in particular interested me. A photo of the thirteenth Dalai Lama. It felt familiar.

Years before, I'd accessed and re-experienced part of a previous life where an aspect of my soul had been a male astrologer to a Dalai Lama in Lhasa. During that life I had been asked by the Tibetan leaders to provide the best date to initiate a war. I handed the task over to my apprentice and did not check his mathematical calculations. Because of my irresponsible and arrogant behaviour, I caused the death of thousands who were sent to war at an incorrect astrological time. Tibet lost that war. From the Potala palace of that time I had looked down on hundreds of wooden carts filled with charred dead bodies passing by on the road underneath the palace. Public disgrace followed. This karma was to be corrected in a future life.

Vague memories associated with this former irresponsibility arose in my body when sitting for the calculation examinations I needed to pass in order to attain my astrology diploma. Even though I'd primed myself with flower essences, special crystals and positive affirmations, the unconscious (at that time) fear of making a mistake and experiencing public disgrace was so great my body became paralysed while writing the exam papers. When completed, I was unable to stand and had to be supported out of the examination room. I'd had a fear of making a mistake all my life and this fear only dissipated a short time before my ascension in October 2000. I detail the ascension experience in my book *I Am an Experiment, An Extraordinary Spiritual Adventure*.

When visiting the Potala Palace in June 2006 I stood at that same place and the visual memories were as clear then as they were hundreds of years before. However, this time it was as if I was witnessing someone else's story because I didn't feel emotion. That issue had been consciously healed years before. Love and forgiveness were the tools. The immutable Universal Law of Karma, of cause and effect, is always operative. We create our own karma every minute of the day by our thoughts, emotions and deeds. Shadow karma always has to be addressed and brought into balance through self-realisation and good deeds, often connected by theme to cause. I realised my passion for teaching astrology was connected to the karma created from that time.

During this adventure, I learned that Tara is the mother of all Tibetan deities, committed to always re-incarnating into female form. A beautiful and large bronze statue of Tara, the Tibetan mother goddess, sits near my front door welcoming all who enter my home. My 2001 class of astrology students gave her to me. Tara is one of my spiritual guides mentioned in the *Experiment* book.

From the Potala Palace we visited the Drepung monastery. Situated on a wall behind the many large golden statues, symbolically representing different aspects of the Buddha, is a huge tapestry depicting the many stages of the Tibetan story of human evolution. The Goddess of the Sea is clearly evident, represented as a mermaid. This monastery accommodates four hundred and forty Tibetan Buddhist monks. Before the Chinese invasion seven hundred monks lived and studied here.

The following day we visited the Summer Palace of the Dalai Lama on the outskirts of Lhasa. We were interested to discover a number of smaller palaces built around beautiful gardens complete with trees, lake, swans and a variety of birds. It was quite lovely. We didn't count the buildings but each one represented the summer home of a former Dalai Lama. I spent time in the larger building, the simple summer palace of the current fourteenth Dalai Lama. I noticed, on the wall above the foot of his single bed, a tapestry woven with the Tibetan story of human evolution. Every morning he visited his holiday home the Dalai Lama would wake up to this tapestry. Mesmerised by the human evolution story woven into the tapestry I sat on the end of his former bed completely absorbed in it. The mermaid again caught my eye. A guard came in to the room interrupting my reverie. My private time was over.

One of the highlights of our journey to Tibet was an unplanned visit to a Tibetan hospital connected to a medical educational facility. Here Tibetan students were trained to become medical doctors. Our tour guide needed to deliver a parcel to someone in the building and Karen and I were asked to wait in a classroom while he did so. On the walls of the large classroom were a series of mandalas – paintings displaying astrological themes. Animals were depicted in each of the paintings. As if the experience was pre-planned by invisible guides, a white-coated medical doctor entered the room greeting us warmly in excellent English. Our Tibetan teacher explained that the astrological method he taught was visual and connected to life associations. The colours depicted in the drawings were indicative of the different psychological states of being that caused illness.

He said that, in Tibetan astrology, there are three main underlying causes of illness, each represented by an animal. The white pig symbolises human ignorance that comes from being unconscious of personal psychology. The pig also connects to the white fluids in the human body. In western astrology, the white fluids in the human body are linked to the sign of Cancer and the Moon. The snake, he said, represents the emotions of jealousy, envy, revenge and betrayal (Scorpio). The cock/rooster symbolises the fire behind the desire to fight with hate and aggression (Aries). Tibetan medicine is a mixture of Indian, Chinese and Tibetan beliefs and is based on the travels to those lands around 708AD by a Tibetan medical scholar. This scholar wrote a manual of his findings, a copy of this manuscript scroll is encased in an incredibly long glass cabinet around this teaching room.

The foetus, we were told, when first conceived, is at the fish stage of development, then the turtle stage, and finally the pig stage. At the pig stage the embryo loses memory of previous lives yet is receptive to education in all forms such as music, language, sound, vibrations, feelings and thoughts. These foetal developmental stages are depicted in an astrological mandala. The five energy centres (chakras) used by Tibetans are also depicted in a mandala. Prana (life-force) energy healing forms a major part of the Tibetan healing practices. In one chart, animals were depicted taking pulses. A horse symbolises a strong pulse and probable high blood pressure. Patients who have this are usually angry and aggressive. This behaviour adversely affects the heart and blood circulation.

During this teaching, I realised where I had learned to view astrology as I do, as an incredibly accurate healing tool. It's the tool I've used to be as healthy, fit and as vital as I am. Unconsciously I've applied the Tibetan medical astrological teachings to my mind and body since I re-discovered astrology, age forty-seven. The teachings work.

A group of approximately twenty medical students suddenly burst into the room and I felt I belonged in their company. I learned that the thirteenth Dalai Lama had built this particular teaching hospital early last century, around 1916.

Tibetan medicine has astrology as its main component. It used to take nine years to become a Tibetan medical practitioner. Three years' study of astrology was mandatory. Now it takes only six years to obtain a medical degree and the study embraces western medicine. The students are taught astrology so they can determine the psychological cause of medical problems, and the best time of the year to seek and find special healing herbs. They learn not to conduct surgery under certain astrological configurations. At the time of a person's death, or immediately after, an astrologer/doctor is consulted to determine what can be done to assist that soul's transition to another world. Astrological dates are calculated for all of life's major events.

Karen and I loved the excitement of the long journey in a four-wheel drive car across the Tibetan plateau from Lhasa to Kathmandu. The Italian couple did not. Nor did our tour guide. Because of the many roads under construction, pot-holes, dust and construction blasting, we had to travel on old river beds over rocky uninhabited territory. We crossed many rivers and streams, fortunately not very deep. A huge hydro-electric power station was under construction not far from Lhasa. We encountered so many roadblocks and detours along the way it became the daily normal. Roadblocks in Tibet are not like those in the western world. There they are actual roadblocks in the form of huge impassable piles of dirt and rubble. They appear unexpectedly and without warning.

Our Tibetan guide spoke poor English and the Italian couple could not speak any. Neither the guide, Karen nor I spoke Italian. Communication was difficult although I could intuit much that was said and felt. On some parts of the rock and roll journey our guide sat nervously hunched in the corner of the back seat fingering his 108 Tibetan beads necklace, muttering the Tibetan chant – Om Mana Padma Hum. At every stop, he had to pee. The poor guy was terrified. There were of course no toilets. Karen and I, having been on many adventures to third world countries, use nature to relieve ourselves when necessary. Not so the Italian tourists. Completely out of their comfort zone they held on tightly to their natural bodily functions.

When we arrived at our first stop, Gyantse, we realised tourists didn't come to this remote area. Karen, being blonde, and I were frequently stared at. When we sat on rocks in the courtyard of the Gyantse Pelkor

Chode Monastery, some curious Tibetan women and children came to join us. I liked this authentic monastery, untainted by modern beliefs and desires for grandeur. Three Buddhist philosophical streams, coming from three different lineages, are taught here so students could make up their own minds as to which one, or all, they choose to study. The many statues of Buddha, symbolising different aspects of the one Buddha, were carved in wood, rather than the ornate gold of the Lhasa monasteries. Relaxed and feeling safe, Karen and I had dinner at a small local restaurant and watched a DVD movie with the Tibetan staff. All of us had fun.

The following day we were scheduled to travel to a high pass and, because of even more road blockages, had to take the only available route to our next destination. The obstacles on this part of the journey were far greater than those of the day before. At the smelly and dirty village of Lhatse we encountered a major road block. The only road out wouldn't be opened to traffic until 7.00pm and it was only 10.00am. It was the day of the Gemini New Moon and there was work for Karen and me to do here, later in the afternoon. We decided we needed to get out of this small town for a few hours. I consulted my trusty guidebook and discovered there was a remote and small Tibetan monastery, the Gelugpa Monastery of Lhatse Chode built in 1200AD, about ten kilometres away.

Having the good fortune to be greeted by a young monk, we were given a guided tour. Later, he played the huge Tibetan drum positioned in pride of place near the entrance. In this monastery was a tapestry depicting the same Tibetan human evolution story as the ones I'd previously seen. Karen and I were delighted to be so warmly welcomed. Later, walking through the nearby small village, we attracted hordes of small children. Fortunately, I'd brought from Australia coloured pencils and pens which I happily distributed to the beautiful children. We asked directions to the school and eventually found it. Only two years old, it had been built by the Chinese. At each end of every classroom were large posters of the three Chinese leaders. Lessons were taught in both Tibetan and Chinese, as is the case in all Tibetan schools now. Even though it was Sunday there were heaps of live-in students at the school. Those children, mostly boys, thronged around us.

Unplanned excursions often turn out to be the most memorable, and this one was no exception. Returning to Lhatse later in the day the four of us walked through the town to the river. Karen and I discovered a side road with a few trees and decided to walk along it beside the river. At such a high altitudes trees are scarce so we were fortunate. I had been guided to facilitate a sacred ceremony so I began with Karen and I facing the snow-capped mountains. High on the mountain summit directly above we noticed Tibetan prayer flags. I gave Karen the stone from Peru and I held the Australian one. A small tree symbolised Tibetan energy. We formed a triangle of force, honouring Mother Earth, Great Spirit, the four directions, the four elements and the mountains. Intent on reconnecting these ancient lands through the triangular force field, we felt the powerful energy gather mass and travel via the triangle to the aligned countries at the time of the New Moon. We followed this with a stone planting ceremony using my silver cake slice as a digging tool. Many years previously I had been asked by my spiritual guides to 'plant' specific crystals or stones into geometric formations at many of the sacred sites I visited. I do this with reverence and love, knowing that the energy generated by intent, loving feelings and thought travels to wherever and whatever we focus upon. When we completed our ceremony a group of small children joined us. They accompanied us for most of our return walk. With still over an hour to go before the road would open, Karen and I braved eating in a Chinese restaurant, recommended by my guidebook. It was surprisingly good.

At a New Moon the sky is dark. We were to travel on an unmade road through unknown, unmarked remote territory to reach our destination – the tiny village of Old Tingri – close to Mt Everest base camp.

We had thought the trip to Gyantse the day before was hair-raising. It was nothing compared to this adventure. Pitch black, with only the car headlights to guide us, we drove through seemingly uninhabitable territory, rocky countryside, creek beds and the unmade road. Our driver couldn't see the many road blockages until we were close to them. We travelled more off the road than on the road. Our Italian friends wondered where the streetlights were. Nature answered, providing the most incredible light and sound show. Lightning flashes, deep and loud rumbles of thunder and torrential rain accompanied us for hours. It was a challenge to our driver's capabilities and he passed nature's test with flying colours.

It was close to midnight when we arrived at Old Tingare and shown our basic cabin lodging. Karen and I piled into our warm beds, following a nature visit to relieve ourselves under a poplar tree. We had discovered there weren't any showers or toilets, at least not ones we could use. Being so close to Mt Everest base camp it was extremely cold.

The toilet theme continued the next day. On waking to brilliant sunshine, I realised there were only four poplar trees on the entire property, all of them growing in a row close to the wooden veranda posts in front of the cabins. Warmly clothed, I was relieving myself underneath one of the trees when I heard the sound of doors slamming followed by heavy footsteps. I looked up to the veranda a metre above and saw two handsome and tall young male British mountain climbers preparing to begin their climb. Whoops! Hastily hitching up my pyjama pants we exchanged greetings.

After Karen awoke we searched the area for a depression, rock or anywhere where we couldn't be seen while we attended to more serious ablutions. We noticed a slight depression containing heaps of garbage a little distance from the cabins and decided this had to do. Totally engaged in our business, we suddenly heard a machine start up. The rumbling noise became closer. We looked up. A huge yellow machine operated by a male driver was preparing to dig into, or cover, the rubbish. The driver probably got as much a surprise as we did. Another hasty retreat!

One of my impressions of this tiny outpost was of a well-used flat and shiny metal disk in front of the small lodge with a black kettle of boiling water on it. The early morning sun's rays heated the metal disk sufficiently for the water to boil. Eggs could also be cooked on it.

At the high pass close to Mt Everest, 5220 metres above sea level, I performed a sacred ceremony, acknowledging Prime Creator for the magnificent beauty of creation, the power and majesty of this huge mountain, and willingly released fears, limitations and control patterns. No longer would I allow them to overtake my life.

We drove on to visit Milarepa's cave. A famous Buddhist, living in the twelfth century, he attained enlightenment by sitting in this cave meditating for three years, and eating only nettles. Situated above a beautiful green valley with Chinese guards, armed with machine guns guarding its entrance, we felt his peace upon entering his small home. Guards were also ensuring that the Tibetan workers, mostly women, who were reconstructing the exterior of the cave with huge boulders, kept up their back-breaking work. The workers had to carry the boulders on their backs for some distance. There was no evidence of machinery. Obvious in the valley below were other Chinese guards, also wielding machine guns. We learned that Tibetans who tried to escape Tibet through this area were shot on the spot.

The Tibetan people are the world's most peaceful and have much to teach westerners. I so enjoyed our encounters with them. No matter their deprivation, the Tibetans we met were happy. Most sang together as they worked. In one construction building somewhere along our adventurous route we noticed a team of Tibetan workers, mostly women, on a roof. Each had a long hand-made broom type of device and were pressing it into the roofing material, singing chants as they worked in unison. Accepting their lot in life they utilise their skills and always seemed to enjoy the menial work allocated.

I noticed the incredible physical likeness of the Tibetan people to the Andean Quechua people. They obviously come from the same root race.

***

A Journey of Remembrance

January 1, 2010: on a Full Moon and Lunar Eclipse in Cancer, I arrived in Israel. Two thousand years ago it was my home. On my return I am to walk this land and remember. Warmly welcomed on arrival at my lodging and invited to join the Jewish family's celebration of the Shabbat, I did so. Now a stranger from another land, the land of the Rainbow Serpent, I realised my lodging was near where I used to live. The Sea of Galilee is close by. I am here to not only remember but also to re-experience soul memories. I will feel these in my body.

After sleeping deeply, I was woken in the early hours of the morning, sensing a memory stirring. In the vision, I walk with my girlfriend to the home of a nearby sound master. While my friend is engaged in animated conversation I see, in the darkened corner of another room, an old man lying, dying on his bed. I go to him and kneel beside his bed. He speaks in a weakened voice: 'I have waited and waited for you to come home my beloved daughter. Now I can pass in peace. You must tell your story. Sing your song. It is time'.

In the land where the divine masculine and feminine were once united in sacred marriage in the bodies and souls of Mary Magdalen and Yeshua, the archetypal father requested his beloved daughter to speak.

Before this adventure we made only two accommodation reservations. The first, close to the Sea of Galilee and the other, at the end of our journey, in Glastonbury, England. The mission given to me was to retrace the steps taken by Mary Magdalen on her escape journey from the Holy Land, after Jesus' crucifixion and resurrection into his light-body. With only my body's sensitivity to guide me, and faith in my *Magdalen Codes* of memory, I completely trusted the pathway would be shown. I would feel and intuit each step of the journey. The only anchor I had was my 1996 experience where Mary seemed to take over my body and I felt I was her, walking along on the sand around the Sea of Galilee, preparing for an important meeting with Yeshua.

Karen, my traveling companion, friend and driver, trusted my guidance. I had hired a car and asked her to drive around the Sea of Galilee so I could tune in to my body's remembrance. My heart responded to land resonance at a certain area and, to ensure what I felt was real, I asked Karen to drive around the lake twice more. Each time, at the exact same place my heart responded with remembrance. This was where the important meeting with Yeshua had taken place. I now had an anchoring point. As we were walking along the sand in this area, we felt incredible peace and lightness of spirit. My heart felt joyful and relaxation was easy. Intuition kicked in and I knew where we were to travel next – Qumran, on the Dead Sea, where many ancient sacred documents had once been stored. This was where the Dead Sea Scrolls had been discovered in 1948. The former home of an Essene gnostic group known to the holy family, it was a peaceful sanctuary where Mary and Yeshua had received support, nourishment and companionship.

A kibbutz close to Qumran was our home for a couple of nights, while I awaited guidance. Qumran is now a tourist site, but it was where Mary had gone to seek support and refuge on her escape from Israel. The Qumran Essenes provided her with a camel, food and water for her trek across the desert. It had been too risky to travel via the coast so she chose the difficult overland route. As I tuned in, I felt in my body that Mary was with child and needed to ride on a camel for support. From Qumran, she journeyed to Egypt. Having been trained as a Priestess of Isis in the temples along the Nile, she wanted to say farewell to her connections there, knowing she could never return.

Karen and I had to get to Egypt. But how? It was January, and winter. There were no boats, not even fishing boats, for hire. We would have to fly. We investigated and were advised that, because of the enmity between Israel and Egypt, no airline would take us from Israel to Egypt. I knew we would find a way but needed to drive to Jerusalem to find it. While walking along a Jerusalem side street, not far from the city centre, Karen spied an American Express travel agency upstairs in a building. We decided to follow this lead. Success. The senior sales lady spoke English extremely well. She told us that she often visits an area close to where I live in Australia and makes all the booking for the Australian military of that area. She organised not only our flight to Cairo but also a tour of the temples along the Nile, and our flight to France afterwards. Had we not booked this flight to France we would not have been able to travel into Egypt.

Four days and nights we travelled along the Nile, visiting places of remembrance. In ancient Egyptian times the temples along the Nile were used as spiritual initiation chambers. The Komombo temple had an underground chamber filled with crocodiles and this initiation involved diving into the pitch-black and dark water-filled cavern and negotiating the way out to a different exit. The purpose for its existence was to assist initiates overcome fear. Memories from another incarnation arose into my conscious mind at this temple. I knew that animals feel or sense human emotions and act accordingly. I had learned to ride a crocodile on its back, holding on to its neck tightly as it did a death- roll three times. Having trained myself to breathe deeply and hold my breath for a long time, and overcome all fear, the practice didn't take long and was relatively easy. I also knew the crocodiles had been well fed.

The Nile temples that had the greatest meaning, and where I experienced the strongest resonant body waves were those of Abydos and Dendera. Some of the temples were where initiates of the sacred esoteric mysteries were trained.

Before entering the Abydos temple, I felt nausea in my stomach, a sure sign that something connected to a past life was emerging. It was a cautionary reminder to be fully 'tuned in" to my body. In the central area of the large temple is a group of smaller temples. These temples used to be an inner sanctum for highly trained spiritual initiates. Walking into the larger room of the inner sanctum, that of Osiris the Egyptian god, my stomach began churning even more. I suddenly became weakened as unconscious memories surfaced. My lower body pained. When moving into the Isis temple the nausea intensified and the pain around my sacral chakra intensified. In the third small temple, the temple of Horus, the divine child birthed from the union of Osiris and Isis, I collapsed. Karen was concerned but I knew I'd be all right as soon as I realised truth.

I knew Mary Magdalen had birthed her child here and had been given refuge by her Egyptian spiritual family and friends until she and the baby were well enough to travel. Following her recovery, Joseph of Arimathea organised a small fishing boat to take her to the South of France where she lived and taught for many years. My body recovered immediately after this realisation.

Covering the entire ceiling of a small upstairs room in the nearby Dendera temple is a copy of an Egyptian zodiac. The original is so priceless the complete ceiling was cut out and taken to the Louvre in Paris.

In this temple spiritual initiates were taught an astrology system dating back to Atlantean times. Mary Magdalen had advanced knowledge of the stars, and of the cosmic system underpinning Egyptian astrology. She would have been trained in this temple. She entered my consciousness when I began studying evolutionary astrology and has guided me ever since. I purchased a papyrus copy of the ceiling model and have worked on interpreting it. Karen and I, the only people in the tiny upper room, lay on the floor attempting to see and understand the amazing depiction above. It wasn't easily decipherable. Many questions entered our minds that couldn't be answered, so we moved on.

There were other temples to explore along the Nile as we made our way back to Cairo. In some temples vague memories stirred, but none with as much impact as those of Dendera and Abydos. However, another memory emerged when visiting a room in the Cairo museum. It was the room set aside for the artefacts connected to Pharaoh Akhenaten. As soon as I walked into the room I felt the refined energy. I knew without a doubt that this man was of the Christ consciousness and the Law of One. His wonderful paintings depicted the beauty of nature, and his unusual sculptures demonstrated the unity between the masculine and feminine within the human body. I knew he was connected in soul essence to Jesus. Much later I learned that Jesus was an incarnation of Akhenaten.

While resting in our hotel room on the night before our early morning flight to Paris, we suddenly realised we would need accommodation in the south of France for the next few nights. What to do? The only connection I had was a brochure, placed into my backpack by a friend the day before I left Australia. It was a small promotional brochure for a shop in the Rennes Le Chateaux in the Languedoc area of France. I phoned the proprietor. Being mid-winter, her business was temporarily closed and she was unavailable to accommodate us but she referred me to her friend. I rang the friend. She just happened to have a Gite (small cottage) on her property for rent. Eager for us to stay, she and her husband picked us up from the train station the next day. It was about an hour's drive from her property. She was the local expert on Mary Magdalen and knew all the sites where she had lived and taught. Most of them were off the tourist trail. Synchronicity, or cosmic design? Our hosts owned a small tour company and acted as tour guide and driver for the five wonderful days we were there.

A joyful reunion with the land followed. The many ruins of Essene dwellings we visited brought up more memories. I recognised an ancient astronomical observatory strategically placed on the top of a nearby small mountain and I wanted to climb it. However, time was not on my side. I also recognised ancient carved monuments similar to those in the Peruvian high Andes. I felt sure the symbolic themes were the same, as was the design. These ancient carved stone monuments indicated a connection between the people of the two lands. While inspecting one ancient sacred site, in a local farmer's sheep paddock, I realised there was a triangular pattern connecting some of the other sites visited. Intuitively

I knew there was something incredibly sacred within the centre of this invisible triangle. I could feel the Magdalen's presence in some of the well-known sites visited, even though many tourists now visit the area.

Our new friends organised our comfortable train trip to England. Reluctantly we left the area. There was so much more exploration we could do but Glastonbury called. Extremely cold and damp, mid-winter in England was a shock. But Glastonbury was where we needed to be. Again, our adventures were guided by invisible forces and, even though nothing had been planned, much was experienced. We were taken to Avebury and other ancient sacred sites seemingly by accident.

There was only one time during the entire adventure we experienced a challenge. And that was in Israel, when driving from Qumran to Jerusalem. We had been given a map by the car hire company that didn't differentiate between Israel and Palestine. Israel is a beautiful country but small by Australian standards. We drove on a road that, on the map, appeared be the closest route to Jerusalem from Qumran. It wasn't the main highway. Whoops! Not a good move. Without realising it we had entered Palestinian territory. Huge barbed wire enclosures surrounded us. Men with machine guns directed their weapons at our car. Karen hastily did a U-turn. We decided the longer highway route to Jerusalem would be the best way. We learned later we were lucky to have escaped.

***

PART TWO

The Weavings Reveal

A Cosmic System through which Consciousness Evolves

Chapter Six

Astrology and Higher Consciousness

Multi-Dimensional Consciousness

In Part One I wrote of my adventures to foreign lands. I also wrote of how my subconscious mind was activated into remembering previous lives spent in the areas visited. Part Two concerns my adventures into higher dimensional realms of consciousness. In one of these higher dimensions I was taught a cosmic system that further advances human consciousness development beyond that of our solar system astrology.

Years ago, during a time of meditative stillness, Tibetan Master Djwhal Khul, (D.K.) telepathically asked me to write a book about a new astrology system for the Aquarian Age. Replying, I said I would gladly do so but was unable to write it academically. For many years I've attempted to read *Esoteric Astrology*, a book transmitted by him to Alice A. Bailey, and it's only now I'm beginning to understand the depth of its wisdom and truth. I said that if I couldn't understand it how could many others? We agreed to co-operate. Saying he would come to me again when it was time to write, I allowed the idea to gestate.

He was the one who asked me to write this book about the three levels of consciousness, because the new astrology system is based on consciousness. The system, as I experienced it, follows.

***

According to astro-physicists in their DVD documentary *Origins* – all atoms of our universe are forged by stars. We are all stars, with iron in our blood. We exist in an interstellar soup and each generation of stars enriches the broth. New stars are continually forming in our Milky Way galaxy and all elements needed for life exist throughout the cosmos.

From an esoteric perspective, there's a universal system of energy, of consciousness, continually permeating all of life and matter. The Creator of this system is known by many names. Source energy is consciousness and is within every atom and cell of our bodies. When Source awakened from a state of bliss a question arose 'Who Am I when not in this state of bliss?'

In the beginning was sound. According to ancient tradition, that sound was AUM or OM. Within sound resides tremendous power because it opens doors to other realities, especially when the sound comes from our heart, through feelings of divine love. When seeking to become clear about something it is beneficial to chant sacred names, feeling into the essence of the names chanted, until the mind becomes calm. In that calm and still place the answer comes.

And, there was light. Light is Source consciousness that permeates all of creation. Many indigenous races worship the great light of the Sun as the Prime Creator. Some other races regard Source as feminine. The Goddess allows all things. She is the energy that holds things together. She invites you to open your hearts to feel her warmth and love coursing through your veins. She asks you to awaken from your deep sleep to feel her creative and loving energy coursing through your minds and bodies.

Source is androgynous; unified masculine and feminine energies. These two unified aspects are energy without form. The masculine energy holds the foci for radiating light, supporting the feminine to create as she pleases. The Elohim creator gods were birthed as a result of the union between the divine masculine and feminine. The Elohim created the Seven Colour Rays of Light that permeate all of creation. These Rays evolve consciousness by receiving and transmitting Source's infinite light and love.

The Great Bear constellation, Sirius and the Pleiades receive these light frequencies and, through a triangle of force, radiate them to our zodiac and solar system. These Colour Rays finally reach earth and her inhabitants. They activate human consciousness through the seven chakras, the main energy centres of the etheric human body. The Elohim also created an energetic system of galaxies and the kingdom of souls. All creation has one purpose. To answer Source's question.

Source essence, which is pure love, permeates all of creation. Great Spirit desired to experience all that could be. When each evolving soul integrates full consciousness through self-awareness a return home ticket becomes available. Each soul has the free-will choice to create its own experience. Every species is unique and contributes to the system. A descent into matter occurred through a step-by-step gradual process. The steps into, and out of consciousness evolution are slow, and not one step can be missed.

For human beings, the purpose of the Divine Plan is to experience, and successfully navigate, many consciousness dimensions, and to disseminate the knowledge learned to other souls. This enables species evolution.

Following immersion into 3D consciousness most souls forget their purpose for being. Now souls are becoming restless as the time for human remembrance is at hand. A return to finer frequencies of light is imminent. The current personality aspects of these souls cannot understand why this is so and acts up, rebelling against the unconscious chains of ignorance that bind them.

The consciousness system is designed to break through third dimensional (3D) barriers. The 'break-through' process begins to take place when a soul is deemed ready. This is ascertained by the level of light embodied by each soul. But who is the 'watcher' of each soul's light levels? The one who deems that soul to be ready?

Each personality has a higher aspect of itself. This Higher Self, is more highly evolved than the personality, or lower self. This higher aspect operates and exists in a finer dimension to that of 3D and acts somewhat like an invisible and wise personal guide or a guardian angel. Learn to trust that it knows what you need, can see a far broader view than your limited 3D perspective, and will guide you to the best way of attaining your potential. Receptivity, trust, faith, and relaxation of the mind are needed to communicate with the soul. This is feminine energy. Impatience, control and force do not work. The process of soul activation works through cosmic time cycles, not man-made time.

Many human souls are in the process of breaking through their 3D illusionary walls. How long it takes is up to each individual. The process requires the willingness to identify, and alchemise, personal psychological density into the light of higher consciousness. Love is the key. It's by identifying clearly, and loving to death, the shadows, that alchemy occurs. Matter is trapped light. The personality needs to surrender its little agendas to enable manifestation of the soul's desire. Easy to say, but not to do! Knowing the Great Plan enables the emergence of the details required to work with it. Understanding the design accelerates the process. The details come into human consciousness through 'Ah-Ha' moments of self-realisation.

Think of a jigsaw puzzle. When we see the cover design of a jigsaw puzzle we have a better understanding of where each piece fits in. We use the whole picture as a guide. My frustration was in not having a cover picture – hence my passion to uncover the system.

My expanded understanding came from my many multi-dimensional experiences into higher realms of light. Being trained by celestial and star light beings in the ascension process increased my body's ability to retain greater light. As each dimensional level of consciousness was mastered I was trained to master the next. I had many more jigsaw pieces, but still did not have a cover picture.

Astrology, used as an accurate psychological tool to uncover aeons of life-times of darkness, was the main tool I used. This tool was deliberately sourced from higher dimensions aeons ago to aid human consciousness development. Used in this way it is a passage out of 3D density. By developing the spiritual will, determination and courage to investigate our shadows, evident in our birth charts, and willingly doing whatever it takes to extract ourselves from it, we raise our frequency.

Imagine it's a dark night and you enter an old unlit house. You open the door of this house and feel around the wall for a light switch. It's not where you think it should be. You feel around some more. Ah-ha! There it is. Press it and on comes the light. You can now see the contents of that room. It's the same process when seeking the light of truth in our subconscious. The important key word is 'feel'.

Consciousness can be likened to electricity. When plugged into a power source, electricity runs through a cord activating a device. Whether the device is a light bulb, computer, or a vacuum cleaner, electricity is what is needed to start-up and fuel the device. In the human body, when plugged into Source, consciousness runs through the synapses of the brain, the meridians and blood vessels of the body activating the body and mind into self-realisation. When we perceive a disconnection from Source we are unconscious, acting as robots, programmed by others to think, act and do as they, religion or society dictates.

One of the most important keys in developing higher consciousness is to create sufficient self-love to allow loving feelings to guide our life journey. Self-love means to love our divine Source essence, resident in every cell of our body. When 'plugged in' to it through acknowledgement, this energy begins to 'spark'. We can tune in to these electrical impulses that become activated when truth is thought or spoken, and act positively upon them. Some people feel truth as goose bumps, or waves of heart-felt warmth and love coursing through their bodies. Being receptive to, and allowing, our loving feminine nature to guide our life through feelings, provides our masculine with the purpose and drive to accomplish tasks.

The consciousness system is fool proof. Willingly confronting our smaller selves and committing to be the best we can be, assists us to move up the dimensional levels. Each level brings its own challenges per favour of the transiting planets and their connections to natal placements in our birth charts. When we are conscious of the content of the challenges we can move through them, with greater clarity and understanding.

Our birth chart also shows the gifts and talents learned in previous lives that can be used to consciously progress our evolutionary growth. Planetary transits and progressions to natal charts enable the astro-alchemical process. When we learn to constructively use the cyclic timing of planetary energies to advance our awakening greater sensitivity opens up other brain centres, enabling access to more highly refined energies. Then the zodiacal energies open us to the refined cosmic frequencies beyond our solar system. We can choose to drink of this light and life-giving nectar, or not. My experiences of these refined cosmic frequencies follow.

***

The Law of One – the Law of Love

I have memories of countless lifetimes, many spent traversing the different dimensions of space through cyclical spirals of time. The memories arise in my body as feelings and sensations. Inner tuition guides me, and I feel truth emerging. During the emergence, my conscious mind switches off and, when understanding integrates, re-engages to make sense of the new reality. I transfer the memories into conscious knowledge through my seemingly elastic right brain.

The timing of consciousness evolution is determined by a system of cosmic energy. In spiritual terms the process can be likened to the in-breath from Source calling her family back to divine union.

According to esoteric psychology, every soul who was part of the second Atlantean epoch with lessons still to learn, is now incarnate on Earth. We're here to master and embody the light of Christ consciousness, known as the Law of One. This third and final Atlantean epoch can then heal its predecessors by releasing this portion of humanity from the limitation of duality. Jesus incarnated to be the great Teacher of Love and to re-establish the Law of One, the Law of Love.

Ultimate responsibility lies with each one of us to take charge of ourselves, to respect each other, and to fulfil our designated role as custodians of the earth. It's important to be grateful for all our blessings and to give to life, rather than take from it.

Consciousness, the essence of Source, is pure unconditional love. Like the Sun, it shines on every living thing, pouring its love-based radiation into the fabric of the universe. In some scientific minds the God particle is the one that completes their understanding of the Universe. Love does make the world go around. It is from divine love we were birthed and it is to this pure love essence we return. The level of light and divine love we embody during each lifetime determines our 3D experiences.

Should your soul desire a return home to Source during this incarnation your personality self will feel it. The journey requires the willingness to confront, and to love to death, the shadows that bind us in 3D chains. It's important to keep our heart's open. I focus on the freedom I will feel when the transformational process is over.

As we begin working through the details involved in the inner process we begin raising our vibration. The mind then expands to enable more light. The journey involves learning to love ourselves as a precious part of divine creation; to love our body for its amazingly intricate design and function, and to love our brain for the increasing clarity that comes from doing the inner work. Our body is the temple that houses our soul and is a barometer for our level of love and light. When we raise our frequencies of love and light to higher levels, everyone in our sphere of influence benefits.

I often reflect on the story of Jesus when he went through this internal alchemising process. He spent forty days and forty nights in the desert working with his inner demons. It is a process each initiate, dedicated to the path of light and love, needs to go through. I wish you well on your journey.

***

Esoteric Astrology

From a spiritual evolutionary perspective, our Solar System was designed as an energetic system to propel humans into higher consciousness, increased light and spiritualised love. Predetermined by the soul before incarnation, the timing of the consciousness growth process is influenced by each individual's willingness to advance spiritually in any one lifetime. The planets act as sub-stations for the power and force of the Sun, each one providing its individual characteristics and qualities. The Sun provides life force energy. Just as each human is a storehouse of differing energetic patterns so too is each planet and star.

Each human, planet, star, constellation and the vastness of space itself are conscious beings. Each one has its own role to play in the evolution of human consciousness. Every being receives, stores and transmits energies, the frequency of which depends upon the amount of light carried and emitted. Beings vibrate according to that level of light. Where the light is great, the frequency is fine and the radiance bright. Where there is psychological shadow, the frequency is slow and the radiation dull. Each being can be likened to a cell in the body of the Prime Creator, whose energetic influence pervades and guides all conscious life. Source's energetic system is infinite, and forever evolving. As electro-magnetic humans, we live in an energy ocean of consciousness. When we realise this, life changes.

Humanity can also be likened to a cell in the body of Source with each human an atom in that cell. The grandeur of the Great Plan is vast and precisely orchestrated. A system of energy, it is an ancient spiritual science.

Each solar system has a central hub, a brilliant Sun containing huge energetic force and radiation. Our solar system is one of the solar systems orbiting around Alcyone, the central star of the Pleiades. The Pleiadians are light beings operating in 5D consciousness. Their system orbits around Sirius, a 6D consciousness. Each level of consciousness is like a frequency wave. The frequency wave of 5D is based on universal love. The frequency wave of Sirius is universal love taken to another level by combining it with sacred geometry. I explain my experiences in these dimensional levels in my book *I Am an Experiment, an Extraordinary Spiritual Adventure.*

During a meditation at the end of August 2005 I was taken by Helios and Vesta, the two great beings of Light who hold the foci for our Sun, into and through the heart of our Sun to view an alignment of two other Suns. The three Suns, Alcyone, Sirius and our Sun were not quite in perfect alignment. This remote viewing visit was repeated during the following ten years.

Geology confirms that around twelve thousand years ago, great cataclysms took place upon our precious planet. From a spiritual evolutionary perspective, the catastrophe was due in the main part to the misuse of human will caused by power abuse. Human shadow energy of self-aggrandisement, manipulation, abuse of scientific technology and greed eventually consumed those in power on the continent of Atlantis. As a consequence, it sank into the Atlantic Ocean. Gaia was in shock, as were all living creatures upon her. Our conscious 'lights' went out. A dense energetic shadow permeated our planet as we humans descended into the ignorance of unconscious robotic thought and behaviour. The story of the Great

Flood, told in so many cultures through legend and sacred text, depicts this time.

Many of us have cellular memories of these times. The energy package containing these memories can be accessed and the shadow emotions released. This requires individual choice and dedication to the light. The releasing process enables mass human consciousness evolution. People dedicated to the light emit a specific radiation and vibrate accordingly. Their energy naturally activates a spark of consciousness in others, who have the choice to develop the same light.

Our body consists of space, atoms and trillions of cells, and is a miniscule version of the universe. Around our body is an energy field. Our field connects to others like a giant spider web. Whatever occurs in the cosmos occurs within each one of us. We can learn to feel the cosmic movements within our bodies and minds if we take the time to stop, observe, and 'smell the roses'. We can also learn to feel nature's elements of fire, earth, air and water operating in our bodies and minds. When we become conscious of these internal energies we can learn to master them. Astrology is a wonderful tool to objectively decode emotions and feelings. Psychological issues arise under transits and progressions to the birth chart. When we consciously work with our birth charts to resolve the issues symbolised by the planets and the zodiacal signs, we pass through initiatory processes and accelerate our evolutionary growth.

Thousands of years ago, masculine energy dominated the Age of Leo, and Atlantis was destroyed. Human values (Taurus) had become distorted and the misuse of technology (Aquarius) and abuse of power (Scorpio) created the downfall.

When we learn to feel, and manage, the cosmic energy currents coursing through our body and mind we are able to attain a state of wholeness and equilibrium as a constant. This is what the Age of Aquarius – the Age of Light – is about. Aquarius is the opposing sign to Leo. During the transformation process, usually experienced through a Pluto/Scorpio metamorphoses, our lower self can symbolically die. The higher aspect of our being, our soul, then governs. The Scorpion finally stops self-destructing and the inner eagle, the second sign of the Scorpio growth process, takes flight.

At this stage of consciousness development, the growth challenges occurring through Saturn, Chiron, Neptune and Pluto have been mastered and the individual allows Uranus and Jupiter to carry them forward and upward on the evolutionary spiral. These two planetary influences further the journey until access to fifth-dimensional consciousness, based on divine love, becomes the individual's constant. It is at this point in human evolution that higher vibrational cosmic bodies ignite dormant light codes.

Through personal interaction with these cosmic bodies, along with penetrating inner research, this work was created. What I write may or may not be deemed correct. It is for you to ascertain truth. If this teaching brings a feeling response and a flash of intuition then accept the teaching for its value and use. If not, let it go.

When a dedicated truth seeker reaches a certain vibratory level of consciousness as a result of internal depth-digging and alchemy, their light radiance can be tuned into by invisible supportive teachers from higher dimensional realms. Like a radio station the teachers - often the spiritual Masters - tune into specific frequency waves. As individuals and as a collective, we humans emit electromagnetic pulses carrying certain coded information. Celestial and stellar light beings offer expansion of consciousness gifts to accelerate the seeker's journey way beyond solar system consciousness. Galactic, or Christ, consciousness is real. It is where humanity is heading.

Consciousness training is ongoing and takes the form of psychological lessons. One that emerged was for me to stop taking responsibility for other people's burdens because, by doing so, I took away their power. Realising I must have played this control game in previous lifetimes, I felt a tremendous hot wash of shame consume my body. I chose to immediately stop.

***

Chiron, A Centaur and Cosmic Guide

Chiron rocked into human consciousness in November 1977. This is when astronomers first discovered its presence in our solar system. In mythology, Chiron chose to give up his immortality to help humans heal their soul wounds by becoming conscious of them. Soul wounds emerge from our subconscious mind into every-day consciousness as feelings and emotions. We feel emotions and we feel body sensations. Our shadow feelings seek recognition and healing. Permeating our subconscious, psychological wounds cause reactive, weakening and disempowering behaviour.

Mythical centaur Chiron was wounded on his left side, the feminine side. He activates us into remembrance of truth through transits to our natal planets or points. Chiron, a master teacher and guide for the spiritual seeker activates our soul's desire to discover the holy grail of higher consciousness. I was given a teaching by Chiron who said he is the key to open closed doors in our subconscious so we can access the cause of our soul's psychological wounds. As we heal our wounds Chiron assists the fusion of our body and mind with spirit and soul.

I liken each placement in our natal chart to an acupuncture point in our bodies. Each point contains a memory package of valuable information. When a transiting planet triggers a birth-chart point, the coded information stored within the cells of activated humans becomes energised. Sparks of memory awaken. The stimulated energetic points release motivations, feelings and behavioural patterns. We unconsciously re-enact old dramas, leaking energy packages that magnetically attract like energy. A previous life psychological game perpetuates, until we become conscious of it. Only then can we change it. We have the choice to learn to understand why we play games that no longer serve our evolutionary conscious development or remain sleeping and continue suffering. Chiron's transits to a natal planet or point in a birth chart provide a symbolic key to open closed doors in our psyche, enabling us to 'wake up' and become aware of self-destructive shadow games, and their origins.

***

Uranus the Illuminator

Uranus brings us to the light of higher consciousness through the many 'Ah-ha" epiphany moments we experience. At these times, especially when we experience shock, it can be as if his flash of light acts like a lightning bolt, shattering the false mirrors of mental shadows and smashing them into tiny fragments. Our mind, emotions and body can take days to recover. We can never be the same again after we realise, and accept as truth, our perpetuating psychological games. Often, we feel a wash of shame or guilt after these 'Ah-Ha' moments. Uranus showed me how, when enlightened consciousness occurs, shattered crystalline patterns of human psychology reform into diamond shapes. A living light sphere, complete with diamond awareness patterns, is a model for advanced human consciousness.

One of my given tasks is to shatter myths. Reflect for a moment on the story of King Arthur, Camelot and the Round Table. When living above a beautiful lake surrounded by a two-hundred-and-seventy-degree view of mountains, plus a thirty-degree view to the ocean, I became aware that, had the site been in the mountains of Peru, it would have been described as a feminine sacred site. A lake symbolises the womb of the Great Mother. A thirty-degree outlet to the sea symbolises her birth canal. While reflecting on this understanding, my attention became focused on the deepest part of the lake. Through my occasional external psychic vision, I saw a large hand emerge above the water, holding aloft King Arthur's Excalibur sword. The Lady of the Lake offered me the sword saying I had earned the right to use it. And, that the information connected to it is lodged in my heart.

I didn't understand the significance of this information at the time. However, at a later date I was told that, when it was the time to write about this experience I'm to imagine the Excalibur sword point entering my crown and moving between my pineal and pituitary glands, descending through my throat and lodging in my heart. The tip of the sword needs to connect to my heart to open the records. The cross bar of the sword is to rest on my crown. The spirit being connected to the sword is a guide, a revealer of truth and wisdom. I did the suggested process before I began writing this book.

There are at least nine dimensions of consciousness currently available to those striving to ascend into higher frequencies of divine light and love. There are many levels to each dimension rather than cut off points. The dimensions are like radio waves. We move in and out of dimensional levels according to our level of consciousness. Our conscious level is based on everyday thoughts and the level of love vibration we embody. These levels can differ day by day until a consistency is maintained. This consistency requires integrating Saturn's teachings.

***

Saturn, the Lord of Karma and Time

Saturn, the Lord of Karma and Time, also rules the structure of consciousness, and mastery of the mind. His energy can be likened to a wise, and often stern teacher, or father figure, who encourages us to take responsibility for our creations and become our own authority. The process involves learning to identify and heal shadow thoughts and emotions especially those based on fear. Fear, and the rigidity of thought attached to the fear that often involves a need to control, plays havoc with our bones and teeth. We can become paralysed with fear, unable to act responsibly on our own behalf. Fear blocks trust and acts as a concrete wall we need to break down before we can move forward in our lives. It's wise to befriend Saturn. He has our best interests at heart. He knows we can attain the potential depicted in our birth chart. Playing small and irresponsible only attracts stronger tests.

There is also a psychic wall that confuses the mind, blocking access to higher dimensional consciousness. It is the psychological content of this psychic wall that creates mental health problems.

***

Neptune's Psychic Wall

According to North American Indian teachings, when we point a finger at someone three fingers point back at us. And, whoever we judge or criticise to be wrong, stronger, weaker, inexperienced or inept, is but a reflection of what we criticise, and judge about self. Developing compassion for the paths others have trodden is part of watery Neptune's teaching. A lack of compassion results in an unforgiving coldness that eats into the heart. A person who cannot forgive self or others cannot grow. When spiritual growth, analogous to the evolution of consciousness, is stultified an inner critical "parent" archetype emerges in our psychology and our body demonstrates this coldness.

Beating oneself up, or blaming others for our struggles, has no value and is an exceedingly low vibration. It can lead to addictions and victim consciousness. Yes, we do create our reality by our thoughts but when we say this comment to another as a cold, hard criticism or judgement, the dense energy behind it eats into our heart, eventually causing disease. Our body is the final repository of our thoughts and is the barometer of our soul.

How healthy is your body? Polluted thoughts create a smoky haze, a grey smoke screen around our aura that some can see, sense or feel. When combined with other humans on the same level of 3D consciousness the 'smoke' gathers mass, circling around our planet. This is humanity's psychic wall that contains the shadows and density of the collective consciousness. This contamination can make sensitive people ill. It is real, although invisible to most. I know it well. It is the main pollutant on this planet.

Neptune is Lord of the Seas and rules our internal ocean of emotion. When our emotions are suppressed and contained, as if in a pea soup reservoir, we are unaware and unconscious of the specific emotions we feel. To become self-aware we need to observe, without judgement, our reactive behaviour and to seek the thought and emotion behind it. Until conscious of our thoughts, we view our world through a dirty lens.

One of the best healing gifts a warm-hearted group of people can give to our planet and to humanity, is to generate the frequency of divine love and light within the group and direct the loving energy to the dense smoke screen lurking around earth. Then, with intent and dedicated purpose, use the generated love energy to pierce through the dark barriers. Many years ago, one of my spiritual guides, Sai Baba, asked me regularly facilitate this practice with my groups. If other group leaders will also do the same much good will be experienced.

On a personal level, this psychic smoke is the barrier each of us needs to individually move through to enable consistent access to higher dimensional levels of experience. When we live our life from a genuinely compassionate, internally clean and pure loving consciousness we infect others who want a bit of what we've got.

Through Neptune transits to our natal chart we have opportunities to leave the smoke behind and clear our mind of the floating psychological debris that contaminates our body. Let self-doubt, confusion and victim status go. Shatter any smoky mirrors that insist on self-importance. Our shadow has immense value because it's the only thing that brings us to the light. Through heart-felt compassion and gratitude for the gift contained within the shadow, decide to love it to death. Detailed self-observation and correction is needed to move through the cloudy mental veils of illusion, self-sabotage, self-doubt, confusion and addictions.

All of creation can only be viewed when we learn to see through the fog of physical illusion into the true nature of reality. Worlds upon worlds can be discovered. Whatever is above us is also within. Every particle, atom and cell in our bodies contains everything we've ever learned over countless lifetimes on Earth. When we identify and heal, through compassionate love and forgiveness our karmic lessons, all cells in our bodies experience the energy release and rejoice. Our vibratory level rises dramatically and our health improves.

Every time the mental haze of illusion and confusion clears, a bright new understanding appears on our mental horizon. We are what we decide to be so why not decide to be the best you can be? Decide to part the mental veils that cloud truth. Decide to quit playing false roles and being fearful of your potential. Choose to be the best you can be and dedicate yourself to this goal.

From the clarity of mind that comes from doing the inner work we begin to move into the higher, and more subtle realms of Neptune's territory, the 4D higher astral plane. Neptune is a gateway to union with Source. Ghosts from the past begin to reveal themselves when we develop mindfulness - present time self-awareness. When we tune in to our body and mind each day, from an observer perspective, we learn to pay attention to finer details, and to be discerning. Concentration and focus are needed for detailed distinctions to become obvious. Through this process we move through and beyond our self-created psychological blocks by easily recognising our illusions and glamorous fantasies. We can now laugh at them.

Through left-brain analytical self-examination and right-brain creative visualisations and meditations, many self-realisations can take place. These lead to enlightened perspectives whereby we can view personal density from a higher perspective.

***

Pluto, the Transformer

Around the time Pluto was discovered in 1930, scientists found a way to split the atom. The consequences of this discovery were clearly demonstrated in World War Two. This momentous external event is analogous to the human ability to split the atoms of personal density contained within cellular memory. This nuclear process releases accumulated density from thousands of years of spiritual amnesia. Also, around that time, experiments began into human genetics.

Pluto's role in the great evolutionary plan is to assist individuals become conscious of, and alchemise, soul density from previous astrological Ages. Hidden within the deep recesses of our subconscious mind lies a treasure chest containing truth and wisdom. This is the realm of the divine feminine serpent. Our Soul's incarnational intent and evolutionary purpose hides in Pluto's realm. In 2007, when transiting Pluto at twenty-seven degrees Sagittarius conjuncted the Galactic Centre, the opportunity was made available for a huge leap forward in human consciousness expansion the effect of which will last for at least two hundred years.

When the soul's incarnational intent and purpose is understood and embodied, the higher Self can consciously work with the Soul's guidance to attain it. Life becomes an effortless harmonious flow. The quick manifestation of thoughts and ideas happens the more we consciously, with ever increasing self-awareness, work in partnership with our Soul's evolutionary purpose for incarnation.

The answers to our personal mysteries reside in our subconscious, in Pluto's realm. Until clarity emerges our power is limited. After accurately decoding the content of this realm, the next step is to take appropriate positive forward action by instantly quitting repetitive dramas and stories. Many people are afraid to take this step even though freedom is the result. The third step is to consciously create a light filled future based on divine love.

***

Chapter Seven

A New Player in the Light Game

Sedna

When a new cosmic body in our solar system, Sedna, was discovered in 2003 I received another clear inner directive. It was loud and clear. *Pay attention. Sedna provides a key to humanity's future.*

New Zealand, the land of the long white cloud, is the landscape for the next part of the story. The long white cloud symbolises Neptune. A few days before Sedna's discovery I was presenting a Chiron workshop in a retreat centre on the shores of Lake Taupo. Following the presentation, I felt the impulse to walk up the hill towards a small building. A large, burly and balding military man stopped me, gave me a huge bear hug and burst into tears after saying that my words on Chiron had triggered the healing of a psychological wound he'd carried all his life. He thanked me profusely.

A few minutes later, in the meditation temple on the hill above the workshop building, I facilitated the birth of a star baby. Is this a Neptune fantasy? No, it was real to the woman giving birth. She was in pain, experiencing intense contractions. It was real to me, the midwife. Even though

I hadn't heard of Sedna's discovery I intuitively knew what was happening. She didn't. Nor did the two other women trying to assist her. I was the first to hold that etheric star baby in my arms. I don't fully understand this etheric birthing process but I have experienced it myself and have acted as mid-wife to others who have also experienced it. I also wrote about it in my *I Am Experiment* book. Such a 'birth' must take place in another consciousness dimension for it to make sense. The 'baby' is an energy baby, not a physical one even though the symptoms of giving birth are the same as if the baby was physical.

Sedna is the name of that baby. I can't ignore her. I even have her in my bedroom in the form of an ancient quartz crystal shaped like a dolphin's head. Inside that rare crystal is a drop of water, three million years old. The dolphin's head provides a clue to much that follows.

Incidentally, the natural shape of Lake Taupo's surrounding mountain is that of a pregnant woman, breasts and all. Synchronicity?

***

The Mermaid

I enjoy fairy stories because there's often an element of truth in them. The story of *The Little Mermaid* illustrates part of the human evolutionary journey. A metaphysical and astrological perspective of the story follows.

Once upon a time merpeople swam happily in the Neptune waters. They especially loved playing with the dolphins and whales, chatting about times past and their memories of life on Sirius. Occasionally, when sitting on the rocks, basking in the sunlight, they had interaction with the humans attracted to their beautiful singing. One mermaid fell in love with a human prince whom she saved from death after his ship struck a rock and sank.

She yearned to be with him for the rest of her life so she visited a witch who offered to make her a horrible brew. Should she drink the brew her fish tail would turn into human legs. However, in payment, she would have to give the witch her voice.

There was no doubt in the little mermaid's mind because her love for the human was so great. She acted on the witch's advice and left her peaceful underwater realm to embrace the 3D material realm. She sacrificed part of herself to become a human. She sacrificed her voice, the voice of the feminine.

Sacrifice is a Piscean theme. The Age of Pisces, with its many themes and issues including those of sacrifice, victim-hood, martyrdom, confusion, deception and illusion needs to be left behind. We no longer have to die physically on a cross of our own creation to be re-born into our light body. The symbol for watery Pisces is that of two fish bound together, symbolising the captivity of the soul in form. However, in ancient Lemuria, the symbol for

Pisces was a Mermaid. It was only in late Atlantean times, when duality arose in humanity's consciousness, that the feminine part of the symbol was dropped.

The fairy story of *The Little Mermaid* veils the truth of the Sirian mermaids' interaction with earthlings. By mating with the star gods, humans were seeded with consciousness and, through the process, developed mental abilities. This information is a major key to understanding human evolutionary development.

The Age of Pisces was an Age of illusion, subterfuge, cover-ups, suffering, worshipping of male deities and a veiling of the Light. Yeshua and Mary, as two great avatars, incarnated in the early Piscean Age to sow the seeds of union and equality between the masculine and feminine, and to activate greater Light upon the planet.

For two thousand years, the truth of their story remained hidden, mostly through the activities of the male authorities advising the Church of Rome. However, the truth cannot remain hidden forever. The seeds of Light (consciousness) that were sown by Yeshua and his beloved counterpart, Mary Magdalen, can be accessed by those ready to receive them.

It is time for the mermaid with her Codes of Light to return. I introduce you to Sedna, The Sea Goddess.

***

Sedna, Our Connection to Multi-dimensionality

An intuitive empath, I sense and feel psychic nuances. This is my feminine. I allow her to guide and inspire my masculine into constructive action. Huge learning experiences, often through suffering, combined with the bliss of divine union, were part of my journey. For twenty-eight years, a Saturn cycle, I needed to live away from cities to bring these internal forces into balance. Through necessity I developed workable spiritual practices. Neptune in Virgo. The birth chart always confirms.

On November 14th 2003, 06.32 UT, Sedna, a red and very bright cosmic body beyond Pluto, was sighted by three astronomers, Mike Brown, Drs Chad Trujillo and David Rabinowitz at Caltech, near San Diego in California. Within a few days this cosmic body was observed from telescopes in Chile, Spain and Arizona. It was sighted in the constellation of Cetus, The Whale. The discovery was not made public until March 15th 2004.

Sedna has a 10,500-year highly elliptical orbit around the Sun and loops out as far as 135 billion kilometres. More than 12 billion kilometres from Earth its size is estimated to be about halfway between that of Pluto and Quaoar, the dwarf planet discovered by the same team in 2002.

Until Sedna was discovered Quaoar was the largest known body beyond Pluto. From Sedna's icy surface, our Sun would appear so small that the head of a pin could block it out. It is well beyond the Kuiper belt, a region of ice and rock just beyond Neptune. Mike Brown and his colleagues believe Sedna is the first known member of the long-hypothesized Oort cloud, a sphere of material orbiting the sun. Initially catalogued as 2003 VB12 the International Astronomical Union eventually approved its name.

Sedna will become closer and brighter over the next 72 years before it turns around to return to the far reaches of our solar system again. It moves only 36 degrees every 1000 years. The last time Sedna was this close to us was when Earth was coming out of the last ice age. According to astronomer Mike Brown, Sedna is totally unlike anything currently discovered in our solar system. It is 'an unknown' and therefore difficult to identify accurately. It apparently does not meet the current definition of a planet.

There are many theories discussed by astronomers as to its origin. According to Brown, Sedna is one of the most pristine objects in the solar system and 'Very little has happened to this object since the beginning of the solar system. Sedna sits all by itself in the very outer reaches of the solar system.'

So, what does this astronomical information mean astrologically? What does it mean to those dedicated to the path of higher consciousness and ascension? How will it affect human mass consciousness and why was this strange cosmic body named Sedna?

***

Sedna, Goddess of Synthesis

Goddess: *The female face, aspect, nature and/or essence of God.*

Sedna is the name of an Inuit goddess who in appearance was similar to a mermaid. She was the daughter of the Creator God, Anguta and his wife, Nerrivik. There are many versions of her earthly exploits before she became the Goddess of the Sea. All tales agree she descended into the depths of the ocean after experiencing deceit and abuse from men. This was brought about by her egocentric wilful and rebellious lower nature. There is a father/daughter theme throughout the different versions.

One version has Sedna rejecting her many male suitors, to her father's chagrin, and choosing instead to marry a large sea bird. Her new husband took her to the bird tribes' home whereupon she was forced to live life in submission and servitude. She called upon her father to save her from her rebellious decision and he did – however the bird tribe followed them, attempting to forcibly retrieve Sedna. To save his daughter from their clutches her father took her to the ocean and rowed her in a boat to deep water. The birds persisted their abusive attempts so Sedna's father pushed her out of the boat. She clung to the sides, holding on tightly with her hands, but her father cut off her fingers. Not once, but three times, at each finger joint. These fingers transformed into sea mammals.

Strong willed Sedna had to surrender to her fate. Descending to the ocean depths, symbolic for the deeper realms of the subconscious, she experienced a transformation. Re-born, she became a revered Goddess of the Sea, the Fish Goddess of ancient Lemurian times. Considered a vital deity, she is worshipped by hunters who depend on her goodwill to supply food. Sedna is connected to all sea creatures, especially seals, whales and dolphins, i.e. the sea mammals.

Possessing superhuman strength and endurance, she can manipulate water in considerable volumes, and command the creatures of the sea, including the large sea dragon. She has a siren call for enthralling mortal men and gods and a fierce dog guards the entrance to her home. Only a shaman can approach her. She is self-sufficient and self-contained.

There is a Gnostic myth with close ties to Sedna, that of the fallen Sophia. Sophia, a favoured daughter, left her celestial home, the house of her benevolent father, to wilfully pursue her own desires, falling deeper and deeper into a life of underworld activities. She became trapped in this world of darkness and eventually called out to her celestial father to rescue her. He did, and she returned to her true spiritual self. This is the story of the redemption of the soul.

Mary Magdalen embodied the Christ Sophia wisdom. Yeshua descended from Divine reality to redeem and restore Sophia, the divine wisdom of the feminine, to its rightful place.

Sedna's discovery was made by a group of three astronomers, a team. Does this sound like an Aquarian effort and somewhat reminiscent, symbolically, of an earlier discovery by 'three wise men' at the beginning of The Age of Pisces?

Sedna will become closer and brighter over the next seventy-two years before it turns around to again sojourn to the far reaches of our solar system again. The last time Sedna was this close was when Earth was coming out of the last ice age.

The last Ice Age and the associated cataclysms are relevant to our story. Our ice mountains are melting now. Our seas are warming. A large cosmic cycle is in process. Before the destruction of Atlantis humans had advanced to a high level of consciousness and technical intellectual brilliance. They understood crystal technology and used their minds to create great scientific advances. However, they ignored their spirituality and natural feminine wisdom. The result of their thought forms is being experienced in our world today. Sedna's discovery and approach activates these memories.

From Sedna's surface the Sun would appear to be the size of a pin. Therefore, any light on Sedna would have to be generated from within. This state of being only comes about when a human has sufficiently evolved in consciousness from a dense form into a being of light, able to generate and radiate light from within. This is the evolutionary purpose of every human being. How long this process takes is the choice of every soul, and their soul group.

Sedna is totally unlike anything ever discovered within our solar system.

It is 'an unknown' and incredibly 'pristine'.

Sedna sits by itself in the outer reaches of our solar system.

These three aspects of Sedna's discovery are unlike anything we have ever known. However, from the broader perspective we are entering another cycle of cosmic timing. All living things are governed by cosmic energy and Sedna is coming closer to Earth. Her energy is clear and *'pristine'*.

In other words, untarnished by negativity of mental and emotional constructs. She traverses the outer regions of the solar system alone, adrift in the soup of creation, maintaining her own inner light through self-sufficiency, self-containment, superhuman strength and endurance.

These are Taurean qualities we humans need in order to traverse the 'soup' of our personal darkness. Through it we habitually create pain and limitation by being unconscious of our psychological games.

This myth is important astrologically as it gives insight into the esoteric reasons for the discovery of Sedna at this current time in human evolution. According to esoteric astrology, a new planet or cosmic body is discovered when humanity's mass consciousness reaches a certain level of spiritual evolution whereby higher consciousness can be accessed. The new cosmic body offers an opportunity to accelerate the journey to a higher and more refined frequency of light. For example, when Pluto was discovered in 1930 the Great Depression created many financial problems. Waves of blackness and fear swept across collective minds and Hitler, Mussolini and Stalin walked the Earth. Scientists began creating nuclear and chemical warfare. Pluto rules the underworld of the human psyche, the dark forces, evolution and the most intense levels of emotions. It also rules the power games people play to obtain personal, financial or political gain. Often these power games are unconscious.

Since Pluto's discovery, our personal psychological 'underworld' began emerging from our subconscious mind. What was the evolutionary purpose? To become conscious of our personal darkness so we can alchemise it through divine love. Divine love is the energy of the infinite, unified consciousness of the Divine Mind, the intelligence behind all of creation. Divine love is the highest frequency of light and heals all. Pluto's discovery was an evolutionary process that acted as the catalyst for each one of us to delve deeply into our subconscious to extract our treasure of truth. We all have these dense forces within us. How many of us are aware of them?

There were other new cosmic bodies discovered in our solar system during last century and Chiron was one of them. Eris another. Since Chiron's discovery huge advances in natural and spiritual healing practices have been made. Chiron was considered one of the greatest astrologers in ancient mythology and his sighting in 1977 heralded the return of this ancient science.

Early in the 21st century Sedna was discovered and named after an Inuit goddess of the sea.

She was the daughter of the Creator God and Goddess.

Sedna is therefore an important archetypal force emerging within the collective consciousness. We have all played male and female roles in previous incarnations and Sedna is showing us we are all 'daughters' of the Creator God/Goddess. We carry the feminine goddess energy regardless of our current life gender.

She descended into the depths of the ocean after experiencing deceit and abuse from men. The ocean is symbolic for the waters of consciousness. Unconscious and suppressed human emotions energetically 'freeze', become ice and develop discordant geometric shapes. When Sedna reached a low enough state of desperation she called upon her father to save her, and he did. Is this not indicative of what happens when we reach that dense psychological state of being and call upon 'Our Father" to rescue us from our self-sabotaging life experiences?

Sedna's father pushed her out of the boat. This may seem unjustly hard however Sedna's father had her best interests at heart. He knew he could not save her from the attacking 'birds', those negative thoughts that we allow to constantly bombard our mind. To allow her to be taken by them again would only cause her greater suffering and despair, so he did the best thing he could and released her to her fate.

She clung to the sides, holding on tightly but her father cut off her fingers. Sedna did not appreciate her father's gift and tried to cling to the boat, her old life. Her father knew what was best for her, and, as she had asked him for help he did the best he could. He released her from her former life so she could experience a higher dimensional state of being. Strong willed Sedna had to surrender to her fate.

At a high level on the initiation path to Christ consciousness we need to surrender our personality will to the will of our soul. Sedna eventually surrendered, 'drowned' as a human, and re-emerged into a new light body, that of a mermaid.

She can manipulate water in considerable volumes and command the creatures of the sea, particularly the large sea dragon. This is a metaphor for individuals who have developed a high level of conscious self-awareness and have reached 'witness' objectivity. At this level of consciousness, the ability to alchemise 'the waters' of our emotions arises, through observing and identifying subconscious themes and issues. From this state of being, we 'command the creatures of our seas', and in particular, our inner 'dragon', resident within our subconscious emotional depths. Water is a conductor of consciousness and is a feminine element.

She also has a siren call for enthralling mortal men and gods.

A 'siren call' is a special sound vibration that resonates and magnetically attracts. Venus, the exoteric planetary ruler of Taurus, rules the throat chakra where sound is expressed through our vocal chords with either resonance or dissonance. When we speak from a place of inner harmony and balance our voice takes on a particular resonant sound that carries high vibrations of love. This energy is transmitted to the receiver. Mercury rules the words and language we speak however Venus rules the quality of sound resonance. When we speak from this place of heart resonance we enthral men and gods.

A fierce dog to guard the entrance to her abode and only a shaman can approach her. The 'fierce dog' is of the star system of Sirius, often referred to as the Dog Star. Anubis is the name given to the guarding dog. It is on Sirius that many of our ascended Masters trained, including Jesus. The mermaids came from Sirius, as did the mammals of the sea, i.e. whales and dolphins. They carry sound frequencies of higher consciousness. These beings came to guide Sedna after she released her 3D suffering.

Only a 'shaman' can approach her abode.

A shaman is an individual who chooses to traverse the inner regions of darkness, experiences a death of the lower self, heals from the discord and attains wisdom. A shaman has contact with spirits from other dimensions. Attaining this shamanic level of consciousness requires the release of our personality will and our surrender to Divine Will. When integrated, a higher vibrational energy of love enters 'our abode', our energy field. A state of Grace is experienced. We experience a 5th dimensional state of being whereby emotional charge has been realised and released, and we lovingly accept others for where they are at in their evolutionary process. We compassionately assist where possible however, we will not, for any reason, lower our personal love vibration by immersing ourselves in their density.

Our brains are designed so that mystical, spiritual or cosmic experiences can be fairly common. We can train our brain to be more responsive to these experiences by consciously clearing our shadows. And by regularly meditating, eating natural and healthy foods, living in calm, peaceful and natural surroundings, engaging in regular exercise, feeding our minds positive thoughts and consciously generating the uplifting and energising emotions of love, compassion, appreciation and gratitude.

Sedna, the ancient Lemurian Fish Goddess, is being re-claimed in our psyche. She is our solar system's link to multi-dimensional, galactic consciousness. A goddess, she is associated with the nurturing, caring and mothering of the sea mammals so a Cancer theme connects to her. She is also connected to the fertility of the sea, so there is a link between Sedna and Ceres, the Asteroid Goddess of fertility.

I selected the birth chart of 13 November, 2003: 10.32 pm, San Diego, California, (UT of 6.32 AM, 14 November). Apparently, this is when and where the team met and first photographed Sedna at Caltech near San Diego. This chart is interesting and fits well with the myth and the story as it places the Moon conjunct Ceres in Cancer in 12th house. The nurturing Goddess of the Sea is adrift in the 12th house Neptune realms.

Astronomically, her position is in the southern sky constellation of Cetus. Her discovery position was 17 degrees Taurus 52 minutes. You'll find an ephemeris for Sedna on the internet, and I suggest you place her position in your birth charts so you can develop your personal understanding of her influence, using the themes mentioned above. You might ask yourself the following question. "Am I ready to surrender my personality will to the greater Will of the Divine or do I still hold on to my old ways that keep me immersed in the density of 3D life?" Your answer will decide your future.

The Sabian Symbol for Sedna's discovery is revealing (18 degrees Taurus).

A woman airing her old bag through the open window of her room.

Keynote: The cleansing of ego-consciousness.

This image symbolically represents the human feminine energy being cleared of 'old baggage'. It is now open and receptive to re-filling, or re-fuelling through the air, or etheric spiritual realms. Purification is now available, as the ego has released attachments to the mental and emotional 'possessions' of the past.

The universe dislikes a vacuum. The collective feminine 'bag' can be now filled with more valuable possessions –i.e. higher consciousness and broader perceptions. This symbol reflects my inner research, as we will see.

Sedna was discovered in the constellation of Cetus, the Whale.

Once upon a time, way back in ancient biblical history, a man called Jonah was asked by God to travel to the great city of Ninevah to cry out against the wickedness of the people. But Jonah, fearful of the consequences of his task, fled from the presence of God and found a ship to take him across the seas. After sailing for some time, a great wind arose upon the sea with huge waves bashing against the ship. The ship was about to break into pieces. Many material possessions were thrown overboard to lighten the load. While this was taking place Jonah, below deck, was sleeping. The captain came to him, shook him awake and told him to call upon his God for help. When Jonah went up on deck the crew cast lots to establish who was the cause of the turmoil on the waters. Jonah was the one selected. He was questioned. Upon admitting his truth, he offered to sacrifice himself to the ocean. As soon as Jonah was thrown overboard the seas calmed down. A great whale swallowed Jonah and he stayed in its belly for three days and three nights – the timing of the crucifixion and resurrection process. Then Jonah prayed to God with thanksgiving for his safety and sincerely asked to be delivered from his fate, vowing he would, in future, always act upon God's will. The Lord spoke to the whale and it vomited Jonah onto dry land. Then Jonah heard once again the word of God saying, for the second time, 'Arise, go to Ninevah, that great city, and proclaim to it the message that I give you. Let them know they must stop their wickedness and turn away from their evil ways'. Jonah acted on the Will of God and saved the city from its approaching demise.

According to D.K. in his book *Esoteric Astrology*, transmitted through Alice A. Bailey, the story of Jonah and the whale is a parable concerned with the Piscean level of consciousness, the awakening of the Christ consciousness and the subsequent dispute it entails. Jonah stands for the hidden imprisoned Christ, alive to the perils of the situation. The huge whale stands for the bondage of incarnation and the personality.

In our story Cetus is the whale, representing the bondage of incarnation and the personality. Both Sedna and Jonah were sacrificed into the deep waters of the ocean, representing the unconscious. Both freed themselves from that bondage, transmuting their former identity by surrendering to Divine Will. The whale played an important role in the holding and containing Jonah's Christ Consciousness until it was time for release. Sedna's discovery in the constellation of Cetus indicates that time is now.

Sedna lies far from the galactic plane so many distant galaxies are visible from her vantage point, unobscured by the dust of the Milky Way.

These words indicate the opportunity is now provided to access galactic or Christ consciousness unobscured by 'dust'.

Mesopotamia identified Cetus with the cosmic dragon, Tiamat. The dragon is a derivation of the serpent and serpent culture is prevalent in most ancient esoteric teachings. The Serpent was known as a Goddess who was birthed from the union of the Creator God/Goddess. As such the dragon/ serpent became the creative force behind the building of the Universe and was the vehicle for Divine Mind.

D.K. says that the dragon/serpent energy was responsible for the influx of mind energy into our solar system. And, it was triple karma which brought in the 'Serpents or Dragons of Wisdom' in Lemurian days. This had to do with planetary kundalini or serpent fire. As I experienced it, the dragon is masculine and the serpent feminine streams of consciousness. This etheric energy dances as one in the cosmos and its life force circulates within Earth's energy grid. After this serpent life force reaches the Earth it enters 'dragon's lairs' or vortex points and circumnavigates the planet through a network of subtle channels. These are referred to as dragon or ley lines. Ancient sacred sites were built over these dragon's lairs to receive and transmit dragon/

serpent energy. Pyramids were/are efficient generators of this serpent life force.

After all this, perhaps it is no surprise that Mary Magdalen should enter the story as a Master of Dragon/Serpent wisdom and a high initiate trained in the Temple of Isis. The star Sirius, symbolic of the goddess Isis, is where many spiritual Masters have been and are still trained. Mary Magdalen used her powerful abilities and serpent wisdom to activate her husband Yeshua in his quest for ascension into his light body. It was through her loving feminine dragon/serpent wisdom and power that the masculine aspect of Christ Consciousness re-seeded on our planet 2000 years ago.

Mary Magdalen carried the codes of the feminine aspect of Christ Consciousness through her lineage from the stars. She was of the lineage of the Dragon/Serpents.

Much of western astrology is based on the mythology from ancient Greece and Rome. However, times are changing. Our human evolutionary story can also be found in the indigenous legends. The myth of Sedna came from the Inuit so it is fitting to incorporate an indigenous understanding of Whale into our story. At this point it is also interesting to remember the Hermetic axiom – *As Above so it is Below. That which has been will return again. As in Heaven, so on earth.*

According to Jamie Sams and David Carson in their *Medicine Cards* the whale was considered to be the Record Keeper, a swimming library who carries the history of Mother Earth within her. The ancients from the Dog Star, Sirius, introduced the whale into our sky and our seas.

Biologists say the whale, a mammal, possibly lived on the land millions of years ago. The native medicine people say that Earth's children will have to unite and honour all ways and all races in order to survive.

This American Indian story fits well with the mythology of Sedna, whose 'siren call' enthralled mortal men and gods. Many people with Sedna in a prominent position in their charts carry this 'whale medicine'. They, as record keepers, carry the codes of the dragon/serpent energy stream I refer to as *The Magdalen Codes*. They know that special sounds bring up soul memories and ancient knowledge of Earth's records.

***

Sedna, Goddess of Synthesis

In meditation I invoked Sedna, as I am used to doing with the other planets, having worked with them in this way for many years. This process bypasses the logical mind allowing access to the intuitive mind. Through this process I learned to decode, understand and resolve many deep psychological issues and ancient cellular density. This powerful process can be done by anyone and I highly recommend it.

In order for the process to be successful a letting go of control of the logical mind is required. One needs to be in a meditative state of inner calm, openness, receptivity, mindfulness and trust.

Sedna appeared to me as a beautiful, seemingly fragile mermaid, with many geometric shapes visible within her transparent light blue form. Radiating, she looked like a diamond under bright light with all facets sparkling. She showed me her connection to astrology and I pass this on for you to embrace, or otherwise.

Sedna's main function is to take us beyond the realms of Pluto into other galaxies and higher dimensions of time/space reality. Pluto cloaks his light. Sedna reveals her light in all its feminine, vulnerable, seemingly fragile but strong magnificence. She is the crystalline connection to other galaxies through the "womb of the mother".

Another of her functions is to assist humans achieve a state of purification, total trust, relaxation, surrender and stillness while fulfilling an active role in our daily life. She brings synthesis to our Neptune and Venus issues after we embrace, own and alchemise, through love, our shadows.

Pluto's process is the willingness to confront the disempowering contents of our subconscious and to alchemise it by acknowledging truth and loving it for its wondrous teaching.

The Neptune process is the dissolution of the ego from a personality-based consciousness to a soul infused, unconditionally loving consciousness. It requires the dissolving of illusion, suffering, martyrdom and victimhood to bring about a state of internal divine union and grace.

The Venus process is about developing self-worth, self-value, self-love and self-respect and to bring the internal feminine into balance with the masculine through trust, receptivity, peace, love of beauty, resonance and harmony.

As a new, enlightened consciousness arises within individuals who have done their inner spiritual work Sedna provides the opportunity to journey into even higher consciousness dimensions. She operates in a different dimension of time and space and introduces us to multi-dimensionality. This is our ability to live our lives on a higher frequency of consciousness, allowing unconditional love and higher mind guidance to rule. Sedna was discovered before transiting Pluto reached the potent galactic centre of our Milky Way galaxy. This centre is the 'womb of the mother' through which our solar system birthed.

Sedna has a crystalline form. A crystal contains codes of information. Within Sedna's clear crystalline form are many codes of light and much information of other galaxies. She assists us to dive into our akashic (soul) records to read our crystalline patterning. She helps bring clarity to our galactic star roots. Her crystalline form contains sound and music, the music of the spheres and the galactic overtones of synthesis. When we clear much of our density our blood changes and becomes light filled. The light develops geometric shapes. These crystals contain our codes and the information we have gathered along our soul's journey. Medical intuitives, with the psychic ability to view inside the body, can see the geometric shapes in our blood but may not understand their significance.

Sedna's glyph is the vertical symbol of infinity – an elongated figure of eight – symbolising limitlessness, timelessness, and oneness with Spirit.

Sedna took me into her deep waters and into, and through, the 'womb of the mother' during another meditation. It felt like I was swimming in embryonic fluid. I birthed into no-thing-ness. Absolute stillness. No movement. No sound. No activity. No feeling. Totally boring! I realized this was how Source must have felt when awakening from her no-thing-ness experience. She chose to create individual sparks of consciousness in order to know herself. Sedna asked if I preferred this state of being, or activity. I said I definitely preferred activity.

She said another of her functions is to assist people achieve a sense of grace and stillness while being active.

At another time Sedna was sitting on a rock and asked me to swim to her. Doing so I basked in her seemingly phosphorescent light. It was warm and 'other worldly'. We sat calmly together and she told me she offers *food for the Soul*. Her fish tail symbolises Pisces/Neptune and her beauty Venus. She is a synthesis of Neptune and Venus – the Goddess of Synthesis.

Sedna, the Sea Goddess, is the cosmic body discovered as humanity reached a sufficient level of evolution to embrace a higher dimension of consciousness.

Co-ruling Libra and Pisces she is a synthesis of Neptune and Venus operating on a higher octave of consciousness.

She was discovered in the zodiacal sign of Taurus and the constellation of Cetus.

Her stone is a diamond.

She is the crystalline connection between our solar system and the galaxies beyond.

Her glyph is the vertical infinity symbol.

Her function in the birth chart is to assist human evolution beyond the confines of solar system consciousness into galactic, or multi-dimensional consciousness.

The process of accelerating our evolutionary journey into higher consciousness requires that we:

- Surrender our personality will to a higher power.
- Strengthen our spiritual Will.
- Become mindful of attacking birds (negative thoughts).
- Alchemise all that is not love enabling emergence of an open and loving heart.
- Practice toning until vibrational resonance occurs between heart and throat.
- Practice internal relaxation during activities.

***

Sedna and the Andes

It is interesting that the word, Sedna, when spelt backwards is Andes, and it is in the Andes at Lake Titicaca that the cosmic Feminine Ray enters our planet. Information accessed through inner experiences when visiting there revealed some of the ancient history of human evolution. The Andes emanates a feminine energy via the feminine Ray. The counterpart is the Himalayas where the masculine Ray entered our planet.

The Bolivian spiritual elders say that these two Rays have joined and now emanate from Lake Titicaca.

The sacred sites in the Andes are different to those of the Egyptian pyramids. Natural rocky formations were chosen to be sacred sites because of their geographical location. Specific symbols were carved into individual mountains, hills, rocks and caves and the carved sites were used for ceremonies and rituals. The additional rocks needed to complete the sacred sites were transported long distances. How? Some of them weighed tonnes and, when placed together, formed meaningful structures. These huge rocks fit so tightly together that a hair could not be placed between them yet there was no mortar used. In my annual journeys to these sites I saw many of these enormous rock structures. It is my understanding that highly evolved conscious beings used advanced vibrational technology, such as sound, to build the sacred sites.

Sedna connects to the Andes and the ancient information stored within the land and sacred sites. I mentioned some of this information in Part One.

It is also interesting that mermaids existed in Lemuria and interacted with the dolphins and whales, and the Andes was a base for Lemurian people. The merpeople, like the dolphins, are intelligent Light Beings from Sirius who came to Earth to create a bridge between the stars and humans. They carry the DNA of dolphins and humans combined.

When visiting the small Island of Molokai, one of the islands of Hawaii and a Lemurian outpost, I sensed the presence of mermaids at a remote and beautiful point where rocky crags met the sea. It was at this point a girl friend and I did a thanksgiving ceremony offering our leis to the ocean. When later visiting The Big Island of Hawaii I learned that mermaids had been seen there in recent years and verified as such by at least three different and highly respected people. They have also been seen near the Islands of the Sun and Moon in Lake Titicaca.

***

Sedna and the Magdalen Codes

Those souls who chose to incarnate towards the end of the Piscean Age and who carried certain light codes were awakened to higher consciousness at a pre-destined time and often under difficult emotional circumstances. Their dedication to their spiritual path and purpose was challenged. Those who chose to commit to their spiritual path of service to the Divine Plan are the forerunners, healers and teachers of the mass consciousness development for the new Age of Aquarius, an Age of Light that brings higher photon frequencies of awakening. People who are unwilling to confront themselves to do their deep inner work are likely to find it difficult to manage the increasingly higher frequencies bombarding our planet.

The Divine Plan will be carried out. It is time for an acceleration of mass human consciousness.

As we enter the Aquarian age the cosmic body, Sedna is discovered and is our solar systems symbolic representation of the feminine Christ consciousness. She offers us the opportunity to achieve the sacred marriage, the divine union between our inner masculine and feminine. She offers this high vibration to all who choose to embrace it.

The Mermaid, woven into the Tibetan tapestries of human evolution, has returned. The star lore from ancient Lemurian days can now be reclaimed. Sedna asked that I bring people to her as their first activation to the new astrology system. I am to teach her myth only in terms of the collective psyche.

It is important to note that Venus plays a prominent role in the acceleration of consciousness at the end of each Age. Hence, the current influence of the goddess. Venus is likened to the Higher Self of Earth and her pathway through the heavens forms a five-pointed star, a pentagram. The most sacred and esoteric of all geometric forms the pentagram is revered by initiates as a talisman of feminine power. Goddess energy. The cosmic job of Venus is to 're-unite the severed lives with no binding thread'. She symbolises the union of the heart and mind and is the esoteric ruler of Gemini.

During my teaching of *The Magdalen Codes* many participants experienced Sedna as I did. Yet, I did not share my experiences, nor did I teach the details before the Sedna meditation. I did this purposefully because I did not want to put images and thoughts into the students' minds. Some students received other details. One observed that Sedna's fish tail was not scaly but slinky, like a seal or snake. She also heard the 'music of the spheres' and identified the sounds as being like the sound one hears when placing a spiral shell to the ear. This was combined with, or alternated with, a high pitched, light and fine resonating EEEE. She also saw the frequency line along which these sounds were transmitted. The sounds made by the cosmos has been known since antiquity as the 'music of the spheres'.

The Sedna chapter was written in 2004/5 and since then I've taught hundreds of spiritual seekers and astrology students to embrace Sedna in their birth charts. I felt it important because, when we discover something for ourselves we know it's true, otherwise its only someone else's words. Sedna had an enlightening effect especially the connection made to the Aquarian Age feminine archetype, Mary Magdalen.

During a 2005 adventure to Peru and Bolivia Sedna instructed me on another part of her role. Revealing herself as a mermaid again, she said she is a 6D geometric sphere of diamond light and was activating my 6D diamond light sphere.

The billions of stars in our Milky Way galaxy are all interconnected by an invisible network of nerve-like pulsations or vibrations much like the intricacies of the human brain. There is a connection between the two. The star vibrations form certain harmonics some call the music of the spheres. Just like the stars in our galaxy, we humans are interconnected by threads of consciousness, of light. What we perceive and experience in our external world is an outer depiction of our consciousness. Sedna aids our evolutionary journey connecting us to worlds beyond our solar system. As we reach the evolutionary stage where the planets in our solar system no longer have a transformative effect on our consciousness development another system becomes available.

***

A Lemurian Treasure

What was the collective mind thinking that created the Lemurian civilisation to fall from grace? My experiences of Lord and Lady Meru were of early Lemurian memories. I must have incurred karma in a later Lemurian life because another memory emerged where I was a curious female, seeking to know the hidden mysteries but banned from doing so because of my gender. Having to walk on my knees as a punishment for my interest, subservient to my dominating father, I realised the goddess had already given her power away. Mother Nature was unhappy. Her waters churned as a result of the penetration of a comet. Her fury unleashed. The Islands of Lemuria tumbled into the Pacific Ocean.

Someday, I vowed, in the cycles of time, the feminine wisdom, knowledge and power will once again be respected, valued and honoured. We will not ever give our power away again. Knowing we are equal, we will not ever reject our inner knowing, the truth behind our sensitivities. We will listen to our guidance and follow it.

Women are the record keepers of ancient wisdom teachings, the star codes. We hold the keys to these codes in our heart. We know we need to live in harmony with Mother Earth because we feel her pulse, her heart beat. We tune in to her rhythms. Intuitively we know, often without conscious comprehension. The memories of gender equality, experienced early in Lemurian times, lie imbedded in our consciousness. Ancient Lemurian wisdom is rising from the Pacific.

When totally connected to the greater 'me' there is no distortion. Not thinking, I allow guidance and life flows in a natural rhythm, like a gentle river flowing down to the sea. Tuned into the Universal Flow I offer no resistance. My trust and faith are strong. According to cosmic timing, an insert from another dimension slots in, and I again begin operating on 3D time. These different states are distinctive, like slipping into and out of different worlds.

Information and ideas enter the mind of the willing and creative writer when they are ready to receive. The cosmic timing is important. The human mind and the cosmos need to be aligned for truth to be downloaded and understood. Specific cosmic configurations take place to enable this process. I had been patiently waiting for specific information and knew something would enter my mind at an upcoming Full Moon because it made a close connection to Sedna in my chart. At that time, I meditated and invoked Sedna. Observing her sitting in the sixth house of my birth chart, the area of life connected to service and work, she beckoned me to approach. When she asked me to dive with her to the depths of the ocean I did so, knowing she would show me something of value. Clearly seeing shells and sea creatures, I became attracted to a pulsating golden cord, a living umbilical cord. The cord, resting on the sand, exuded bright golden light and connected two things. I couldn't see what they were.

We swam further and I found a treasure chest. Sedna asked me to open it. Inside the treasure chest was a large black pearl of a colour found only in Tahitian pearls. I realised that the myth behind Mission Three - *Resurrect an ancient archetype from the soul of humanity* - was connected to the ancient land of Lemuria, and the early origins of humanity. Tahiti was part of Lemuria. Sedna asked me to remember this connection and to find the large 'pearl of wisdom' inside my memory banks. With stomach churning and nauseous from overwhelm, I felt the importance of a truth to be revealed. I won't allow fear to hold me back. I intend to uncover the information. I've been killed before, and a serious attempt made on my life while writing my *Experiment* book in Bolivia. I'm not afraid of death, knowing it's simply a transition from one dimension to another. However, I do not want to pass on without uncovering and revealing the third part of the mission.

Sedna suggested I open my akashic book of records. All souls have them. I opened at page 176.

And it came to pass that the joining together of two specific strands of genetic material resulted in a creature that could live under the sea and walk upon the land. The combination of three strands of genetic material formed the basic material structure of the current human race. Inherently, within our geometric structure is a triangle. Humans were created with three strands of genetic material, two strands originating from the stars and one from an existing earth species. The two strands were of the beings from the Pleiades and Sirius. Ancient Tahitian myth carries within it a small vestige of truth. The memory of the genetic splicing is stored in a specific gland in the human brain that connects to the stomach. The back of the head energises when the memory cell activates. Research well.

Whew. Mystic Neptune was having a party!

Where to start? I must go for a walk. I need to be surrounded by nature to ground my mental energies and calm my emotions. I also need to be mindful of symbols.

Nature is a wonderful teacher and healer. As I walked along the banks of a canal I noticed two ducks. They flew into the water a distance apart from each other creating two large expanding circles. The rippling circles grew in size as they approached the canal boundaries. There was an overlap in the centre of the two circles forming a geometric egg shape known as a *vesica pisces*. A vesica pisces is the interpenetration of two circles, or spheres, and is a birthing place where people, ideas (or genetic material?) join in mutual understanding and common ground.

Let's take this a bit further. If evolved scientists from two different star species decided to jointly seed an existing race to fulfil a part of the Creator's Plan and both understood sacred geometry, then it's likely this is how we are made. I get this. Do you? Thanks for the lesson, ducks.

What earth species was the third component needed to birth a human race through a 'watery' *vesica pisces*? The third genetic component would form a triangle and a triangle is the most stable geometric form. Many things come in threes. There's the trinity of mother, father and child. A beginning, a middle and an end. The subconscious, conscious and super-conscious mind. Then there's the synthesis of body, mind and spirit, or body, soul and spirit. Synthesis brings balance, strength and completion to our human experience.

As I was reflecting on the triangle theme two words flashed into my head. *Triple karma*. D.K. in Alice A. Bailey's book, *Esoteric Astrology*, speaks of triple karma. I couldn't understand it when I first read it. Now it makes sense. There would have to be karma associated with the two species that seeded the human race through genetic manipulation. I've read that the Pleiadians realised their evolution stopped because they had ancient karma with the human race to overcome. That's why they've come back into our midst. It stands to reason that the Sirians also have karma to work through and that's why they've returned. What was the third species? I have the records inside me. What vestige of truth resides in the Tahitian myths?

Immediately my mind flashed back to an old movie titled *Cocoon*. The movie stirred memories I didn't understand at the time of viewing. The cocoons were sent to Earth by star beings. They landed in an ocean, resting on the ocean floor until ready to hatch. What if they were Sirian and Pleiadian embryos and one of them was seeded with the genetics of an ocean creature, such as a fish or dolphin? Recently, I was given a wonderful drawing, created many years ago by a brilliant and intuitive spiritual artist, Bryan de Flores. It is of a dolphin transforming into a human, with human arms and legs. The depiction stirs my heart with warm and loving feelings.

In the Bolivian museums, two particular kinds of artefacts attracted me. One was of the large elongated skulls of the ancient Andeans. These are similar in size and shape to the early pharaohs of ancient Egypt. The other was the numerous carvings of large backbones of fish-like creatures. These were carved into rocks at temple sites in Peru and Bolivia. I've puzzled over them for years. I've even seen a small version carved into a rock and placed above a hotel entrance.

On one journey to Copacabana in Bolivia I climbed up the high rocky hill behind the fishing village to discover an outdoor museum filled with ancient history. A plethora of ancient knowledge had been carved into the giant rocks. Some carvings appeared to be zodiacal symbols. Close to the summit, I noticed a huge carved frog and felt I needed to lie on top of it. Because it is amphibious and its genetics are untainted, the frog is still highly regarded by the older wise ones. Our human genetics is tainted because of the splicing of our original DNA. Were we once amphibious, coming from the sea? The Andeans believe that, when a frog is milked, and its juice placed upon the palms of our hands to dry, and our hands placed on each of our chakras, our knowledge of creation is activated.

This part of my story connects to the following discovery mentioned in the Preface.

On 19 October /2006 SBS World News reported that Nature magazine detailed the findings of a 400-million-year old fossil, complete with fin. This fin has the same components as a human arm. The fish is referred to as *gogonasis*. It never stepped on land. This fossil find throws new light on human evolution that began in the sea.

***

Chapter Eight

Human Connections to the Stars

The Pleiades

Earth is a zone of duality. We have North and South poles, an axis upon which our Earth spins and rotates. The purpose of human consciousness evolution is to resolve duality through re-uniting, integrating and balancing our internal polarities. I teach my students to do this balancing process by working with the opposing zodiacal signs. Once this is resolved, a triangular force is created. A triangle represents the integration of two polarities through a third influence. We have no guidelines for our evolution. Those in other realms are truly amazed at our ability to burst through the limitation contained within duality. We do this through a natural yearning for integration and union with our perception of God/Goddess. The journey towards integration, or Christ Consciousness, has been played out for astrological Ages of time.

The radiation emanations from our Sun apparently change according to the consciousness level of collective humans. As our Sun releases solar bursts, the polar regions of our planet are affected. Earth's magnetic poles catch the energy and create a cylinder of vibrational energy, a lightning rod that travels through earth. In previous time, when the balance of earth was at stake pole shifts occurred. Geologists know a pole shift will occur again. They also know that comets have hit the earth before and will do so again.

A three-fold solar force connected our Sun with Alcyone, the Sun of the Pleiadian system, and the Great Central Sun of the Sirius system when these suns were closely aligned between 2005 and 2015. I was taken to view this alignment and saw it clearly with my inner vision through a process known by NASA as remote viewing. I was asked to record and share the details of the experiences. The effect of the radiating force from the three Suns in major alignment may be too much for some people to handle. Those self-aware, with uncluttered psychology, are able to house this extra solar light in their bodies. Those filled with negative thoughts feel the effects of the increased density in their body and life and react to it.

Plants thrive when they receive sufficient sunlight and so do humans. Sensitive individuals feel the extra sun bursts. Each time they occur we have the opportunity to open our hearts and minds to increases in intuition, psychic potential, divine love and the ability to decode our DNA.

Our Sun pours light into the planets of our solar system. It receives its light from Alcyone the brightest star of the Pleiades, and Sirius. These light codes are filled with love, the essence of our Mother Goddess, she who birthed our souls. Love is the highest vibratory force in creation and heals all. Without light and love humans couldn't survive as a species.

During the three Sun's alignment three cosmic sisters, Gaia, Alcyone and Isis, symbolising the Sirius star system, united. During quiet times a friend of mine received a repeated message: 'The sisters are reuniting'. When I led a group of women to Hawaii to dance the sacred circle dance Paneurythmy at sacred sites on the Big Island, this same phrase kept resounding in my head. At first, I didn't understand its symbolic meaning.

A major cosmic change heralds change on all frequencies. The feminine is once again becoming the major force of creation and the masculine will do well to be guided by her. The three sisters do not approve of war. They want to play and love rather than fight. They want to restore natural balance and harmony to all of existence and create beautiful music, art and beauty. They choose to share their joy with all of humankind and they encourage group participation in goodwill projects.

There are some four hundred stars in the Pleiadian system. The seven main stars are often referred to as the Seven Sisters. I often visited Alcyone and experienced their library, which contains the records of Earth. A peaceful and enjoyable experience, I learned to trust the Pleaidians. They have been major players in the great experiment of human evolution on Earth and are intricately tied to our evolutionary development. In our far distant past they made the mistake of genetically interfering with our natural evolution. Now they want to correct this mistake so their collective karma can be healed. Anxious for humanity not to make the same mistake they see clearly how it could happen. By working with channels such as Barbara Hand Clow, Barbara Marciniak and Amorah Quan Yin the Pleiadians attempt to bring awareness to humans. The books written by these authors are truly enlightening and I recommend them for your further study.

Alcyone is known in the East as Brahma, the seat of creative power or universal magnetism. It operates at a 5D frequency of light that resonates with heart felt universal love. Our Sun, and its related zodiacal sign, Leo, rules the heart in the western astrological model. Sirius resonates with both the heart and the wisdom of sacred geometry. This once in approximately two-hundred and thirty-million-year alignment is provided as a spiritual pathway to ascension for those who choose to take it. Hopefully it will be a well-trodden pathway with masses of humans walking it. This pathway leads to divine union with Source through the dedicated development of Christ consciousness.

As our solar system traverses the photon band, the great band of photonic light emanating from Alcyone through the zodiacal signs of Aquarius and Leo, the Pleiadian frequencies will become stronger within the minds and hearts of humanity. Alcyone continually resides in this photon band. The Pleiadians are doing their utmost to assist us open our hearts so we can heal our galactic wounds and access the prime cause of our fall from grace, our former Christ consciousness. They want us to play, have fun and spontaneously create from a place of joy. They also want us to honour the feminine through our hearts.

***

The Pleiades and the Andes Mountains of Peru and Bolivia

In South America, specifically Peru, the ancient Incas honoured the Pleiades and followed carefully its passage in the night sky. They knew that everything in the world carried consciousness containing the seeds of divinity. They were able to access their cellular memory and sacred knowledge whenever it was needed. The equinoxes, solstices and return of the Pleiades were observed, celebrated and revered as important spiritual occasions. The Pleiades was also important to the Inca for determining the seasons. At certain times of the year specific stars or constellations appear invisible because of their close proximity to the Sun. The date of their reappearance is known as its heliacal rise.

The day the Pleiades became visible before the Sun rose was the date of the Return of the Pleiades. This event was an important tool for measuring the Incan calendar. The ancient astronomers referred to the Pleiades as The Granary. In Quechua, the indigenous language of Peru, the Pleiades system is referred to as Collca, which means granary. A granary stores precious seeds. In northern Bolivia, the Quechua word for the Pleiades is Coto, meaning a handful of seeds. The 'handful of seeds' symbolise the light codes, or spiritual DNA within every human. These lie dormant until the planetary energies activate them into awakening. The fruit from awakening these seeds is Christ Consciousness.

The Mesoamerican and Peruvian sacred sites were built as spiritual initiation temples and to connect the Earth plane with the higher worlds. Considerable resources were used in their construction. The particular movement of the luminaries, constellations and planets, along with the equinoxes, solstices and eclipses, provided gateways of cosmic energy that could be utilised to access higher states of consciousness. The ancients understood and worked with this energy.

The Maya created an important calendar that defines the spiritual progression of humanity throughout the precessional Ages of astrological time. During the course of a precessional cycle of approximately twenty-six thousand years, the equinox and solstice suns align with the centre of the Milky Way galaxy. The alignment of a solstice sun with the Milky Way occurred on the December solstice, 2012. This completed one huge precessional cycle of human spiritual evolution. The crossing point is the Galactic Centre, 27 degrees Sagittarius. To the Maya this crossing point is called the sacred tree and is the birthplace of creation, the cosmic womb. My experience connects to this ancient knowledge. That story comes later.

At the 2012 December Solstice, a potent spiritual gateway opened. The opportunity was made available for another huge leap forward in human consciousness evolution. This is one of the reasons for the huge wave of spirituality and consciousness acceleration sweeping the planet. Between 2005 and 2008 Pluto formed a conjunction to the galactic centre. The effect of a Pluto transit can be likened to that of a caterpillar metamorphosing into a butterfly. A 'cocoon' time is experienced deep within the individual's psychology. All that is no longer needed for the next level of spiritual growth needs to be realised and released. Some aspect of consciousness, usually a part of our comfort zone, has to 'die' before a rebirth can take place. If this process is not undergone consciously then ill health, sometimes in the form of debilitating disease, occurs. The soul's desire for spiritual growth through evolution of consciousness is paramount.

A well carved ancient monument referred to by the Peruvian Quechua people as *The Granary* looms tall and imposing, looking like a fortress. Proudly standing on a steep and rugged mountain opposite the ancient sacred site of Ollyantaytambo at the entrance to the Sacred Valley of the Incas, this monument fascinated me.

This monument was built as a granary to store seeds because of its perfect location perched high on one side of a steep mountain. The grain seeds would be kept dry by the wind. The ancient building is untouched by archaeologists and will probably remain so because of its inaccessibility. A few local people, who climb these steep mountains like mountain goats, can access it. Terraces were built on the slopes beneath the building to grow crops from the stored corn seeds. The Quechua believe that this technology was given to them by the Pleaidians. Their influence is strong in the high mountains of Peru and Bolivia.

***

Sirius

Astrologically, Sirius is situated at 13 degrees Cancer. My natal chart's Sun and Mercury conjunct Sirius in the 8th house. What does this mean? Within my subconscious I carry soul memories of the Sirius mysteries, and the knowledge of its cosmology. It is to Sirius I regularly space travel to receive guidance and instruction as to the next step of my earthly experience.

The light of Sirius, the brightest star in our night sky, is sometimes referred to as the RA light and the energy of this great light being is androgynous, i.e. balanced masculine and feminine. Author and astrologer Barbara Hand Clow, in her book *The Pleiadian Agenda*, has a lot to say about Sirius that helped me make sense of my reality. She says the Great Central Sun, Sirius, is an advanced trinary system. Astronomers discovered its third star in 1985. These three cosmic bodies are one consciousness.

Clow says that our Sun lost its twin, Sirius, after being birthed through the Galactic Centre. Separation through duality was the theme. This is the theme we humans have been playing out over countless incarnations. I expand on this theme, believing it is based on our perceived separation from divine Spirit. Sirius returned recently to align once again with our Sun and, using my inner vision, I was fortunate to clearly view this alignment over a number of years from 2005 to 2016.

Once we humans have awakened, re-membered and ignited our internal Sun and embraced our twin, the soul or higher self, we are able to reconnect to divinity through feelings of all-encompassing love and gratitude. We choose to shine our light daily and are determined to never again descend into darkness. We have a strong moral and ethical code and are in integrity with our truth. We take responsibility for our creations.

At this stage of consciousness development many initiations have been passed that tested our integrity and faith. We now operate through our heart and higher mind at the witness level of higher consciousness. We are so grateful for the transformational teachings. From our witness perspective, we laugh at our former unconscious reactive antics. I refer to this perception as a cosmic joke. I chuckle when I'm tempted to repeat old self-sabotaging behaviour, realising its just another test. Our solar system has done its work and we are ready to embrace higher refined frequencies. Our cells contain these star codes - *The Magdalen Codes*.

Our current time is a most incredible period of accelerating human evolution. Cosmic alignments create permanent change. A quantum leap unlike anything humans have ever experienced is taking place, involving a huge shift in mass human consciousness. Just as our solar system orbits around Alcyone, the central Sun of the Pleiades, the galaxy itself moves through space in a form of continual circles and spirals. We are experiencing the energy of the completion of a multi-billion-year single circular orbit around the greater Central Sun Sirius. We are so fortunate to be living at this time of accelerated change.

Sirius, the Dog Star, is associated with the goddess of resurrection, Isis. Many female initiates were trained in the Isis mysteries of ecstatic and transformative sexual union. Sirius, a bright star in the heavens, is a member of the constellation of Canis Major.

The Sirians gave the Egyptians, as well as other earthly cultures, advanced astronomical information. For example, the African Dogon tribe understands, and can demonstrate, the Sirius orbital patterns. The Sirians left clues about Earth's past and have been a guiding force for the development of our civilisation. They are also prime characters in the creation of the human species.

According to Clow, the Sirians built the Sphinx in 17,800 BC and it was constructed over an ancient Sirian sacred site. When I visited the sphinx, I felt a tremendous affinity with her. She was beautiful, serene and calm, exuding feminine grace. I became excited when I noticed at her base a similar ancient building technique to that of the ancient Andean sacred sites. I knew that the same advanced consciousness had built both structures. I also realised the Egyptians pyramids were built much later than those of the Andean sites.

Sacred sites, mostly built on dragon lairs, or ley lines, hold ancient knowledge and the wisdom of the stars. The Sirian records are available for downloading within the minds of those with a receptive consciousness. Implanted during the Age of Taurus when Osiris and Isis came to Earth, they are being re-ignited in human consciousness. It is time to remember them.

***

Human Connection to Sirius

Over a period of many years, and during my daily mediation practice, I was taken to Sirius for training. My meditations begin with deep regular focused breathing. This enables my mind and body to relax so I can descend my consciousness to my heart. Heart-consciousness, different to the intellect, is receptive and allowing. When the human body, heart-intelligence and soul work in unison, they become a finely tuned instrument for receiving direct communication from higher spheres of light.

A group of advanced light beings from Sirius conducted my training, referring to themselves as the Council of Nine. Omega, the spokesperson for this collective consciousness appeared incredibly tall, slim, silvery and strong. On my first Sirius visit Omega introduced me to the other members of the Council of Nine and invited me to sit in the central position of the horseshoe formation directly opposite him. I felt completely 'at home' and relaxed. To my right were my star brothers and sister who had chosen not to incarnate upon Earth. To my left were ascended Masters who had experienced time on Earth.

Curious, I wondered why I was there. The training, of which I am now aware, involved identifying each Council member, accepting and developing the feeling of equality with each one, and finally realising each is a soul aspect within me. I learned to identify each one through my senses. They trained me to re-awaken my inner eyes and to hear telepathically. The training process took many earth years.

My greatest difficulty was with feeling equal to one of the ascended Masters. As the awareness of his identity washed over me, like a giant wave, I wanted to prostrate myself at his feet. When I finally identified him, I experienced profound shock. Jesus looked deeply into my eyes and spoke directly to my soul with the words 'I know you'. I felt these powerful words resonate deeply in my heart and soul and knew them to be true.

I first space-travelled to Sirius under the protection of two angels, Uriel and Gabriel. Later it was via a spaceship. Inter-dimensional travel and remote viewing came naturally, as if I'd done it many times before. Upon entering my first space vehicle I was greeted by three Sirian beings. Slightly light blue in colour they emitted soft fluorescence radiance. I noticed how their extremely large thin hands seemed disproportionate to the rest of their semi-etheric body. Their heads were elongated, much like the skull shape of Akhenaton, one of the Egyptian Pharaohs.

The Sirians I met at that time had large penetrating dark almond shaped eyes. All the beings on this ship were androgynous yet chose to portray themselves as male or female. All were slim, elegant, beautifully formed, light (semi-etheric), and moved gracefully. They were warmly welcoming yet intent on their individual tasks. One female played the role of tour guide.

The space vehicle seemed to expand as we walked through it. It also emanated a soothing light blue colour. Advised I was free to go into whichever rooms I chose I did so, feeling safe and secure. As I approached each room it seemed to expand according to my desire to investigate. The ship emanated a calming glow. It felt huge, as if it was housing the entire population of a city. I noticed people working in relaxed harmony in each space visited. In the 'cockpit' was a group of individuals, intent on task, each with a screen in front of them. They were seated in a horseshoe shape. The desk was clean, without wires, cords or connections. The screens appeared to change according to thought. When I ventured into their space the Sirians warmly welcomed me and then resumed their tasks.

Mary Magdalen's esoteric training in the Egyptian temples connected to star lore, the energy centres (chakras) within the human body and those of Mother Earth. These energy centres receive and transmit subtle cosmic energies. When the chakras are cleared of psychological density the sacred sexual practices between highly evolved and loving couples can be practiced. A 'sacred marriage' between the inner divine masculine and feminine energies can be experienced within each participant when both are attuned to Divine Source - the third point of the triangle. In the ancient Egyptian spiritual tradition Isis, the Mother Goddess, is the Creatrix of all matter and an equal counterpart to the masculine God (Osiris). Yeshua could not have ascended into his light body without the divine love and wisdom of Mary Magdalen.

Yeshua was a multi-dimensional being of immense light. Following his birth into this dense 3D world, his light body had to be contained by the Magi astrologers through the application of pure gold to his energy field. Sourced from higher dimensions, he incarnated for a specific purpose; to assist humanity evolve in consciousness and apply his teachings of love for all of nature (the Goddess). He revered women and initiated them along with men. He also set up processes so that higher dimensional beings could incarnate more frequently on Earth. He planted seeds of higher consciousness around the globe. The Sirians engineered his arrival.

Reflect on earth's position in our solar system, sandwiched between Venus (feminine and magnetic) and Mars, (masculine and electric). Each of us has the challenge to bring into balance our internal masculine and feminine energies. When able to do so, and maintain this balance as a constant, we pave the way to experience Christ or multi-dimensional consciousness. Our energy field expands to encompass greater light and we attract according to the frequency contained within that light. The greater the love within the light the greater becomes our magnetism.

Many of the ascended Masters were, and still are, trained on Sirius. Isis is the divine feminine archetype of the ancient Egyptian esoteric mysteries and is connected to Sirius. During a 2009 meditation on Sirius she invited me to energetically merge with her.

Sirius is now the central Sun for our arm of the galaxy. The three stars of Sirius form a triangular shape, providing the way out of 3D duality. The Pleiades are part of the Sirius star system and our solar system is a part of the Pleiadian system. This system adjustment was made when the three Suns of these systems aligned between 2006 and 2016.

***

My Training on Antares

I wrote about my Antares training in my *Experiment* book but it is relevant to include some of it here. My cosmic travels there were frequent, taking place in deep meditation during most of 2000.

Taken to a light 'room' on Antares, I noticed five, almost invisible light beings sitting cross-legged in space way above a 'floor'. All around me were gentle vibrating waves of energy. The light beings invited me to sit on an extension stool I could feel and sense, but not see. When I sat, it took me up to their level. Welcoming me, they advised they were to be my next group of trainers, if I would accept them. I asked three times if they were working with the Will of God/Goddess and they said a firm 'yes' each time. I felt comfortable with them, even though the experience seemed strange and mystical. Individually they gave me an energy infusion. Their role, they said, was to take me further up the spiritual ladder.

Operating on a higher vibration to the Sirians, they said I was deemed ready to move to this new level. That evening, I made a note in my journal that transiting Pluto in Sagittarius was conjunct with the bright star Antares when this experience took place. I realised how our spiritual guides use the planetary transits as cosmic channels to expand human consciousness.

On my next visit, and while seated on the training stool, the same light beings told me I had a specific role to play in the 3D world, and their role was to prepare, and test me, for it. They knew I was ready to meet the challenges, otherwise I would not be with them. Following this conversation, they blended individually with me, and then as a collective. Questioning my awareness of their collective energy, they asked me to describe what it felt like.

Replying, I said it looked like the shape of a butterfly, vertical in the centre and then winging out into two semi-circles. Congratulating me on my accuracy they tested me again. Each one played with the energy of the butterfly shape, moving out further into its wings from the centre. Pausing, they moved even further out. I felt the movement in my mind and body each time and said so. I passed their test. When they individually merged into one, I felt the difference in each of their energies, but then went into doubt, wondering if I would get it right the next time round. They immediately picked up on my doubt, and referred me to my previous observation, saying it had been correct.

On the next visit, I noticed brilliant pink and purple colours. My five trainers hoisted my stool up higher, then lower, and then higher again. I was asked to relax, accept an infusion of the colour rays and to realise that the colours emitted a fine and high frequency. They told me that a 3D X-ray is of very low frequency and the human body is adversely affected by it. They lowered me, so each one could merge into me. Then they explained that the Sirians were my soul group and had experienced 9D and beyond infusions from this group of Antares trainers. The Sirians had chosen to remain in 6D. I was to remain in 3D and be infused with the higher dimensional frequencies of 9D in order to fulfil my potential, and they were the instruments for this process.

On my next visit, while seated on the stool, I was asked to focus on the domed roof of the building and report on what I saw. Reporting that the roof appeared to be constructed of a transparent membrane or skin, they asked me to look at them, and report on all I observed. I saw them as outlines of smiling faces with one very loving large eye in the centre of their respective foreheads. The love and joy pouring from them was a delight to experience. All five merged into me individually, and as one unit, we moved in an anti-clockwise direction, building up speed until it seemed we were like a top, becoming one strand of highly charged energy. The spinning ceased, the energy dissipated and they returned to their respective stools. I was again asked to look at them closely, and saw beams of soft fluorescent pink and violet, with an occasional beam of gold emanating from their crown. I felt I was experiencing a magnificent light show. Asked to look at their hands I observed the same colour rays radiating from them. They then directed their hands towards me and I observed the colour rays cross the space, and felt the differing vibrations enter me. They bowed their heads again and I saw and felt the energy rays change. They told me I could now 'read' energy and they were pleased with my progress. I could also see how I had learned to let go of old control patterns and was happily allowing the process to unfold.

The merging process occurred again, and this time I noticed the first Antarian had masculine energy, the second feminine, and the third androgynous. I observed another male and female. They wound around me at great speed until we became one beam of light then moved back to their seats to beam energy to me from their hands. I felt the light frequencies enter my body. They formed a joint ball of light that came to me, entering my third eye where I could feel this chakra pulsate. I understood I was experiencing perturbation that would continue because the light would explode existing density of beliefs carried within my cells, drenching them with information and knowledge. At another training, I noticed how the light seemed almost blinding with brilliant colour waves of pink and mauve. Observing the domed building to be lighter and more sparkling than previously, I realised my internal light had increased.

Then I observed the five Antareans had doubles. They were now ten. The ten formed a circle around me and asked if I wanted to move my stool so I could see each of them, or whether they should move. Sitting still, I suggested they move. Quizzing me, they asked me to tell them about the quality of group energy emanating from them. Initially they were calm, then agitated, and then were dancing lightly, like fairies. Anger, aggression, and finally love were the next emotions I felt from them. When I felt their anger and aggression my body became agitated and my stomach heaved in fear. Then I was asked to absorb their love. I felt this vibrational flow enter my heart as a warm and nourishing wash. Congratulating me, they said I was learning to read, and feel, energy. I was being trained and would be totally equipped to deal with the 'flood gates' when they opened. I didn't know what they meant but felt it could be connected to humanity's future.

Travelling again to Antares, I was invited into another room, higher up in the building. This room contained many lights in the form of waves and transparent blobs. Relaxing, and breathing more deeply, I began to see more clearly and the waves and blobs morphed into beings of light. Masses of light beings had gathered in the room. Sitting in a chair that moved upwards I became higher than the assembled group, above them in the centre. A voice, appearing to come from above, resounded around the room, embracing everyone present. Welcoming me, it said how great an honour it was to have me there.

I expressed gratitude for the opportunity to be trained by them. The speaker replied, saying they would bestow a blessing on me, somewhat like a baptism. He said they were going to sprinkle a substance over me that would positively affect my etheric field. I felt myself being lowered, as if going deep down into a nebulous mass of an unknown soft and pliable substance. Feeling completely comfortable and at ease, I was raised up again, and, at the same time, felt something being sprinkled over me, a little like drops of oil. Raised higher I was told my life would never be the same again because the substance would work on my etheric field first, and then move into my physical body.

A few days later I again visited Antares and was asked to look around. I saw three different rays of colour as red, orange and green. These three beams of light played with my energy. First together and then individually. I realised these Rays had a consciousness and were highly evolved entities. Merging into me they said I needed the three colours: red for power and confidence: orange for creativity: and green for harmony. Noticing a female being prostrating in front of an enormous light being, I was asked how I felt about it. Replying, I said that it didn't feel appropriate because we are all equal. I was invited to join the women in the experience and, as I did so, felt loving energy wash all over my spine, in waves of warmth. "This is why people prostrate", I was told, "because they receive a gift". My trainers told me that I was being prepared for an exciting and broadening experience that would have far reaching effects. I had the image of transiting Jupiter approaching to conjunct with my natal Uranus.

The broadening experience was my experience of ascension, and all that followed from it.

The next time, as I sat on my stool, I was asked to look closely at the group of five. I saw they had their doubles, trebles, quadruples and more, on and on as far as my inner eyes could see. Each being had a great number of etheric 'doubles'. I was asked to understand and integrate this energetic system. Each being allowed their 'doubles' to move around separately, and then brought them back into the one at the centre. This is when I felt their energy to be the strongest.

My trainers said that when focus and healing is needed, I am to call in all my etheric doubles so that the greatest energetic force can be given out to whoever needs healing. Each of the doubles blended with me, and I could distinguish the subtle energetic differences in my body. I was again congratulated and asked to remember the lesson.

I understood that the lesson being taught was one of unity. Each of us has doubles, trebles etc. operating in different dimensions of time and space and, as we evolve spiritually and gain higher conscious understanding, we can become aware of, and learn to manage, these aspects of self. We are all one, operating as cells in the great 'body' of God/Goddess/All That Is.

The book, *The Source Field Investigations* by David Wilcock, explains how scientists, in particular Dr Peter Gariaev, discovered that our DNA has an energetic 'duplicate' and, by extension, so too does our body. Wilcock also said how Dr Glen Rein, a biochemist, discovered that our DNA behaves in direct response to our consciousness, and that love generates coherence in our brain waves that directly affects our DNA. It's pleasing to know that modern scientists are proving sacred wisdom teachings. I recommend you read David Wilcock's informative book. His website is www.DivineCosmos.com and Dr Peter Gariaev's website is www.wavegenetic.ru

On my next visit to Antares the colours seemed much brighter. There appeared to be more space and clearer light. This was because my vibration was higher, so my perception and inner vision had naturally changed. I saw neon colours, purple, pink and gold, in streams or rays. The building also seemed different. It appeared to have greater space and clearer light. The training room, invisible at first, manifested only when I stopped at the right spot. It appeared more solid, made from material that looked like white crystal. It was built on a 'stem' that had a mechanism inside it.

The light beings came very close, asking me to close my inner eyes and tell them what I felt when they began to work on my energy field. I felt their touch invade it, and said so, but my curiosity and trust were greater than my fear of invasion. They moved closer and eventually merged into me. I felt it. They asked if I had any requests. Replying "yes" I asked if they would help me fulfil my intention to continually be in a state of love, trust, peace and harmony. They seemed delighted with this request and immediately agreed to it. Asking me to close my eyes again they made adjustments to my energy field. Again, they questioned as to what I had felt. I felt them first adjust my throat and then my thymus. My heart was next, where they spent a long time making many adjustments. Then they moved to my solar plexus. Apparently, I passed their test because they told me there was still work to be done before the 'big event'.

At the next training, I was taken to a large and seemingly important room, higher than anywhere they'd taken me before. They asked me to stand in the centre of a horseshoe formation to face them. Behind me, at the rear of the room, was a large group of other light beings. My trainers moved in a line behind me and then merged into one. I could both sense and feel this, as if I had sensing eyes at the back of my head. The five formed a semi-circle in front of me and merged into one again. I realised we are all one, and that each person we meet or interact with is a reflection of a part of us. I was asked to fully integrate this truth. They then merged into one again, and that one merged into me. I felt it as a finer vibration.

I understand that all the people in my life are out-picturings of parts of myself. They show me, just by being themselves, my many and varied aspects.

Journeying again to Antares, I was guided to a different room and asked to focus on the domed ceiling. As I did I sensed and saw the room expand and contract according to my thought. Some light beings formed a pillar within me. They then become blobs in front of me. The 'blobs' became larger, forming human-like beings. They reduced to blobs and again into a pillar, as one. This process was repeated. I was tested on this process, always reporting by telepathic communication what I was seeing and feeling.

A single eye appeared, which blinked. I reported it to my trainers. I was then asked to comment on the qualities and characteristics behind the eye. It appeared to me to be detached and without emotion. It was simply observing. It blinked sometimes. The eye was dark brown and fathomless. This was the All-Seeing Eye, and I felt I was the Eye and the Eye was me. I was told my lesson was over, that I had done well and was a good student.

At my next training the five beings merged into one, and, as one, merged into me. I was asked to feel this process as they repeated it three times. Once again, they were insistent that I understood it. Then I was asked to swivel around on my stool so my back was to them. They then merged with me from behind. Again, I was asked to feel the point of impact. I did this easily, feeling their different vibrations enter me.

As a result of this training I have an unshakeable awareness that we are all one, and the light beings represented the out-picturing of the Antares part of me operating in the 9th dimension and beyond. They told me their training program would end soon because I had learnt well. They also said my evolutionary process is to be further accelerated and I will be introduced to yet another group of trainers when the time was right. I felt sad when they said this and expressed it. They replied there was little more they could teach me because I understand we are all one. I am part of them and they me, and what more is there?

***

Adventures into the Unknown

The writing of this book is a process of 'connecting the dots'. I enjoy playing detective, uncovering clues and remembering my ancient roots. It gives my life meaning and purpose. One of my Sirian guides, RA, tells me he is only with me while I research and write about the section on Sirius and will come again to assist in the conclusion and publication of this book. I have faith, along with a strong conviction, that the book needs to be written. I understand the process is also a journey into myself, to reclaim my stellar identity and to extract my 'treasure of truth' buried within the depths of my astrological birth chart's 8th house.

Reclaiming identity and remembering parts of one's soul that were cut off or split, is part of the spiritual ascension training process. In the ancient Egyptian mystery schools, high-level initiates were placed, for a certain period of time, in a closed sarcophagus in order to remember their soul's origins. A few died because they became so involved in the emotionally weakening experiences of a former life they were unable to extract themselves from it.

Jupiter and Uranus transits provide opportunities to expand our consciousness and open new doorways of perception. I wrote this chapter at Sedona, a small desert town in Arizona USA where the masculine and feminine dragon lairs are balanced.

On 25th November 2005, I awakened from a dream that ended with the words, 'it's time to go through the Sirian portal'. Being curious, I invoked my then travelling guide, Uni, a unicorn, who told me there was much work to be done. I hopped on his back and he asked me to close my inner eyes in order to feel and 'see' through my other senses. I sensed us travelling at incredible speed through a 'worm-hole', an open tunnel of light that created a wave as we journeyed. It seemed as if we were parting the waters of light. Suddenly we emerged from the light tunnel into the most brilliant, radiating huge ball of light – our Sun.

We travelled straight to its heart centre and then through it, intense bright light and radiance filling us. Suddenly we left this light to emerge into another light tunnel. This time the light was softer and more refined. It felt luminous, a little like moonlight. I could see clearly. It felt as if we were travelling through a liquid light water tunnel and, as we moved, the gentle light water opened up before us, as if we were magnetic.

We were being pulled towards a different cosmic body, one not as brilliant and radiant as our Sun but one that felt more like a womb, a black hole. As we approached its field we were sucked into a vortex, travelling clockwise, spinning downwards into a whirlpool of fluid darkness, being sucked closer and closer to the centre. It felt comforting and safe.

We spun into the centre and were sucked into the womb. It was like a dark cave, a place of absolute stillness. It felt calm, peaceful, safe and nurturing. We were then catapulted from this place straight out into space. I felt I could observe from the womb, and travel on the fine light beam at amazing speed. Uni and I went on and on into a vast region of space. We took a right-hand turn, creating a huge great circle.

After making sure I had integrated all he was showing me, Uni turned and re-entered the light beam travelling back into the black hole/cave/womb. He told me that what he had shown was my new playground. I understood him to mean that this was the area in space of a new astrology system I was to work with and introduce to my students and readers. It was huge and seemingly empty. He not only outlined my new playground but also the process.

- Become the reflective, intuitive, introspective Moon in all her feminine attributes.
- Become a radiant Sun. Attain the child-like joy, wonder, spontaneity, openness, light, warmth, generosity of spirit and an all-encompassing love for all of creation and integrate the higher consciousness that comes through the process.
- Unite the internal Sun and Moon, the sacred feminine and masculine principles.
- Allow your highest guidance to lead. The timing is always according to the giant cosmic clock, i.e. when planetary transits are in particular aspect to the natal chart, and when the outer planets involved in that aspect move in direct motion.
- Without resistance, be willing to travel on beams of brilliant radiating light through our Sun into unknown regions and light tunnels to feel and sense new wonders. Allow fluidity, and the magnetic attraction of the soft luminous light, the Cosmic Mother, to draw you into the womb of creation, the Galactic Centre. Be willing to enter the black swirling vortex, totally trusting, relaxed and at ease.
- Be willing to observe, from a higher dimensional perspective, your new playground.

***

Sound and Sacred Geometry

Geometry is the form consciousness takes when sound waves move away from creation. Groups of Buddhist monks frequently demonstrate this natural vibrational process when they purposefully create peace sand mandalas. When the group repeatedly and harmoniously chant the sacred sound of OM, geometric shapes form in the sand. Sounds can stimulate deterioration, or regeneration of body organs. Disharmonious sounds cause body deterioration. Harmonious sounds activate the body into healing. Our bodies are filled with sacred geometry and some medical intuitives can see these shapes.

In time, our medical profession will realise the healing value of sound and will play specific combinations of sound to regenerate the different organs. Some energy healers are already doing so - using specifically created tuning forks to positively change the vibratory tone of body organs. Our entire body can to be mapped and tuned, much like a piano. Our internal geometric shapes change as we grow into higher consciousness. This evolutionary process comes as a result of passing initiations that enable the development of meaningful spirituality and purposeful psychological alchemy. Before birth our over-soul created an idealised blueprint for our body and it naturally seeks to grow into it. Harmonious sounds assist body healing. As we raise our consciousness and choose to love our body as an incredible temple that houses our soul, it begins to morph into its original blueprint.

Sound is the primal energy used to create.

In an initiation, we pass through the bowels of darkness. Pluto transits to our natal chart placements activate this evolutionary growth process. Throughout the descent journey into our underworld, our subconscious, we are offered opportunities to face our fears. We are the ones who energise our fearful thought forms into being. When we view our life from a holistic and broader perspective, realising we are an immortal soul having a 3D growth experience, we can more easily confront our fears and love them to death.

When our energy field no longer holds the fear, what we have feared no longer has the life to take us down into the abyss of darkness again. We emerge from the experience stronger, with greater vitality and increased self-awareness. As we learn to love ourselves and to trust our feelings, body sensations and intuitive higher mind we learn to let go of emotional attachments and meaningless materialism. We are moved to take care of ourselves, our life and health. We learn to allow our internal loving spirit to guide our mind and activities.

It is through transmuting our earthly density and accessing our stellar heritage that we become multi-dimensional beings of light.

When on earth the Sirians left behind many time capsules and puzzles for future generations to discover. Some believed they had the right to manipulate genetics and were interested in establishing a primitive humanoid race on earth. The Sirian group who interfered with human genetics became karmically tied to human development.

We were programmed to develop through limitation, without knowledge of our galactic roots. Through our descent into the darkness of ignorance, we've evolved through struggle, victim hood, and self-destruction. What an incredible journey it has been. This period is ending. For those willing to see, and be the light, it is there. The Sirians are willing to assist those prepared to act on spiritual will and determination to clear their limitation and density. They are our neighbours, offering a friendly hand to all who choose to reach out for it. Will you take it? Will you do the necessary inner work? I do hope so. Our future depends on it.

Our third dimension is that of linear space and time. In order for us to evolve beyond our limited 3D consciousness we need an accelerator in which to do so. Our solar system planets act as substations, or power-houses, for human evolution out of the 3D state of being. Saturn and beyond are the key players. Planet Earth (Gaia), is evolving and changing frequency. This is a fact determined by many researchers. Prolific author Greg Braden is one of the main proponents who bridges science and spirituality. He says that Nature gives us the turning points we need to shift life's extremes of struggle into life-affirming choices. As Gaia evolves her frequency we humans have the opportunity to also evolve to a higher frequency of light. When enough humans have willingly penetrated, and mastered, the illusionary and sticky 4th dimensional state of being and evolved through it, a fifth dimensional world awaits. This is the dimensional experience of universal love that connects to the heart chakra and involves the higher mind.

In the frequency range of the lower fourth dimension resides the conglomeration of human emotional density built up over the past 12,500 years. This dimension needs to be mastered before 5D consciousness can emerge.

4D is often referred to as the astral plane and experienced as a sticky mass of subtle psychic energy that veils higher consciousness. There is a lot of confusion, illusion, deception and self-sabotage on this plane. It connects to Neptune.

Sedna is our connection to galactic or Christ consciousness and, through the understanding and integration of her energy, we can experience a 5D state of being as a constant.

***

Chapter Nine

A Cosmic System Reveals

The Great Bear

As a regular meditator for many years I've learned to trust my inner guidance. Often, I need to decode the given symbols. Early in my astrological journey I learned to invoke the archetypes of the planets while meditating. This regular process taught me to develop my mental telepathy and visionary skills. The process involves visualising myself in the centre of my birth chart and carefully viewing each placement in it, beginning at the Ascendant. This trains my mind to stay calm and focused. From the centre I invoke a planet that has a message for me. I never know which one will appear. Often Chiron appeared, offering to take me on a space journey. I always accepted his offer.

Years ago, I did a similar process except that I purposefully invoked Chiron. He took me down into a deep cave where I felt totally protected. Chiron and I have been on many journeys together. We entered a large, very dark and dingy cave filled with unsavoury smells. Slumped into a corner was the outline of a huge shape. We walked to this shape so I could see it more clearly. The shape was an enormous great bear and, as I looked, it began to stir.

It slowly stretched making loud guttural noises. We stood and watched.

The Great Bear awakened and stood up. She was starving after her long hibernation and needed food badly. She looked directly into my eyes and I felt she was considering eating me for breakfast. I looked back, steadily with focus, emanating love. The bear continued to look at me intensely, then shrugged and lumbered away to the outside of the cave. I decided to energetically clean up the mess in the cave so it would be pristine for her return. I filled the cave with light, which followed the bear as it moved through the tunnel to the outside world.

I understood the Great Bear awakening was a symbolic message related to this book. The Great Bear constellation is awakening to purpose, that of activating human consciousness into galactic frequencies of light. The cave symbolically represents the subconscious mind.

Ursa Major, The Great Bear constellation, was involved in Earth's planetary pole shift at the time of the great cataclysm, when the last Ice Age began. Sedna links in, with her connection to the Arctic Circle, the place of the Inuit/Eskimos. The Ice Age occurred during the Age of Leo following the great cataclysm caused when Atlantis sank. Our new Age is Aquarius, the opposing sign to Leo. Just as the Full Moon brings up emotions and memories relating to the opposing sign it is passing through, so too will the Age of Aquarius bring up the individual and collective soul memories of experiences during the Age of Leo. The ancient memory of the wisdom teachings, based on the Law of One is being awakened. The Great Bear wants her story told.

In her book *Catastrophobia* Clow explains how the orientation of the Earth's circumpolar circle is now shifting to the influence of the Great Bear constellation. She explains how this shift heralds the beginning of the time of paradise. I understand this is when we will find our way back to the Garden of Eden that existed in our pre-cataclysmic history. This is early Lemuria times when we humans lived in a state of galactic or Christ consciousness, fully connected to Source. Our ancestors worked with, and understood natural Law, the Law of One, and knew how the great cosmic theatre replicated on Earth.

The great cataclysm changed our level of consciousness. We descended into the darkness of ignorance and illusion, losing the memories of our star heritage and the wisdom of higher perceptions. This was our fall from Grace into amnesia. This amnesia also occurs on a personal level whenever a significant trauma occurs in life. At these times, our brain shuts down and we momentarily stop breathing, unable to integrate the shock. We hold our breath. Within that action, the psychological energy of the trauma experienced is tightly condensed into dense matter. We separate from the part of us that was hurt. Yet the memory of the emotional experience is embedded in our cells as energetic density. It can be accessed through re-birthing therapy. Sincere intent and focused continual deep circular breathing is a release factor. Separation from love is an Aquarian theme, as is the illumination of cause and the subsequent healing of that separation. Heart-felt divine love (Leo) is the healer.

After the great cataclysm, we struggled with dense emotions, and fear enveloped many souls. Survival was of utmost importance. Trust flew out the symbolic window of our psyche.

The Great Bear has significance in the human evolutionary spiral. However, there must be more to the unfolding story. A few days after having written the above experience I invoked Chiron again, and he appeared as Pegasus. He emphasised this point. I'd not experienced Pegasus before. Pegasus, a white horse with wings, took me again to the Great Bear and asked me what it would do after it awakened. I said it would want food, company and maybe a mate to explore its new life.

Astrology and astronomy used to be one subject. Astrology gave meaning to the science of astronomy and the study and integration of it was necessary for evolutionary purposes. The understanding of this natural Law is in the collective psyche of human souls. During the last Age of Aquarius, approximately 26,000 years ago, many highly evolved humans had the ability to manage the elements. They understood natural Law and the energetic system of the universe. Understanding that our solar system planets act as energy sub-stations for stellar influences, they were conscious of receiving and transmitting the frequencies of light contained within the Sun's rays. The Sun in our solar system is a life giver.

There are an infinite number of Suns in the universe, all receiving and transmitting life-giving energy from Source. This is why many ancient cultures worshipped the Sun.

When we choose to raise our frequency by gaining greater self-awareness, and willingly taking affirmative action on our findings, our mind begins to expand. Ancient wisdom and knowledge arises from our cellular memory, initially in the form of sensations, emotions and feelings. Our right brain expands as we become more conscious and then our left brain organises the data. Should you choose to acknowledge, trust and consciously work with your inner knowing, greater expansion of intelligence can take place. When the body is relaxed and the mind calm, open and receptive, an energetic channel is available for downloads of information from the Soul.

After the cataclysm of around 12,500 years ago a great flood enveloped much of the known world. Small islands appeared where there once had been land mass. Around Glastonbury in Britain, there were seven islands and upon each was constructed, in later times, a small wooden chapel, purportedly built by Joseph of Aramithea. He was my first spiritual guide. He came to me early in my inner journey when I was participating in a sound workshop. I had no idea who he was. Joseph was an uncle and secret disciple of Jesus and a benevolent benefactor to him, Mary Magdalen and other family members. A wealthy tin merchant, he travelled to many distant places including England on trade missions. Sometimes he took Jesus with him on his travels. In England they befriended the Druids. Joseph also made friends with the important dignitaries of the lands visited. A spiritual agenda was behind many of his movements.

After Jesus' Last Supper, attended by twelve disciples including Mary Magdalen, the holy chalice, a cup said to contain the blood of Christ, was handed to Joseph for safekeeping. His task was to take this cup to a holy place and bury it so that the high frequency of the Christ consciousness contained within it could be accessed when the time was right. Joseph travelled to Britain where the holy chalice was anchored into the planetary heart chakra at the Isle of Avalon, now Glastonbury, England. The area around Glastonbury is one of Mother Earth's chakra points and is an ancient sacred site.

When these seven islands are plotted on a map they form a pattern that replicates the seven stars of the Great

Bear constellation. Glastonbury corresponds to the star Dubhe, upon which the constellation pivots. The wisdom stored in these islands pre-dates Christian times, i.e. well before the Age of Pisces, so it is highly likely there were remnants of earlier sacred sites on these seven islands when Joseph arrived. The myth of Camelot, King Arthur and the Round Table, is associated with the Great Bear constellation. Arcturus, the brightest star in the northern hemisphere, whose position in the sky is indicated by the last two stars in the tail of the Great Bear, is also a player in our cosmic theatre. In Greek, Arcturus means the Keeper of the Great Bear. Is Arcturus or Arthur, the Keeper of the Great Bear who carries the Holy Grail of Christ Consciousness, preparing to re-activate his mission?

The Great Bear constellation was often referred to in ancient times as Arthur's wagon, being seen as the vehicle in which Arthur circled the north celestial pole. Because of Earth's wobble on its axis, the celestial pole describes a near circle among the stars over a period of 25,920 years known as the Great Year. It is this Great Year that divides into twelve, creating astrological Ages of approximately 2160 years. A new Age has begun, bringing with it different frequencies to those we have experienced. We now have the opportunity to awaken to our galactic heritage.

Arthur was referred to as the spirit guardian of the seven islands. His legendary cosmic adventures with his twelve knights of the Round Table questing for the Holy Grail were ritually enacted on Earth as the people in their tribes moved around the central pole of their territory. Their central pole imitated the revolutions of the Great Bear around the pole star, the star nearest the imaginary line through the cosmos produced by the northern extension of the Earth's axis.

To these ancient people the Tor at Glastonbury symbolised the pole star and the bear was their totem animal. The Round Table symbolised both the world and the huge sky circle made by the Great Bear constellation as it moved around the celestial North Pole. The bear is a symbol of great strength and bravery.

The stars Dubhe and Merak, two of the stars in the Great Bear constellation are known as the "Pointers". They are sometimes referred to as the major stars of direction because through them flow the will to unify all aspects of self. Synthesis results from this unification and brings about 'at-one-ment' between the personality and soul. This is a process of consciousness evolution.

According to Native American story the bear symbolises the power of introspection. In the winter, the time of ice and snow, bear enters the cave/womb to hibernate and digest the recent season's experiences. The bear seeks to know truth. In its cave, it receives nourishment through the placenta of the Great Cosmic Mother, the Galactic Centre. It is in this place of stillness that all questions are answered and truth is revealed.

***

Pegasus, the White Winged Horse

Why had Chiron, my spiritual guide for many years, transformed into a flying white horse in the process of taking me on another dimensional journey? And why was he insistent I record it? Pegasus was a new player in my reality but who was he?

Ancient cultures used storytelling as a means of communicating myths, legends and experiences. These stories were re-told down through the ages. The star myths were given to us as stories that depict the evolution of human consciousness and the pathway to spiritual ascension through multi-dimensional consciousness. The memories and truth underlying these stories exist eternally and are accessible to those who have the desire and the consciousness to de-code. Their truths are found through right brain intuition, insight, feeling and inner knowing.

In Greek Mythology Pegasus was a white winged horse with a mane of gold. He sprang from the neck of the gorgon Medusa when Perseus beheaded her. The horse is the animal symbol of intuition and of instinct, the unseen forces that can carry us to freedom. Because he can soar into vast space Pegasus stands for inspiration and imagination. He is the power of the creative spirit within us all. As the white winged stallion, he symbolises the human desire to take to the air. Pegasus can take us into the unknown regions of our brain and broaden our minds to greater realities.

In the human brain the place of memory is called the hippocampus. This word means sea horse. Stedman's medical dictionary defines the hippocampus as a white eminence. Therefore, does Pegasus symbolise our soul's ancient memory? Is he the key to our akashic records and our stellar heritage? Our brain is an incredible organ, mostly untapped and idle. It is an organ for experiencing and understanding consciousness. However, consciousness is not something that can be studied under a microscope. Scientific research into consciousness is still in its infancy. What is known is that 85% of our brains are not being used. Brain imaging studies have shown that chronic stress shrinks the hippocampus.

Through Pegasus we can reclaim lost aspects of self and remember our star heritage. In modern times Pegasus is a symbol for the immortality of the soul.

Pegasus was connected to the Muses, nine entities of mythology who lived on Mt. Helicon, the sacred Mountain of Apollo the Sun God. Pegasus created a fountain for them. The word 'muse' connects to the art of meditation. One of the muses, Mnemosyne, is the goddess of memory and, through her, our clairvoyant insights and intuitive skills develop, all attributes of feminine states of consciousness.

How can this mythology be interpreted in our everyday world? Is the white fluid secreted through the hippocampus the sacred amrit, the 'nectar of immortality' of the ancient Sanskrit teachings? Is the fountain water connected to the glyph for Aquarius, the water-bearer? The Aquarius symbol does not represent water in its literal form. It symbolises the frequency waves of consciousness we can access through objective self-awareness underpinned by our love of, and respect for, Divinity.

Pegasus is a galactic instrument through which ancient human memory can be activated. To do so requires we become a regular meditator, willing to still our mind from internal chatter. As a result of this regular practice clairvoyant, clairaudient and clairsentient gifts develop, along with the ability to travel inter-dimensionally in the mind. As this occurs, multi-dimensional consciousness awakens.

As we become awakened to our akashic records, our soul's ancient 'lost' memory, our consciousness rises and we begin to perceive our world differently. Illusions gradually fade. This state of being is often referred to in religious texts as The Second Coming, or Christ consciousness. *The Book of Revelations* in the Bible says that Jesus will return on a white horse. Jesus attained this Christ level of consciousness and said that whatever he did we could also do.

Christ consciousness is also known as Krishna or God consciousness. When we reach this elevated state of consciousness immortality is available.

Within the centre of the hippocampus is an organ called Ammon's Horn. Another name for Ammon is Amen. *The Book of Revelations* refers to Jesus as The Amen. Akhenaton, mentioned previously, was an enlightened Egyptian pharaoh. Seeded from Sirius he carried the Christ consciousness codes. He sometimes referred to himself as 'The Amen'. He introduced monotheism, The Law of One, to his subjects. Some say Jesus was an incarnation of Akhenaton.

The myth of Pegasus connects to Yeshua/Jesus, who carried the light of Christ consciousness. Mary Magdalen carried the codes of the feminine Christ consciousness. These codes were 'sacred nectar' to the people they taught. Parables were their method because they enabled complex themes to be understood. They anchored the codes of ancient wisdom teachings to accelerate our evolution to the light of galactic or Christ consciousness, our birth right.

Pegasus can take us to the highest heights to retrieve our star codes. When committed to, and advancing on our inner journey the kundalini force, the dual etheric serpents coiled at the base of the spine, begin to rise on each side of the spine. Eventually they emerge at the crown chakra. This is an energetic force connected to the consciousness of each individual. When it is ignited through remembering and experiences of truth, the individual begins to realise that all of creation is connected, as one hologram.

For some the kundalini force will never awaken in their current lifetime. For those who are dedicated to their spiritual evolutionary growth, both Sedna and Pegasus provide vehicles for its activation. I feel that Pegasus and another travelling guide, Uni, a unicorn, are connected.

The treasure hunt to unravel an ancient knowledge system continues.

***

Draco, the Dragon

Some years ago, when visiting the sacred site of Chichen Itza in the Yucatan Peninsula of Mexico, a high pyramid resembling the great pyramids of Egypt, I walked by the Temple of the Skeletons. Immediately, I felt a mass of dense, psychic energy descend upon me and unexpectedly take me over. This was a consequence of my early morning negative thoughts and emotional turmoil. I had unconsciously lowered my vibration and the dark thoughts and emotions acted as a magnet. Becoming extremely nauseous and weak, I wasn't able to climb the outside steps of the pyramid, nor could I contemplate the offer made by the tour guide to go inside the pyramid. It took me several days to recover from this psychic attack, having collapsed and lost consciousness in the next place visited. I tend to learn the hard way!

Years later, while meditating at my home, I received the telepathic message I was to prepare a sacred ceremony at the exact time of the upcoming New Moon. And, I was to follow my inner guidance. I lit candles, placed special crystals on my round table altar and was guided to circle around my table in a clockwise direction first, and then three times in an anti-clockwise direction, intoning a Tibetan chant during the process.

At the conclusion, I sat down at my round altar, deep in meditation, and was asked to return to Chichen Itza and enter inside the pyramid. Advised I would need to take a celestial being with me I invoked Lord Maitreya, an over-lighting celestial presence in my life, to accompany me. I was not to contemplate entering the pyramid if I felt the slightest fear. Totally confident with Lord Maitreya by my side, I entered the pyramid and climbed the steps to a huge, dark cavern.

The light emanating from within Lord Maitreya enabled me to see reasonably well. Hearing terrible heart wrenching moaning, accompanied by distressing gulping sounds, I realised something or someone was deeply upset. Then heart-felt sobs filled the cavern. Feeling my heart fill with compassion I walked to the cries to see if I could help. I made out the shape of a distressed huge dragon, curled around the internal cavern walls. Holding in its paws a limp and relaxed feminine serpent, the dragon gently and lovingly licked it while at the same time sobbing giant tears of grief.

Intuitively I understood my role. I was to take the serpent from the dragon and hold her for safekeeping. The dragon knew it was time to release his hold on the sacred feminine yet was reluctant to do so, hence its tears. I lovingly stroked the dragon and, looking deep into his eyes, spoke to him gently. I assured him that the sacred feminine, the serpent, would be safe with me. I asked the dragon what he would like as a gift for his efforts in guarding the goddess for so long. He said he would like to return to the Light.

I advised him that I couldn't give him this request but, if his desire was strong enough, and if he chose to generate genuine love in his heart, it could happen. I carefully took the large serpent from him and placed her around my neck. She raised her head and looked at me with intense focus, as if testing me. I didn't feel the slightest fear, only love and compassion. The serpent relaxed and rested on my body.

Lord Maitreya and I turned to descend the steps. Some steps down I became aware of bright light filling the cavern above and I knew the dragon had received his greatest gift. He had returned home to the Light. Lord Maitreya urged me on and, as we reached the bottom steps, he suggested I place the serpent somewhere other than around my neck. I placed it at the base of my spine, symbolic for the kundalini energy.

I then saw, and sensed, the above inner cavern exploding through the fusion of great light. The dragon, Draco, symbolising the masculine force, had relinquished his hold on the sacred feminine and, by willingly doing so, opened to the Light.

The Age of Aquarius is the cosmic timing for the Divine Goddess to emerge once again and be honoured for her intuition, insights, psychic gifts and oracular abilities as she had been during the Age of Taurus. The dragon does not need to guard her anymore because she is now capable of being her own power source.

At the centre of the celestial wanderings is the constellation of Draco, the Dragon. King Arthur's father was known as the Pendragon, meaning the Dragon's Head. A divine dragon is a symbol for the universal life force breathed into humanity as the element of fire, or spirit. It teaches us to master our lower mind to allow emergence of the intuitive higher mind.

The story about King Arthur being sired by Pendragon indicates it was when the pole star was located at the head of Draco, the dragon, about 12,000 years ago, that the Arthurian legend began. Male supremacy dominated the people of Earth. Atlantis sunk around this time due to masculine control, greed and power plays.

Draco, the cosmic dragon, opened to the light. The feminine serpent is free. She holds the Excalibur sword, given to her by the Lady of the Lake. The sleeping Great

Bear has awakened. The idyllic state of Camelot, the prophesied Golden Age, is preparing to emerge. The Grail Quest, upon which the myths and legends of King Arthur are based, is the search for the ancient esoteric secrets, knowledge and wisdom that enables direct connection to the stars, and to Source. The journey to super, or multi-dimensional consciousness, requires the dissolution of duality. How interesting that this lost state of Camelot was previously experienced on Earth well before Jesus's teachings of the Holy Grail.

The Ageless Wisdom teachings align to the Law of One, the Law of Love. Honouring and respecting Earth, as our mother, is part of the remembrance journey all souls take. A Camelot, or Garden of Eden on Earth, is reached when a critical mass of humanity chooses to revere nature in all her many forms, and to live lives daily attuned to Spirit, natural harmony, joy and love.

When connecting this story with the research of Englishman Robert Coon an interesting phenomenon is revealed. Robert Coon realised that 'dragon lines' intersected the Earth at sacred sites in the form of a figure of eight, or infinity symbol, the one given to me for Sedna. At some time in their soul's history Mary Magdalen and Yeshua walked some of these dragon lines planting their seeds of Christ consciousness and divine love into the land so that, when the Age of Aquarius flowered, these seeds would ignite ancient soul memories within the minds of the awakened individuals who visited.

In southern England, the country said to store the Holy Grail, the chalice of Christ Consciousness, there exists a smaller infinity symbol. The two currents meet at Glastonbury and Avebury, and Glastonbury is the reflection of the Great Bear constellation. The two lines represent the masculine and feminine energies joining together at these sacred places through the auspices of the Great Bear. These lines would have been, and may still be, initiation places for the Druids.

A stone zodiacal wheel can be seen from the air around the Glastonbury Tor that appears to be the creation of an ancient civilisation. It lies in a circle from Glastonbury in the north to Somerton in the south. Glastonbury is positioned in the area of Aquarius and represented by a phoenix. Glastonbury Tor is situated in the eye of the phoenix. Pisces has a whale situated between the two fish. Just outside the circle sits a Great Dog. Is this symbolic of Anubis, the Sirius dog star, guarding the great circle of life?

Capricorn, the mystical point of ascension from the zodiacal wheel, is depicted as a goat that looks like a unicorn. The goat represents an individual who, sure footedly, chooses to climb the symbolic spiritual mountain towards ascension. The esoteric symbol, the unicorn, symbolises the inner transformation that occurs within an individual when the sacred marriage, the *hieros gamos*, is experienced within the four bodies; spiritual, mental, emotional and physical. D.K. refers to it as a symbol for the triumphant initiate, the 'unicorn of God', in which the one single 'eye of God' is depicted as a single horn.

What message were those ancient builders attempting to convey to their future generations? The zodiacal wheel and the constellations of stars are intimately connected to the story of Mary and Yeshua and the re-awakening of Christ Consciousness.

***

Aquila, the Eagle

Aquila, the Eagle, lies on the border of our Milky Way galaxy, inviting humanity to know and experience the star realms beyond. The Eagle, king of the birds, is a symbol of spirit and the sun, the masculine elements of air and fire. The eagle stands for noble aspiration and the highest spiritual discerning power in humans. It represents the power of the spirit to soar upwards to the stars to become immortal, overcoming death and bondage to earthly things. The eagle is known for its nobility, speed and sharpness of vision and is a symbol for the brilliance of intelligence that enables insight and intuition. Because it flies so high it can be used as a metaphor for the power of spirit to transcend and conquer lower and baser forces. It can see wider horizons than other birds.

To the North American Indians, the eagle represents Great Spirit and enlightenment. It offers the ability to live in the realm of the Great Spirit yet remain connected and balanced within the material realm of Earth. Eagle offers the ability to quickly observe life from an expansive and unlimited perspective. Eagle feathers are considered to be sacred healing tools. Shamans use them to cleanse the energy field of people needing healing. The South American Indians substitute the condor for the eagle.

Eagle represents the state of grace achieved through much inner work. Eagle medicine has to be earned. From pre-historic days until now the soaring eagle is in polarity to the serpent. Because the serpent slithers along the ground it is a symbol for the earth, the Mother Goddess. In ancient cultures, she was depicted as wearing a serpent around her neck, symbolising the power of the feminine to 'shed one's skin' in order to attain immortality through rebirth.

The star Altair, situated in the constellation of The Eagle, Alpha Aquilae, marks the Eagle's throat. Altair is sometimes referred to as The Redeemer or the Ox-herder.

When I introduced a group of students to Altair, one of them saw a huge egg on the throat of the Eagle and said it wasn't yet ready to hatch. My intuitive response was that it needed more nurturing. Is a new seed of Eagle consciousness preparing to birth?

Another of my students received the message: "Note the eagles' cry". The Eagle doesn't 'cry' as it advances on its prey. It cries out with joy as it advances towards the Sun, the source of all Light.

Uni took me to the bright star Altair to view the cosmos from the Eagle's perspective. He placed me upon the throat of the Eagle so I could see and feel what it was like. I felt I was sitting on a nest. I could see the people on Earth wandering senselessly and aimlessly in groups, and individually, without direction or purpose. They were like un-herded cattle. I understood then that, after the divine masculine and feminine streams of energy have united the next step up the evolutionary ladder is to focus on group unity and purpose. A single-minded and heart-felt goal for the 'herd' needs to be created and implemented.

Altair, a radiant star and a cosmic being of great light can assist. He is The Redeemer and Ox-herder of humankind through his ability to activate and anchor group unity aligned with group purpose. This is a true Aquarian Age theme.

In Bolivia on a rocky hill above Copacabana, a small fishing village beside the sacred lake, Titicaca, there is an ancient Sun temple. Above this temple, carved into the rocky mountain outcrop by the wise ancients, is a huge symbol of Aquila, the Eagle. The energy there is incredible. On one of my South American tours, a male participant remembered this site. An old soul, he recalled a time when, as a spiritual initiate, he had been trained at this place to master the air element. Once again, in a meditative state, he symbolised the eagle, arms widely outstretched, embracing the highest heavens. With eyes closed, he intuitively directed his body towards Australia, indicating it was to here he must fly. It was here, he said, that eagle knowledge would be remembered.

***

Arachne, Spider Woman

Arachne had no equal as a weaver. She was a master of her trade. It was often said she must have been taught weaving by Pallas Athena herself, who was the goddess of weaving, but Arachne denied this. Through arrogance, she declared Pallas Athena could come and compete against her any time if she wished. If the goddess should prove the better, Arachne declared, she was prepared to suffer any penalty.

One day, an old woman came to visit advising Arachne to reconsider her rash words because there was still time to avert the goddess's wrath. Arachne told the woman she had lived too long to be given advice and suggested she leave. The old woman stood up, her guise of decrepit old age vanished and she revealed herself as the goddess, Pallas Athena.

A contest followed and Arachne's work proved flawless and far better than the goddess's weaving. However, she had chosen as her theme the amorous misdeeds of the gods, and the squalid tricks they used to get their own way. She depicted the rapes perpetrated on humans by the disguised gods and wove this theme through her depiction of the twelve signs of the zodiac. She added a scene showing Jupiter, disguised as part man and part bull, lustfully pursuing a beautiful woman. Her weaving depicted truth. She knew the gods and goddesses played a part in creating the imbalances experienced on Earth between human masculine and feminine energies. Truth was depicted in her weaving.

Pallas Athena wove a scene of a mortal man strapped into a harness that supported wings made of feathers. The man had clearly flown too close to the sun, for the feathers were already aflame. This, she said, was an image of human arrogance. From her goddess perspective, humans were unconscious and therefore lowly. She thought they were arrogant to believe they could 'fly into the sun' to attain the light of higher consciousness. She showed how they would be strapped and burned if they tried to emulate the consciousness of the gods.

The gods, through their ability to shape shift into whatever form they desired, and their ability to genetically manipulate to get their own way, were graphically and clearly depicted in Arachne's weaving.

Pallas was furious. Jealous of Arachne's weaving, and the truth of her depiction, she chose to view it as a mockery. Angrily, she destroyed the brilliant work and the loom. She was, after all, goddess of War as well as goddess of Weaving and the Arts.

Arachne was in utter despair, but Pallas' revenge was incomplete. She turned Arachne into a spider. The gods took pity on Arachne and elevated her to star status. They assigned her the task of weaving humanity's karma into the individual tapestry of each life. This karma is depicted in an individual's birth chart. She weaves threads of starlight into her designs and this starlight acts as a guide for human souls on their evolutionary journey home to the stars.

This myth is not only told in the western world but also by the North American Indians who revere Spider Woman as a wise crone. To them, her medicine is the ability to weave the web that brought humans the first picture of the alphabet. As she was weaving the letters she told deer it was time for Earth's children to make records of their progress. She held the dream of the world within her and created symbols within her web for humans to understand. When it is the cosmic timing for a part of the dream to manifest in the physical world, she offers these symbols to us through dreams and visions.

Spider's body has eight legs. The number eight is the symbol of infinity and the elongated symbol of eight is Sedna's symbol. In numerology eight is the number of power. Spider Woman is a symbol for the infinite possibilities of creation. Her eight legs represent the four elements and the four directions. She patiently and lovingly weaves the most intricate and beautiful web of life. When we get caught up in her web through illusionary thoughts and unconscious shadow emotions, she has us for her dinner. When we follow the path of the heart we consciously create a light filled and loving future.

Arachne holds the secret key for accessing this state of being and is mysteriously connected to the Galactic Centre, the womb of the Great Mother.

A star within the Auriga constellation, Arachne is positioned directly above Orion. She weaves humanity's karma into the individual tapestry of each life. She creates from a central source. I experienced this source as the Galactic Centre of our Milky Way galaxy.

***

The Sacred Pathway

Restful sounds of running water waken me. Outside my Sedona motel room is a garden stream and my senses are finely attuned. My stomach gurgles in synchronicity with the water. The image of Jonah inside the stomach of the whale comes to mind as well as the story of Pegasus and how it connects to the white fluids of the brain. I feel my body sensitised and vibrating and know the Moon has moved into Cancer. It is time to fly once again with Uni, my unicorn.

He nuzzles my feet. I jump on his back and bend down to hug his neck. He is my current space vehicle and a member of my galactic family. I care for him greatly. He straightens and takes off on a now familiar pathway through the heart of our Sun, into the light tunnel and to the vortex of the Galactic Centre, the black hole cave of the Galactic Mother. I want to stay here a while because it feels so comforting and familiar however Uni continues flying on. Energised, I stand on his back, a triumphant space traveller embracing the freedom of my galactic home.

Travelling quickly to the Sirius Great Central Sun we are greeted by RA. He welcomes us to his home and motions me to sit beside him. Holding my hand, he asks that I close my inner eyes and focus on the sensations inside my body. I do so and feel my stomach lightly churning, like waves upon the sea. The energy moves in a channel from my stomach into my heart and throat. The sensations heighten. The energy continues into my head where a specific area at the back of my head is pulsating strongly. Is this the spot referred to in the Pegasus story?

While concentrating on internal sensations I sense the presence of Grandmother Spider Woman. She appears as a wizened, small and bitter crone, bent over almost horizontally, using a stick to aid her. She says her bitterness comes from being forced to stop her life's work of weaving a giant galactic web because of the jealousy and envy of another woman. This woman was the goddess, Pallas Athena, a warrior woman who sided with men. She led men into battle and fought as one of them. The web was of creation, with all the threads connecting in perfect geometric harmony and being made in accordance with cosmic design. Her weaving was deliberately sliced and cut to shreds because it was a grander and more perfect weaving of truth than the one goddess Pallas Athena was able to make.

Pallas Athena destroyed Spider Woman's creativity and relegated her to a dark cave to live out her life for eternity. However, she says, she has a secret. Within the bowels of her cave is a vital piece of the cosmic jigsaw and only someone unafraid of the dark can find it. She buried it well.

I am in her cave. Instantly and intuitively, I know her secret and go straight to its hiding place. I dig in the earth and uncover the lost phallus of Osiris.

The return of the higher frequency energies is imminent. His phallus found, Osiris can once again be made whole. Spider woman can spin a web that will never again be broken.

***

Hope Creation Myth

According to a Hopi Creation myth, way back in the distant past of human development our ancestors lived below in a world under the earth. They weren't human and lived in darkness. Great Spirit watched over everything and some say he was the Sun. He saw how things were down under the earth, so he sent his messenger, old Spider Woman, to talk to our ancestors. She told them the Sun Spirit wished better for them and that she would lead them to another world. They listened and followed her path. When they emerged onto the surface of the Earth they became humans.

The Hopi Indians tell other stories of Spider Woman and I've seen some wonderful paintings of her. I wrote this part of my story in magnificent Hopi Indian land in Arizona. To them Spider Woman is a metaphor for she who creates from a central source. They believe that one day she will magnetise all of creation to her. Some say she represents the Galactic Centre, the great womb of the Cosmic Mother. She is representative of the dark and moist abyss and the rich and fertile earth into which seeds are planted ready to be nourished and nurtured. From her centre life develops.

The female force of creation, she joins all nations, tribes and galactic families together in her web. The Hopi's believe that what happens in one part of the web influences all parts of the web. Spider Woman is linked to dream catchers. These are tools purposefully made to hang near a bed head in order to catch dark energy from dreams. During dream time part of our consciousness removes itself from physical reality and ventures into Spider Woman's web, to explore different levels of reality.

As I was sitting and meditating on a rock at the airport vortex in Sedona I was asked by a Hopi Spirit-being to write about the Hopi prophesies. I agreed to do so. The wise Hopi elders pass on warnings and prophecies from generation to generation through oral traditions and storytelling. Some of their ancient rock pictographs and tablets tell of the prophecies. There were nine of them. Until this point in time the Hopi Indian prophecies through White Feather, (A Hopi of the ancient Bear Clan), have come true. There is only one more prophecy still to come:

From the sky will come a blue star that will travel close to earth. The waves from it will rock the earth to and fro. When the earth is sick and animals have disappeared, there will come a tribe of people from all cultures who believe in deeds not words, and who will restore the earth to her former beauty. This tribe will be called Warriors of the Rainbow. They say this tribe represents the thirteenth tribe and will be a new breed of humans. This new breed will be androgynous; internally balanced masculine and feminine.

Twelve tribes, or source races, are spoken about in the bible and other ancient texts. The Hopis, and Australia's first people, also refer to these tribes. The thirteenth tribe will be made up of all colours, races, creeds and cultures around the globe. They herald the return of Quetzalcoatl/Kukulkan, the lost white brother and feathered serpent. Quetzalcoatl represents Christ Consciousness and the kundalini, the etheric twin serpents coiled at the base chakra of the human spine and known in the yoga philosophy as Ida and Pingala. When awakened through the energy of divine love and Christ Consciousness, the serpents begin to uncoil to eventually reach the crown chakra. It is then the individual merges with divine consciousness and the Higher Self.

Arachne also has a prophecy, along with the secret she had been hiding for aeons of time. As the weaver of the magical web of life she knows how to repair and re-weave her intricate designs. She will not do this until the timing is right. Her secret has now been uncovered. She knows it is time to begin a new weaving. She found, and buried Osiris's phallus in her deep dark cave, the cosmic womb of the Great Mother Goddess, for a special purpose. She knew that the gods and goddesses were using their lustful ways and powers to manipulate the humans under their care. They were acting abusively, irresponsibly and childishly rather than as wise parents. She did her best to warn Pallas Athena, the warrior woman daughter of Zeus. Pallas, in her arrogance and jealousy, would not admit the truth. The game of devolution perpetuated.

The feminine denied the truth of masculine power abuse. The masculine used the phallus to perpetuate this abuse. Spider Woman, with her ability to see clearly, knew the outcome of these actions. When she observed Set - Osiris's brother- cutting Osiris's phallus she devoured that member, burying it deep within her womb. She knew it would remain hidden until mortals and the fallen immortals changed their ways. She told no one her secret. It was up to the beings playing in the 3D realms of consciousness to come fully into balance through synchronising their feminine and masculine aspects. Unconditional love was the key. This state would bring with it the ability to understand and experience life from a higher and broader perspective. Wisdom would follow.

When Yeshua and Mary Magdalen were born at the beginning of the Age of Pisces Spider Woman knew the time for a new weaving was imminent. Isis carried the wisdom of Spider Woman and prepared accordingly. Isis trained her priestesses well. She vowed that, through her training, the understanding of feminine sexual power would be practiced from only the highest motivations. She would not allow sexual manipulation and prostitution in her temples of learning. She would not allow abuse of the intuitive and feeling senses of feminine power.

The sacred sexual act was taught only as a vehicle for attaining elevated states of consciousness and unity with All That Is. Divine union would result and a Horus – a Christ child -would be born. Two thousand years later Osiris's phallus was uncovered in the cave womb of the Cosmic Mother. The cave's guardian is Spider Woman.

New Moon in Aquarius conjunct Uranus: Propelled by inner guidance I flew to the Galactic Centre. Spinning fast, and then letting go, I experienced tremendous calm and peace. Nothingness. Stillness. A profound connection to All That Is. I rested in the cave of the Great Cosmic Mother. Noticing slight activity on the other side of the womb cave, I observed Spider Woman preparing something beside her hearth. A beautiful white rectangular box with gold around it containing the sacred phallus, the one Isis couldn't find, was offered to me. Spider Woman had been guarding this symbol of the divine masculine for aeons of time. She told me I had been tested many times and had not been found wanting. I found the phallus when others could not, therefore I was its rightful custodian. She asked me to guard it well. I accepted her gift. She asked that I kneel so she could bless me. As I did so I felt her presence envelop me from my crown to all around my body. Her body was on the top of my head and her eight arms wrapped around me. She gave me permission to tell her story.

***

The Sensual Woman

It is still early, around 7.15 am. My 'cave', my Sedona motel room is warm and nurturing. Sedona – O, Sedna!

I nuzzle into my pillow. Questions arise in my mind. Who or what was the cause for the fall of the gods? Who was the female who taught them the sexual ways of earthly women? I racked my brains. No answer. However, I knew the answer was buried deep within. I remembered one of the many gifts Jupiter had given me in 2004 – a book of knowledge containing my akashic records. I decided to open this large, beautiful and ancient book. On its cover is a Star of David, two triangles each interlacing the other symbolising the integration of spirit and matter. At each of the six points of this sacred geometric pattern are three bright stars. When Jupiter gave me the book he said I could open it at any time to find answers to my questions. I have only opened it twice before. Now was the time to do so again.

I held the centre of the six-pointed star formation under my right hand and turned it to the right to open the book. As I did so a spinning vortex appeared. When the vortex stopped spinning the book opens. I flicked through a myriad of pages until I pause, more than halfway through the book. I intuit this is the page I need. As it is still dark outside and it's comfortable in bed I ask Jupiter to read the page for me. I wait. I see an image of a serpent, the Rainbow Serpent, slithering over the Earth. Gaia is involved in the story. Uraeus is the sacred serpent and is so connected to Mother Earth she feels her heartbeat. They are one and the same.

I see Gaia as a most radiant, beautiful and sensual woman, curvaceous yet slim, wearing a circle of flowers and leaves on her long brown hair and vines with fragrant flowers draped over her naked body. Absolutely gorgeous, her beauty reflects the beauty of her home. She is so inviting. Her joy is great. She loves being in nature, playing in the forests, swimming in the streams and dancing beside the sea. Her pleasure in experiencing all of creation is contagious. She was born of Uranus with a highly-developed consciousness.

She invites the gods from other realms to visit her. Enjoying playing the tour guide, she shares her joy of nature's unique manifestations. Knowing where there are the special places of high energy, known as dragons' lairs, she takes her visitors to them. Through her sensual magnetic attraction and joy the gods from other realms feel something stirring within them they'd never experienced before.

This is a new game for them. Just by being in her joyful presence change occurs for them. She can sense and feel this yet does not give it energy. A group of beings from Sirius and the Pleiades visited her beautiful outpost on the edge of the Milky Way Galaxy, arriving as a result of her magnetics. These beings carry a different vibrational energy, a different consciousness, and came from star systems, not a planet. Their stars did not have the wonders, splendour and beauty of Mother Nature. Gaia was enticing. Innocently, she flaunted her sensual beauty, offering herself to the visitors for their pleasure, anchoring them to the earthly plane. She offered them her body for mutual pleasure and took them into realms of indescribable ecstasy. Never had they experienced such joy and pleasure. They wanted more. And more.

The Earth was continually bathed in sunlight at this time of creation. Darkness and the Moon occurred later, after the first fall.

The visitors wanted more of Gaia. She became conscious of the game she had so innocently played and could no longer play it the same way. She saw how she had created lustful desire within the star gods. She saw how they desired more sex, not for the sake of experiencing divine loving union, but for the sake of earthly pleasure. She had something they wanted. She wanted their company and knowledge.

A shift occurred. She gave of herself from a different perspective. She wanted to get, not give. Self-aware, she prostituted herself sexually for personal gain, playing the game of selfish irresponsibility. Divinity, joy and love were sacrificed for selfish desire. Shadow enveloped the land. The original fall took place. Karma ensued.

***

Our Galactic Heritage

Our Soul, a created bundle of light energy containing memory, is connected to Source. Energy created cannot be destroyed however it can change form. Everything in our universe is energy, vibrating at different rates of speed. Matter is dense energy vibrating at a slower rate. Human beings, as individual packages of energy, operate on different frequencies of sound and light, much like a radio. Receivers and transmitters of cosmic vibration, we can choose to tune up to be receivers of greater light or tune out and devolve into deeper density.

Science is becoming closer to esoteric understanding and scientists with tunnel vision are being challenged to open their eyes. Our ancestors, evolved semi-etheric beings of light, came from the stars. Higher consciousness informed their knowledge and wisdom. The stories of these giant gods and goddesses form many global cultural myths.

When an individual opens their four higher chakras to multi-dimensional consciousness their form subtly changes. Light emanates and can be felt, and often seen, by others. Humanity is evolving rapidly as the energy of the Aquarian Age of Light envelops our planet. In order to consciously experience a lighter future, we need to understand our past. What was the origin of our species? Where did the humanoid species come from?

In our current evolutionary state of being most people operate on a 3D level through the personality, the false or lower self. There is a wonderful opportunity for spiritual growth available at this level of consciousness. More people than ever before are taking this growth opportunity.

When we embrace spiritual evolutionary acceleration by willingly identifying, owning and taking responsibility for personal psychology our vibratory rate increases. Our perception of past, present and future becomes more fluid as we experience life in present time. It becomes increasingly difficult to maintain a negative consciousness because all is accepted as a personal creation. This results in an increased desire for internal unity, unconditional love and peace. When the understanding and experience of spiritual Will increases, light codes of ancient memory ignite.

As we pass through the lower 4D archetypal level of sticky psychic pollution we begin to accept responsibility for our life creations. This passage can be challenging and take a long time. However, it can be accelerated when we learn to understand, and positively use, Neptune's transits to our birth chart placements. I've found that greater clarity of mind emerges as the result of a Neptune transit. Mental clarity is a sacred gift.

Developing full consciousness through self-awareness is a choice. However, the results of internal unity, harmony, happiness, peace and good health are so worthwhile. Spending relaxed and appreciative time in nature greatly assists our journey. Nature is a wonderful healer.

When we dedicate ourselves to our spiritual growth we learn to live life from a place of universal love for all beings, including love of our own divine internal spirit. And, we see the cosmic joke of our creations. The laugh is on us. And the childish games we used to play and maybe still do. We become conscious of them and choose never to repeat them. This 5D consciousness level takes time to develop. Devotion and dedication to the spiritual path of higher consciousness, and regular associated practices of meditation, healing and clearing density, are necessary to keep us on track. Opening our hearts to divine love and sharing our light become important practices in our lives. Some people who have evolved to this level are not bound by linear time. They know time is cyclic and live their lives according to the planetary cycles of time. The Pleiadians, through their central star Alcyone, can connect with us at this consciousness level.

The entire ascension process used to take lifetimes but during the Age of Aquarius we have the opportunity to attain it in one. Learning to understand and integrate - through feeling and intuition, - the different dimensional levels of consciousness, we become acutely self-aware. Some of us choose to be teachers and spiritual guides. When we willingly, and lovingly, share our knowledge and the wisdom we have gained, without thought of material benefit, we begin to operate at the vibratory level of Sirius. This is a 6D level, the frequency level from which sacred geometric forms create 3D reality.

When evolving through the consciousness levels we experience a merging with our Higher Self, or Over-soul. Remembering our galactic heritage is also part of the process. In this higher dimensional realm, non-physical experiences occur regularly. Dedicated and one-pointed effort is needed to reach this consciousness level and eventually full soul remembrance occurs. The next level is the awareness of multi-dimensionality along with the realisation and integration of the understanding we are all One.

This is the level of Christ and Buddha Consciousness. (Christ – love: Buddha – wisdom). It is at this level the individual begins taking responsibility for the whole, rather than only the self. Spiritually evolving the self and the whole become one and the same. There are many other dimensional levels we can experience through which we return to merge again with the One Great Spirit. However, the great cycle of earthly experience is completing and the next level of light beckons.

***

Archangel Michael and the Obelisk

When Sedna was discovered in 2003 the vibrational waves became available to open our minds to experience multi-dimensional consciousness. Astrology is a natural vibrational healing tool, and a pathway to ascension and immortality.

The Unicorn is the higher symbol for Capricorn and Capricorn is the soul's gateway out of incarnation according to Esoteric Astrology. The Unicorn helps us to access higher dimensional realms so we can progress our human evolutionary journey. To do so we need to take responsibility for our creations. Many people don't want to do this. They'd rather blame others for their experiences. Uni, the unicorn, can take us to, and through, the Galactic Centre, the realm of Spider Woman and the void of creation. By doing so we seed the resurrection of our light body. We are responsible for fuelling our body and mind with divine love. Sacred geometric shapes form in our blood as we purify our psychology and are consciousness indicators.

Pegasus, the cosmic white flying horse, created a fountain for the Muses, nine mythological entities living on the sacred mountain of Apollo, the Sun god. Are the nine Muses archetypal symbols of our spiritual evolution through nine dimensions of consciousness? Barbara Hand Clow, created a nine-dimensional consciousness model for her book, *The Alchemy of Nine Dimensions*. What if this 9D vertical human consciousness axis connects to Mother Earth's off-centre axis, the North and South poles, and the stars that inform the axis? What if, as the human collective mind develops higher consciousness and becomes lighter, this axis becomes so light filled it is no longer needed as a support mechanism?

Archangel Michael provided an interesting experience during one of my training sessions that throws light on this question. I felt totally safe and secure when he took me travelling vertically into space. Pausing, he asked me to open my inner eyes to look around. I saw a huge column of egg-shaped light emitting from a long obelisk. It had a solid, dark form but the bright light around and within it appeared to change the form. The light filled obelisk stretched upwards as far as I could see. Intuitively I knew the obelisk was the axis of a sphere. I was shown how the sphere spun on the light filled obelisk axis. At first it wobbled, just as our Earth wobbles on its axis as it orbits around the Sun. The wobbling sphere gradually gathered momentum to become more balanced and, as its balanced spin increased in speed, the obelisk became so consumed by light it disappeared. I could feel the resultant harmony, peace and balance in every cell of my body. Archangel Michael showed me a transmutation process applicable to all spheres, including our precious planet. On a miniscule level, every atom or cell is a sphere, spinning on an axis. When the bright light of human Christ consciousness infuses each sphere's axis, the form dissolves into greater light. We humans have two energy poles, the North and South.

Cosmic timing is the reason for the human consciousness explosion. The human acceleration into higher consciousness is shifting the Earth's axis. This understanding personifies the responsibility each one of us has for the changing conditions on Earth. When each of us makes the decision, and takes the appropriate action, to raise our consciousness to embody greater light and spiritualised love, Mother Earth rejoices. We have the individual and collective power to prevent further degradation and destruction.

Reflect for a moment on the thick grey fog emanating from the density of human thoughts, emotions and deeds that permeates our globe. This is the main threat to our survival. Pause for a moment and take an eagle view of 3D reality. Global change is occurring. Ice is melting, and fast. Many more humans are reaching for the light. On the other hand, cities are being destroyed. Violence of all kinds occurs daily. Brainwashing, greed, control and domination are rampant. Disease and illness is on the rise. The disease of ignorance and apathy are the two greatest threats to our survival as a species. It really is 'wake-up' time.

The gods and goddesses left clues about human spiritual evolution and our ascension process through their myths and legends. Our bodies contain density created through lower vibrational thoughts, emotions and beliefs. Shadow psychological content accumulates and magnetically attracts greater density. Over time, dis-ease and death take place. Death is the physical body's reaction to frozen consciousness. To access good health and higher vibrational levels of consciousness personal density needs to be remembered, owned, accepted, and healed. The light of consciousness then replaces former amnesia.

Working with the stars and de-coding their myths accelerates our journey to higher frequencies of light. Crack the codes, bust the myths and truth is revealed. Truth sets us free from karmic chains. Reclaiming our true identity is part of the spiritual ascension process. When claimed our Soul is free to fly like the eagle into Sun's light - super-consciousness.

Jesus demonstrated equality of the feminine through love of his counter-part and wife, Mary Magdalen. The Church of Rome, a masculine stronghold, denied this union. For two thousand years the truth was suppressed. But now, in the Age of Aquarius, the situation is changing. Cosmic currents are activating 'wake up' calls. Divine union has the opportunity to manifest within the hearts and souls of those willing to do the inner work.

***

Orion

'What is the content for the next section. Where to from here?' I ask myself. Intermingled came the knowledge waves about the Pleiades and triangles. So far in this journey I have connected many mental dots by playing cosmic detective. I sense triangles and other sacred geometric forms being created as I work, yet I am unclear exactly how the cosmic jigsaw pieces fit together.

Our Sun, the Pleiades Sun and the Great Central Sun of Sirius have connected and re-united. The Great Bear, Sirius and the Pleiades are an over-arching triangular force connected to the human evolution of consciousness. Aquila, Pegasus and Arachne are important players in the human evolutionary game.

The two bright guiding stars in the Orion constellation are Rigel and Betelgeuse. Rigel is said to be the home of the Dark Lords. I understand that Orion is the anchor for duality and it is where there is a concentration of the darkest and the lightest energies in our galaxy. About halfway between these two great stars is an area of overlap where the energies of light and dark merge. The three stars in the belt of Orion are contained within this overlap. The Council of Light, the Elohim, is responsible for the three stars in the belt of Orion.

I have had many experiences on Orion. My first was early in my conscious spiritual journey, during the early 1990s. I chose to go there and confront the Dark Lords to ask that an ancient soul contract I had made with them be terminated. I was in a healing session where it was discovered this contract was creating life difficulties. Having served its purpose, it was time to render it null and void. There was much negotiating and eventually agreement was reached. Part of the contract involved experiencing Orion implants. I wanted them removed. Over the following years these implants dissolved, and my life changed for the better. Orion implants are triggers that stimulate dense emotion. The dark forces need food to energise them, and human negative emotions are their food. They eat well when humans wallow in mental and emotional density.

Years later I became involved in a decision-making process with both the dark and light Orion Lords, and was party to some of their deliberations, serving as an impartial observer. At an even later time, I was privileged to be present at a great gathering when the representatives of both forces united through one Lord who held the balance of light and dark within him, through his third eye. The Galactic hierarchy rejoiced at the wisdom of the decision made at that time.

Orion is linked with the new astrology system and is in the process of undergoing a complete upheaval with much spiritual house cleaning taking place. I feel it is the celestial playground of the wars, disease and power plays reflected on Earth. Huge changes are occurring in its system, as they are on Earth.

On one of my celestial journeys I was invited to pass through the central star of Orion's belt. Observing a huge being of immense light at the entrance of the belt, appearing as one giant eye, I concentrated and, with focus and spiritual will I passed through the centre of its eye. It was done in 'the twinkling of an eye'. The eye appeared similar to the single eye of the Cyclopean race of giants who inhabited our earth long before Lemurian times.

I reflect upon recent meditations. One of my current practices is to send an imaginary laser beam of violet light from between my eyebrows into my head and lodge in my third eye to make sure this passage way is clean and clear. The third eye connects to a gland. On some of these occasions I am aware of a large, single, unblinking eye where I believe a gland to be. With the aid of the fine laser light I easily pass through this eye to activate another chakra at the back of my head. From this experience, occurring many times, I conclude that Orion rules our third eye chakra.

Our Milky Way galaxy spirals through space around its centre, the Galactic Centre. In western astrology, this is 27 degrees Sagittarius. Known as Hunab K'u in Mayan cosmology this centre is regarded as the giver of movement and measure, and the womb of creation. Our solar system is on the outer reaches of the galaxy and forms a sidereal arc or arm that connects to Orion.

The spiral formation is a fundamental form in nature. A spiral represents the migration from the centre, the womb, into a whirlwind of ascending frequencies. It is a passage of transcendence. It can also represent a gateway between worlds and dimensions, a doorway through which a spiritual devotee begins the quest from the physical to the spiritual plane.

The time is 3.07am. There is another part of the Orion story to be told. Memories stir. Many initiations took place in the Great Pyramid of Giza over which the belt of Orion was positioned around the time of its building. A special chamber inside the pyramid had a tunnel built to allow the light frequencies of Orion entry to the chamber.

In later Egyptian times it was believed that when a Pharaoh was ready to make the transition to a higher world, the soul of that Pharaoh would ascend to Orion and be positioned forever in the stars. Part of the transitioning process was for a young and beautiful female virgin to mount a specially made metal phallus attached to the body of the dead Pharaoh. The metal phallus was long and sharp and the female was drugged before her sacrifice, as she would not survive the piercing experience. The female initiate believed she was rendering a service to the great Pharaoh so his soul would ascend to the stars. She was programmed to believe it was a great privilege to be chosen.

***

The Comet

Walking down the hill to the village of West Sedona, a journey of one and a half miles, I had a task. Not only did I want to enjoy myself with a great lunch I also wanted to buy a copy of *The Mountain Astrologer*, a magazine I used to subscribe to many years ago. Having learned to trust and follow my intuitional feelings I felt there would be something in that magazine that would activate the next part of my story. I wondered what the article could be. Perhaps one about connecting the northern and southern hemispheres?

On the return walk I began to sing and dance. The moon must be in Leo, I thought. It was a beautiful winter day, bright sun, very little cloud and relatively warm. In my room, I eagerly skimmed through the articles but could not find anything pertaining to this story. Undeterred, I began to read each article carefully and, as I did so, began to feel restless. There was nothing here. Maybe my intuition was letting me down. No, I would not embrace that thought. I just wasn't seeing it yet. A Vedic Astrologer, Linda Johnsen, wrote the only article that interested me. I like her work. However, the article was towards the end of the magazine and I was feeling tired. Briefly scanning the article, I made the decision to read it thoroughly on the plane the following day.

During my evening meditation, I was given the image of a scene from years ago. I had been visiting my son, daughter-in-law and grandchildren and was travelling with them to holiday at a ranch in eastern Washington State. It was the middle of winter and the mountains were covered with snow. Driving to our destination on the night before a full Moon and lunar eclipse, we could see the road clearly and didn't need car lights. Never before had I experienced such brilliant moonlight and, when combined with the snow-covered mountains, it made an incredibly memorable sight.

Even more memorable was what transpired the following night. The comet Hale-Bopp passed close to Earth and was visible more clearly in the northern hemisphere than the south. I felt so privileged to be with some of my Australian family visiting my American family at this time.

Through the large ranch telescope, we watched the passage of a total lunar eclipse in one part of the night sky, while the comet passed by in the other. Never before in physicality had I seen such an amazing celestial phenomenon. We could not have had a grander viewing place, because of the location and the pristine clarity. My grandchildren were young at the time, ranging from between two to six years of age, yet they took part in the unfolding celestial light show. The Earth's shadow took hours to move across the face of the Moon, and every moment was an absolute delight.

Why was I given this image when I was nearly asleep, snug in my cosy Sedona motel room, preparing for my last night here? On the day of the winter solstice I would be travelling to Park City in Utah for a white Christmas with my American family and some members of my Australian family who were flying to USA for a family reunion. All the family who were present in East Washington during the time of the lunar eclipse and comet fly-by would be there, plus a few more.

I was shown how there is to be a repeat of a comet fly-by in the future, only this time the comet will be so close to Earth its light will be blinding. The comet will appear huge and its energy 'waves' will create chaos. It will by-pass Earth. This information connects to the Hopi prophecy. I wrote about this snapshot vision in my bedside notebook and drifted again into relaxation, my mind blank. From the emptiness of this void emerged a whirlwind vortex that became a spiral. From its centre emerged a small fish. As I was focusing on it the fish grew to become huge. It faced me. We were eye to eye. We were two beings totally at ease with one another. What was its message?

I wrote this down and again drifted into a totally relaxed state, my mind blank. A large mountain appeared. A red rock mountain, bright with sunlight. As I watched, streams of brilliant white light exuded from two sides of this mountain as if the mountain was cracking open. The light became stronger as the vertical cracks grew larger. The light appeared to encompass most of the front face of the red rock mountain. Truly a magnificent sight.

I wrote this vision in my notebook and again rested. From the void of my blank mind arose another vision. It was the head of a man with wild, dark up-swept hair. His hair was covered with white 'plaster' and he was shaking his head to free himself from its dust and debris. He appeared confused as if 'waking up'. I wrote this and fell asleep.

***

The Southern Fish – *Pisces Austrinus*

On waking, I was reminded of an earlier part in this story, that of Jonah and the Whale and how D.K. places importance on this parable. I have more clarity now. I intuit it's related to the fish in my last night's vision. I remember Linda Johnsen's article. In it a fish is mentioned. I eagerly reached for the magazine. I can't remember the title of her article however she wrote of the great flood written about in most ancient myths, and how it has significance for the Age of Aquarius. In both Hindu and Tibetan astrology, the ancient flood myth is connected to the constellation of Aquarius and the second coming of Christ. This second coming is the arising of Christ Consciousness within the hearts and minds of the mass population on Earth. A 'flood' of multi-dimensional Christ consciousness is 'washing' over the world.

The ancient Greeks envisioned the constellation of Aquarius as Ganymede, the beautiful boy Zeus selected to be his cupbearer. The cup or jar contained nectar. In the Hindu tradition, this nectar is called amrit. It is the sacred nectar created within the region of the third eye chakra when a spiritual initiate has reached a higher level of consciousness. Ganymede pours the sacred nectar of advanced consciousness to the awaiting mortals on Earth. The Aquarian sky-boy with the water jar pours 'life-giving rain" or amrit, to a thirsty earth.

Through the influence of Pegasus, the hippocampus is activated enabling memory retrieval of our soul's heritage. When conscious of our divine heritage, a special white fluid develops within our brain. This fluid is amrit.

Linda Johnsen writes about ancient Hindu mythology saying that, early in creation the gods and goddesses decided to create a sacred nectar in order to unite their different natures. Using their wooden spoon, they churned the celestial milk of the Milky Way galaxy.

All kinds of amazing things emerged from this interesting mix, including a dazzling white horse, Pegasus. After more churning the great Aquarius, the legendary father of India's Ayurveda medical science, emerged holding a jar filled with the most sacred of nectar, the nectar of immortality. When the angels rushed to hold the jar he accidentally spilled four drops of it onto earth. These four drops became the elements of fire, air, earth and water, the elements needed for the creation of human life. Fire and air are masculine elements and earth and water are feminine. These elements rule the four human bodies as the fire of spirit, air of the mental body, water of the emotional body and earth, the physical body. When we learn to master, and bring harmony to our four elemental bodies, we earn the right to immortality.

Remember the obelisk teaching where I was shown a vision of a sphere spinning on an obelisk/axis? Obelisks were a creation of the Egyptians. This vision can tie in with the Hindu myth. Perhaps the obelisk is a similar symbol to the giant wooden spoon? Maybe the sphere is the area in space Uni demonstrated as my new playground? And, or maybe the obelisk symbolises the axis of Mother Earth?

The word soma in Sanskrit means nectar but it also means Moon. The Moon is feminine, and in astrology, rules our past and our soul's memories. One of Mary Magdalen's pictographs I purchased in Copacabana has a crescent Moon at her feet, depicting a Moon Goddess. A crescent Moon symbolises the power of the goddess to understand, and to heal, the past and to move away from it. The Moon also rules the 'waters of life' and Mary was sometimes referred to as 'mistress of the waters'.

Aquarius relates to androgyny, the balanced masculine and feminine through which a third force can be created, a super conscious Christ child – a Horus. The Moon's transit through Aquarius is said to be the best time to administer medicine. Maybe Amrit, the nectar of immortality and eternal life, is the medicine? Mary Magdalen, as the divine feminine avatar for the Age of Aquarius, carries the amrit, the nectar of ancient sacred wisdom that provides medicine and healing to those who willingly embrace and embody her teachings.

Let's refer again to the Hindu fish story. The great flood is an important part of this story. According to Linda Johnsen, the earliest known reference to the Great Flood appears in the Rig Veda, a large Hindu scripture compiled around 3100 B.C.E. In the Hindu version Noah's name is Manu. We are all descendants of Manu who survived the Great Flood and repopulated the Earth. Our words, 'man', 'woman' and 'human' come from this root word. Hu-man means God-man.

One day Manu was bathing in a river when a tiny fish swam to him and said 'Please save me from these waters. If I stay here a bigger fish will come and eat me'. Manu compassionately carried the little fish home in a small jar of water. As the fish grew it had to be transferred into larger jars. Eventually it needed to be taken to the ocean. Manu released the fish to its fate, having nurtured it for a long time. The fish, grateful for Manu's care and loving attention, offered to reciprocate the kindness. It spoke of a great flood coming that would inundate and cleanse the land of human psychological pollution. The big fish suggested Manu build a protective ark so he and his family would be safe. And to move into the ark at the first sign of rain. The fish would then come and tow the boat to safety.

Manu followed the instructions. With the advent of the heavy rains he attached a cable to the fish's horn. Slowly the giant fish pulled the ark to the Himalayas, a stronghold of the masculine Ray. There, Manu anchored it to a mountain and released a bird to see whether it could find dry land. The bird returned carrying the stalk of the sacred soma plant. The soma plant is symbolic for sacred feminine nectar. Manu climbed out of the ark and performed a thanksgiving ceremony, realising the fish was the great Goddess in disguise.

In southern India the word mina means fish. It also means star. From a southern latitude perspective, there is a huge fish in the night sky called Piscis Austrinus approximately 30 degrees south of the equator. The 'horn' or mouth of this fish, the bright star at its head, Formalhaut, is one of the major marker stars used by sailors to find their way across the sea. This bright star was considered one of the four Royal Stars, or heavenly 'watchers' identified in ancient Mesopotamia. The fish constellation appears in the part of the sky between Capricorn and Pisces the ancients call 'the cosmic waters'. In myth, the gigantic fish turned back to speak to the Aquarian man who had released it from its jar into the celestial ocean. In some flood myths, the act of swallowing the 'water', the amrit, flowing from the Aquarian vessel, was seen as salvation from the deluge.

Pisces Austrinus, sometimes referred to as *Pisces Australis*, has been identified as a parent to the two fish of Pisces. The two fish, bound by a cord depicted in the Pisces glyph, becomes one fish in Pisces Australis. D.K. says that, in ancient Lemuria, the symbol for Pisces was a woman with a tail of a fish. A mermaid. In later Atlantean times, when duality became present in the minds of humanity, the tail was dropped and the existing two fish symbol was used. The Fish Saviour or Avatar was called Ea in Mesopotamia and Ea, pronounced EE.AY. and is an ancient word attributed to Sirius.

In ancient Hindu astronomy, specific mountains, such as the one where the ark came to rest, were technical terms for the north celestial pole. The four points along the ecliptic is where the solstices and equinoxes occur. The sprig of soma that the bird brought back to Manu symbolises the crescent Moon. The Crescent Moon phase follows the New Moon phase which is a time when the Sun (masculine) and Moon (feminine) join together and the sky is dark. The Crescent phase symbolises the stepping out of the feminine Moon ahead of the masculine Sun.

Linda Johnsen suggests that it is possible the Great Flood symbology refers to a period of pre-history when ancient calendars had to be radically readjusted because the old ones had become obsolete due to the Earth's precessional cycles. 'Time' had changed. Astrology no longer reflected the cosmos. A 'flood' was needed to clear the old ways to make way for the new. Is this not the case now?

Manu represents the constellation of Aquarius. The Aquarian Age is a time of change and enlightenment. Great time cycles have drawn to a close. A new awareness is dawning in the consciousness of humans. A bright light is breaking free from within the huge red rock Capricorn mountain of matter. What will emerge from that red rock mountain? Red rock mountains are found in the desert and Australia has a sacred red rock mountain, Uluru, at its centre. It is a powerful dragon lair situated on one of Mother Earth's chakra points. Sedona connects to it through intersecting ley lines.

During my last day in Sedona I visited a special place at the airport vortex. With my eyes open I saw a large cluster of red rocks morph into a Lemurian Temple of Light. I viewed it from many different angles. Psychic experiences with my physical eyes open are rare for me. I self-questioned, but the Sedona temple scene in front of my eyes remained – even though I walked, for at least forty-five minutes, to four different locations to view the phenomena. Are the red-rock mountains of Sedona an ancient Lemurian library? I wondered. On my return home to Australia I delved into my library and found a small book about Sedona, written by Tom Dongo. In it he explains how Sedona was once an ancient Lemurian city of Light with many temples at certain vortexes. He had drawn an illustration of one of the temples. It was as I had seen. He also wrote that other people had seen the same phenomena.

There is another ancient legend about Piscis Australis. It commemorates the transformation of Venus, the goddess of love and beauty, into the shape of a fish while she was bathing in the waters of life. There is an esoteric truth that says Venus is prominent at the beginning of each new Age. There is much sacred wisdom contained within myths and fairy tales.

Let's take a side-track for a moment and return to the Andes. After a great flood, the Andean creator god Wiraccocha travelled to Tiahaunaco in Bolivia, bringing light into the darkness and re-populating the world. Wiraccocha appeared to manifest from Lake Titicaca and was a giant light being of immense power. He travelled far, opening dimensional gateways, transmitting seeds of consciousness, language and sacred songs. He taught people to live in harmony with the land and the sea. Wiracocha was often referred to as 'the feathered snake' or serpent, there being a similarity between the first Australians, Andean and Maya legends. Some of the Andean legends say that Wiracocha was a great spiritual teacher, a white (semi-etheric) man with a beard, who performed miracles.

The Andean prophecies speak of the return of a New Age. A new beginning and a stepping beyond 3D constructs. They have a timing system that suggests the Age change began in 1992. According to their understanding this new age is characterised by the growing strength of the feminine. They believe all people on Earth will be influenced to progressively recognise, develop and bring into balance the feminine aspects of their personalities. As this occurs, higher consciousness emerges from the darkness of the past and humans will again begin to radiate a higher frequency of light. Ancient codes will be remembered, often activated by visits to sacred sites.

Many happenings on Earth appear to be beyond the average human understanding. Our planet is undergoing massive energetic change, as are the people upon her. A huge leap in spiritual evolution is taking place. Those who hold the ancient codes open the gateways to other dimensions and do their best to awaken those still sleeping.

***

Chapter Ten

A New Astrology for the Aquarian Age

Cosmic Triangles

When a new student first viewed a birth chart she became excited. A natural therapist specializing in iridology, she immediately connected the divisions of the twelve houses in the birth chart to the iris, intuiting there was a correspondence. That evening, when casually reading notes taken from the book *Earth a Living Library* by Barbara Marciniak, this same view was expressed. There are twelve divisions in the birth chart, representing areas of life referred to as 'houses'. These twelve divisions also represent twelve strands of DNA. It is these twelve strands that will eventually show themselves in the iris of the eye. We'll be able to read the genetic codes of purpose and intent stored in the blood. Many so-called mysteries will be revealed within the iris. When the iris is divided into the twelve astrological houses, each house will correspond to its own place in the body, much as it corresponds to an individual's astrological imprinting of planetary and stellar energies at birth. Truly, the eyes are the window of the soul.

Now it's time to share a new technology I was taught during my regular meditation practices. I have been resisting sharing for ten years. You may remember the story earlier written in the section on Tibet? About a former life as an astrologer? No excuses any more. Roll up your sleeves Ashtara and begin.

It has been scientifically proved that our brains are so designed that mystical or spiritual experiences can occur frequently. We can train our brain to develop these experiences through the process of regular meditation, deep slow and rhythmic breathing, stilling the mind and daily generating the positive feelings of love, compassion and appreciation. Sincere prayers of gratitude each morning and night assist the process. This regular practice enabled this story to be written.

Thirty years of astrological study, and the application of it as a healing tool for self-exploration and self-realisation, led to my understanding of the three levels of consciousness. A persistent question entered my mind during those years. *What cosmic system is available that continues to promote human consciousness evolution after we have worked through our Solar System's planetary challenges and themes depicted in our birth charts?* It's as if my soul knew of a cosmic system to accelerate human consciousness beyond that of our Solar System's influence.

The first answer took the form of spiritual ascension and walk-in experience. I viewed this experience as the birth of a different personality and created a natal chart for the time, date and place of it. Now I had another chart, and the psychological issues contained within it, to work through. The cosmic joke was on me! I thought I'd worked through my incarnational issues! Not so! I tackled the psychological challenges indicated in this chart with as much dedication and commitment as I had done with my natal chart. The lessons were different. This time the element to master was air - the mind. It's a work in progress.

Sometime through this next learning phase, Lord Maitreya taught me about the energy of triangles, and how a trinary system is the way out of duality. D.K. taught me similarly. Each player in the triangle operates at a different frequency of light. When Lord Maitreya was establishing a mutually manageable frequency between himself, Kuthumi and me he said that, as my infusion stabilised I would cease to be concerned about some things in my life. He enquired if I was ready to move on, and I said yes. He then said: *The amount of resistance you have determines the degree of forward movement. It can be easy – or not.* Beaming love and light through his eyes he also touched my third eye saying I would not be as resistant as previously. I noticed that Lord Maitreya had the seven colour Rays emanating from his wings. Light-filled, he infused Kuthumi and me with divine love.

I've noticed that, soon after experiencing progress into a higher level of light (consciousness), we are tested as to whether we can sustain it. The challenges may not be pleasant. It's as if those around us cannot comprehend our increased light and are threatened by it. They react, often aggressively and defensively. Our faith and trust are often tested during these times. Passing this test leads to a more responsible task.

In 2007 I again asked the same question of my Higher Self. The answer came in the form of mystery school training.

***

Arcturus Training

During many meditations throughout 2008 Arcturus light-beings trained me to view clear images of the zodiac engraved into a round board room table.

I was not alone in this training. At first, there were twelve students around the board-room table. Four were from Australia. One man was from France. I do not know where the others came from. All had progressed to a certain frequency of light and love and were deemed ready to be taught at this etheric mystery school. We had one Arcturus instructor.

During the first visit we were advised that this is a place where the Masters work, and what we were viewing was the wheel of life. Our Sun was in the centre of the wheel. Following close observation of the current astrological model on the table, I intuitively looked up, and, on the ceiling, noticed another model with the three stars of Sirius in the centre. This system beamed light rays through triangular forms to our zodiac. We were told we were viewing a system of cosmic management.

On the next visit, we were asked to look more carefully at the engravings on the board-room table. This time we saw a mirror reversed zodiac. Our instructor taught us that, once the wheel of karma stops spinning, the rotational movement of the soul's journey changes. This can only take place within an individual when there is balance between the inner masculine and feminine, the heart is love-filled, and allowance is made for internal spirit to guide. I experienced this directional change in my brain and body years ago, when transiting Saturn passed through Libra so understood the concept taught. Now, we were told, the rotational movement is clockwise, from

Libra. The soul is responsible for the timing of directional change. This balance emerges when responsibility is taken for all we create.

We humans have experienced a retrograde motion in consciousness for some 26,000 years. Atlanteans created the model of our current astrological system of duality. I believe Thoth was the main creator. Maybe their agenda was for power and control? Or, as a tool to help us reclaim our sovereignty as super conscious human beings? The mirror-reversed zodiac was apparently developed earlier, in Lemurian times, before humanity's fall.

We were told that the reversal of the wheel was allowed as part of the divine plan for human evolution. There was an opportunity 12,500 years ago to correct the imbalance, but it wasn't successful. All it will take this time around to correct is a handful of people willing to spread the word. Who was willing to do this? I raised my hand and so did a few others. 'It will be done,' said our teacher.

Arcturus, in the constellation Alpha Bootis, is the guardian of the Great Bear and earth's circumpolar circle is now shifting to the influence of the Great Bear. *We, on Arcturus, are now the foci for beaming light to others. There was a rotational system and Arcturus received light emanations from other sources. These light emanations transmit the radiation to other star systems. It is an energetic system.*

At the next visit, I experienced stomach nausea when looking up above the board room zodiac. I felt something wasn't right. The light beaming down was different. There was only one triangle of energies pouring into the zodiac forming three streams of light at each point, beaming down to a single light focus. As I watched I saw a giant hand reach into the centre of the triangle. It grabbed hold of the sticky substance and pulled it upwards from the centre of the triangle. The substance was held aloft in the giant hand. The triangle changed its location in space, becoming distorted. It swivelled and the three points of it were on a flat plane with the centre still being held up by the hand. I again looked at the table. It now had a sheet covering it. A 'cover-up' had taken place at some point in time. The original blueprint for humanity's evolution into higher consciousness was covered over. Was this the exposure Thoth was referring to when he told me he had my blessing to reveal a hidden secret? Asked to look at the table again, I saw a solid white sheet covering the original zodiac. As I watched, the zodiac we know today was placed over the top of the white sheet.

We were taught that, since Atlantis, there's been a cover-up and we humans have been manipulated and controlled by a duality system. We were also told- *It is time for the truth to be revealed. The reversed zodiac you saw is the correct one. It was purposefully changed in Atlantean times to keep humans in darkness and ignorance of truth.* We were asked to look up.

Now the light beams above seemed to emanate from a gently moving prism. A prism is a spectrum produced by refraction that creates seven beams or rays of different coloured light. These lights are the same colours as a rainbow and the seven Rays that energise the human chakra centres. Esoteric astrology is based on a system of seven rays of energy beamed into our solar system and zodiac through specific stellar systems.

The brilliant light beams appeared to slightly move in sync with the prism and then hold steady. We were told to research, practice and know this information to be true, and then to share it. When the time was right we would be called back to Arcturus to learn more. On a subsequent visit, we were taught that the zodiac we are currently using is a cover-up, created by Thoth as a distortion.

On a later visit, when the cover was again rolled back, I noticed a change. In the centre was a living, bright pulsating heart appearing to breath. Blinding light was around the pulsating heart. Nine cosmic bodies were around the Sirius central heart hub of this wheel. The entire system was alive. The light from above was like moonlight. It was soft, feminine and luminous. A Frenchman and I were the only students at this training.

The next time we were taught how the nine spokes of the stellar wheel went to nine different parts of the human body, and these parts could only be discovered by accessing memory, and through inner experience. My self-questioning was: What organs do the spokes from the heart connect to? We were told the class would resume when we had come up with the answer.

While playing with this question for a few days two images with a connecting theme emerged:

- Within the human body is a universal network of love created through an interconnected web of light. Divine Love is the fabric of the Universe.
- Images of red roses. The rose is a symbol of love. The rose is Mary Magdalen's symbol. Within my body a tree of roses, like the kabbala tree of life, has been seen by three different female healers, at three different times. That image now begins to make sense. I also became aware of different parts of my brain being activated but need to do more inner research on the specifics. Sirius rules Christ consciousness, and probably some parts of the brain.

A month or so later I was taken by an Arcturian being of light to a large empty field. Standing in the centre, a Camelot began forming around us. Music, dancing, laughter and joy abounded. A Golden Age was being shown and I momentarily experienced it. It already exists in the etheric. When will it manifest on Earth? When we are ready. Will it manifest? It's up to us.

I was the only student on a return visit to Arcturus and connected, through feeling, to the pulsating heart on the boardroom table. It was alive. I felt my heart not only beating in unison with it, but also warming and expanding. The heart feels only truth. The stomach can perceive truth by digesting information. Often, the stomach doesn't want to digest the negativity contained in the information fed to it, so the stomach spasms. Knots form. The stomach can also act up when it attempts to digest thoughts of overwhelm. The overwhelm is a Neptune wash of psychic residue containing resistance. I know it well. It's a warning signal to become more aware of negative thoughts such as self-doubt, overwhelm, fear and control, and to relax, have faith and trust. The stomach is an organ of perception. There are others. We perceive life through our senses. Through our eyes, ears, nose and skin. Then, there's the brain. What are the perceptive organs or glands in the brain? And what about memory? Something stores and releases memory. Memory is encoded with feeling.

I wonder if I'm on the right track? Is there more?

To Arcturus again. This time there were five Arcturian teachers. I was the first student to return. They were expecting another, the Frenchman. The board-room table had disappeared. The Arcturians told me they operate on a different frequency to that of the Sirians, and work as one consciousness. That was all the teaching given on that day. A few days later they began training me as had the Antarians, prior to ascension. The training was in mental mastery. They demonstrated how the five Arcturians became one simply through their thoughts and feelings. As with the Antarians, this group of trainers morphed into one and asked me to close my eyes and feel when unity took place, and then to feel when they took the form of five again by separating. I telepathically reported on my experiences. I realised they were testing my sensitivity. I passed their tests.

On my next visit, when again I was the only student, a white cloth covered the board-room table. Removing it, the Arcturians exposed a thin layer of water. Something was under the water. It looked like a photograph being processed from a negative. My attention was drawn to the shimmering waves of the water surrounding the negative. Something is to be revealed in the photograph, and the waves of higher consciousness will active it.

I was told we humans are forming our life picture and can create a Camelot. We have been immersed in fluid, like a photographic negative, and hung out to dry in the dark. The light of consciousness will reveal the whole picture.

My next Arcturus training concerned an egg. I was asked to focus on the egg. My trainers broke it. Out poured the yolk, surrounded by the attached white substance. A spot, a seed, was in the centre of the yolk. 'What came first' they asked. 'The chicken or the egg?' My guides enjoy humour, and know I also enjoy it. What came first? The egg of course, the substance of the Universe. In the beginning was the substance of darkness, a void into which a seed was planted. This substance was impregnated by a seed of consciousness, and a ripple effect created. Change occurred. The seed will grow if nourished. God seeds create god-men and god-women.

A few days later and following a yoga nidra meditation, I became aware I was in a small cave deep within my heart, holding a key in my hand. Walking around a bend in the cave, I encountered a locked door. I used the key to open it. Inside, the faintly lit room was filled with cobwebs, dirt and dust. It obviously hadn't been entered for a long time. Creating a bright torch light, I shone its beam through the dust. Noticing hieroglyphs on the ceiling, walls and the mosaic floor I wanted to see more. Creating a whirlwind, I cleaned the whole area. The small room was a round temple. Brilliant gold was the main colour depicted on the ceiling and walls. On the floor was a magnificent ten-pointed star with the galactic centre in its centre. I stepped into the centre and was whirled clockwise into a downward spiral. When the spinning stopped, I stepped onto a black platform where I encountered a spiritual authority. He placed a royal blue cloak over me, and a white scarf around my neck, advising me that I hold a treasure in my hands. What did he mean? Maybe it's this book?

My final Arcturus training connected to unity. This time there were many players. Like the training received on Antares, I stood in the centre of the circle with many Arcturians surrounding me. On the in-breath of God we merged as one and, on the out-breath separated into individual parts. The Arcturus message was: There is only one life, and it is eternal. An individual can play out a life in a variety of ways, and all are part of a great circle of wholeness. We are all One. I visualise this as a hologram. Each of us is a cell in the God/Goddess hologram, and each one of us has a part to play in the evolutionary process of this great Light Being. When one part is 'out of tune' all other parts experience it, just like an out of tune instrument in a symphony orchestra. Eventually, all cells become harmonised, uniting as one. And then, a new Camelot is born.

When we begin working with higher vibrational cosmic codes we receive energy blessings and experience initiations. Even though they are challenging the initiations are encoded to bring us closer to our purpose for being.

***

The Living Light of Love

Once upon a time when our Earth was young many beings from other star systems enjoyed their holidays here. It was a paradise, a haven, a respite from their normal lives. These beings, of semi-etheric form, appreciated and valued Gaia's beauty and bounty.

A Great Plan was created whereby a species of life form would live permanently in this wonderland. It was decided to impregnate an already existing species with certain formulas that would enable this particular life-form to evolve and grow in accord with nature. This life-form became known as human.

Over aeons of time the species was impregnated with different codes that were dependent upon which visiting species worked the experiment. We are a result of these genetic experiments. We now have the ability to genetically modify other species just as we were once genetically modified. The wheel has turned full circle. Those who implanted the genetic material can now see clearly the results of their work.

In the 21st Century implants are commonplace. Some of these implants are used for research in an attempt to understand animal behaviour and instinct. As was once done to humans, humans are now doing to animal species.

The zodiacal system in use today is a system of duality. Prior to the tampering of this system there was a trinary system. It was this trinary system that created the paradise on Earth. The understanding of this trinary system is known to some people, and this knowledge will spread. It is time for humans to wake up from their amnesia to know the truth of their heritage from the stars. We are a mixture of genetic material from other star systems, and we are an experiment. We are a genetic experiment and, as such, are mutating into distinct polarities. In our zone of duality there is always darkness and light. The battle between the dark and light is intensifying. The dark will do its best to maintain its position and keep on perpetuating amnesia. It does this through the media and misinformation.

The Light is doing its best to awaken humans to truth and it does this through love. The self-generation of love within human hearts and minds is a spiritual technology that is now being practised by millions. As this wave of love sweeps across the planet its light will become too bright for the dark to handle. The dark forces operate behind closed doors. The Light operates in nature where there are no doors. The dark desecrates nature. The light honours and respects nature.

Within the hearts of all humans is a divine spark. This spark becomes a strong flame when the decision is made to follow the Way of the Heart. Heart intelligence slowly begins to take supremacy over the mental aspect. Heart intelligence is connected to the Laws of Nature. Throughout the Ages of human existence there have always been great spiritual teachers. All have said the same thing. The living light of love is the necessary ingredient to fuel a healthy and fulfilled life. It is so simple. The living light of love does not abuse, maim, destroy, hate or fight. The living light of love accepts, respects, and appreciates all of nature for its inherent teachings. The Way is easy to follow when people are awakened and aware of nature's wonders.

The early morning birds sing their song joyfully and their high vibration sends waves of love to the plants. They open their leaves and flowers to the new dawn with eagerness and joy. Where nature is encouraged to flourish the light of consciousness grows strongly in the human soul. The opposite is true. Nature uplifts the human spirit. Will you allow it to uplift your spirit?

***

A Review

The Galactic Centre: Arachne kept hidden a mysterious and important secret that, once revealed, would recreate the divine union of Isis and Osiris, symbolic for the divine masculine and feminine. Arachne sits in the heart of her cosmic web, the Galactic Centre, spinning the truth of the human evolutionary story. Her secret is out in the open. Osiris's phallus has been recovered.

Sirius operates at a 6D dimensional level and forms a cosmic triangle to the Pleiades and Great Bear. Sirius is the great central Sun of the new astrology system that aids humans to grow into super, or galactic, consciousness. This is the highest human attainment possible.

During a harmonising experience with the Sirian Council, I became aware of how the individual members demonstrated the qualities we need in order to experience totality of beingness. When we embody these aspects a merging with the unified field, often referred to as the Goddess, takes place. At one of my recent reunions the Sirians told me: *We are of the Goddess, and we are One.* Isis is the great goddess of the ancient Egyptian mystery schools and sourced from Sirius.

Draco, the Celestial Dragon, is a mythical animal appearing in ancient cultures. A former guardian of the feminine serpent, he kept the goddess hostage, fell in love with her, and willingly relinquished the hold he'd had on her since enticing her from the Garden of Eden. His cosmic task had been to hold her, as a sacred treasure, in safe-keeping until the change of the Ages. He did his job well. Draco's stars were the Pole Stars from 4500 B.C.E to around 2000 B.C.E. The Dragon's job is done, and he ascended through an explosion of divine light. The serpent goddess is again capable of being her own power source.

The Great Bear showed me how she was awakening from a deep sleep. Glastonbury is a reflection of the Great Bear constellation and was, and probably still is, a spiritual initiation place for the Druids. There is an ancient western style stone zodiac circling around Glastonbury that can be clearly seen from the air. It places Glastonbury in the area of Aquarius, represented by a phoenix, the mythical bird that rises out of the ashes of its former self. The story of King Arthur and his twelve knights of the round table connect to Arcturus. The round table symbolises the zodiac. King Arthur sent his twelve knights, symbolising the twelve signs of the zodiac, on a quest to discover the Holy Grail. He created Camelot.

The Arcturians, guardians of the great She-Bear, taught me to experience, and embody, unity. We are all One. At each earthly incarnation, we separate into different fragments of our over-soul in order to experience and learn. After discordant shadows are identified and transmuted, we return to unity with Source. The Arcturians also taught me a new astrology system. My task is to share and teach it.

Polaris, the obelisk, symbolising not only Earth's North/South pole but also our human magnetic/electric poles, when filled with divine love and light overcomes duality.

Pegasus was my travelling guide and wings, until I reclaimed my own. Without his love and guidance, this book could not have been written.

Aquila, the Eagle showed me how humans need a loving, all-seeing leader of light to unite them as one 'herd'.

Orion: Al Nilam – the central star of Orion's belt. Our consciousness raising process accelerates when we pass through the central star in the belt of Orion to experience the all-seeing eye. We then have the eyes to see, and experience, the infinite dimensions beyond.

The great fish, *Pisces Australis*, symbolises the power of the 'cosmic waters', the Mother Goddess. Jonah, swallowed by the whale and released because of his decision to focus on spiritual guidance, rebirthed into a light body through spiritual conversion in the cosmic ocean of the Goddess. The big fish is the great goddess in disguise, situated between Capricorn and Pisces is the area of space referred to by the ancients as the 'cosmic waters'. In the Glastonbury zodiac Pisces is represented by a whale situated between two fish.

A great dog sits outside the Glastonbury zodiacal circle. Is this Anubis, who also guards Sedna?

The Egyptian zodiac shows four pairs of spirits, at each of the cardinal points of Aries, Cancer, Libra and Capricorn, and four women holding up the heavenly circle at the fixed cross points of Taurus, Leo, Scorpio and Aquarius. Inside the wheel are thirty-six images of neters (aspects of the gods), a conglomeration of single humans wandering aimlessly around the zodiac, unaware of their potential that comes from taking the internal adventure into higher consciousness. A couple walk together. All walk in an anti-clockwise direction. There are three spheres seemingly randomly placed inside the inner circle (the three stars of Sirius?) and, close to the centre, the signs of the zodiac. Was this zodiac created to depict human evolution through cycles of time?

Pallas Athena, the goddess who turned Arachne into a spider, tearing up her perfectly woven tapestry depicting the gods' misdeeds and the truth of human evolution, told me she was now ready to receive love. She'd fought too many battles and was tired of them. I asked if she was willing to forgive herself for her jealousy and dark deeds towards Arachne. She said she was. I took her through a forgiveness process and felt an enormous weight lift from her. Apologising to Arachne, she removed the mantle of a black, wizened, bent-over old woman and replaced it with a cloth of bright red. Acknowledging Arachne as the master weaver, she asked her to wear the new mantle with pride, and to accept a leadership role. Pallas Athena told us she was now ready to write a new script.

Part of our human evolutionary ascension process is to re-member the parts of ourselves that were cut off and separated in times past. This soul retrieval process enables us to re-claim our true identity. We were each designed as a unified being of light connected to Divine Intelligence through universal love. The human heart holds the pearls of wisdom and is the key to an illumined, fully conscious mind.

***

Ten - a Perfect Number

And it came to pass that, in the fullness of time, a system emerged relative to the raising of human consciousness through a vibrational sequence. When sufficient training and trust was developed the human brain would be receptive to alternating currents. The downloading of data could take place. The data, from discarnate sources, provided stepping stones that awakened yet another closed door in the human psyche. This process requires a calm and blank mind, much like a still lake. Early mornings are often best because of reduced static. Utilizing specific cosmic currents can enhance clarity of transmission.

The model I was shown consists of ten stars, symbolically demonstrated as red hearts. Sirius, the central star, depicted as a vibrant and pulsating heart, had nine 'satellite' hearts orbiting around it. This model connects to mystical Judaism and the Kabbalah, the Tree of Life, which contains instructions for conscious self-exploration. The tree of life is also encoded with the Flower of Life.

We humans have been granted the free will to choose, at every moment of every day, our personal pathway. The choice is between the dark and the light. Eventually, all souls will choose the light. Our current astrology system was given thousands of years ago for a specific purpose. To aid human consciousness evolution. This system was a deliberate cover-up of a more ancient system. Because we fell from grace following the Atlantis disaster, we needed a guiding system to reclaim our former light. In this Age of Aquarius, we have the opportunity to reclaim this light, the light of galactic or Christ consciousness. Some are already doing so. It's the final stage of the human evolutionary experiment. The players in an ancient cosmic system enabling and accelerating this process has been revealed.

Number ten perfects all numbers, and within it is the nature of all that exists. Its essence is a return to unity. In ten exists the perfect triangle, referred to by Pythagoreans as the Sacred Tetractys. Ten symbolises a state of perfection whereby the human becomes God/Goddess. This is the next stage of human consciousness evolution. Those who have done the deep inner work of transmuting their shadows into light now operate at 5D frequencies. Brighter light beckons in the form of Christ consciousness. This consciousness developmental process leads to a reunion with our galactic family.

Ten stars are involved in the system, each with their own light codes. Sirius, the Great Central Sun, holds the frequencies of Christ Consciousness and sacred geometry. It transmits these frequencies to the other nine, and these in turn transmit to our zodiac. This system, plus the vibrational forces of the Seven Rays, are the cosmic tools we humans have available to accelerate our ascension into super, multi-dimensional or Christ Consciousness.

***

The Journey Ends

21 August, 2017: 4.00am. Meditation to Sirius: Omega, spokesperson for the Sirian Council of Nine, greeted me warmly as did the other seven members. Each of them symbolically represents an aspect in me. Finally, I realised that the one light being I couldn't understand, who I referred to in my *Experiment* book as 'cow's head, tap dancing shoes' was a symbolic representation of my Hathor heritage. The Hathors came from Venus and I began my earthly incarnations into this solar system through Venus. What a ride it's been. On Venus, I fell from grace. Heavily. Karma ensued, for seemingly endless lifetimes. It's over.

All nine players connected as one on Sirius, now the central star for our arm of the Milky Way galaxy. From there, I travelled to Arcturus. Again, I viewed the boardroom. The white cloth had been taken away. What was under it? Nothing. The mystery had been solved.

Orion was the next part of my journey. Through the symbolic 'eye of the needle', the central star in Orion's belt, I travelled to join the Orion Council, which works under the auspices of the Galactic Federation of Light. From my position at the top of the horseshoe formation, with two Orion Lords each side, I quickly observed the other council members. Joy and elation arose in my heart. Since my previous visit each council member had developed a bright light in their third eye. None of them now favoured the dark over the light. The galactic wars involving Orion would now cease.

Following a joyful unification process with the Council Lords, I viewed a large ghostly image emerging above the centre of the Orion group. Osiris, in his majesty and magnificence, showed himself as a huge, maybe forty feet tall giant, as big as the Egyptians statues depict him to be. Then a giant Isis emerged to stand beside him. She showed me the phallus symbolically attached to her sacral chakra. I understood that Osiris had re-developed his feminine side, Isis her masculine and both were demonstrating the power and majesty of the androgynous divine feminine and masculine in harmony with each other. Symbolically, the upper and lower parts of Egypt united as one.

As Above so it is Below. That which has been will return again. As in Heaven, so on earth. A Golden Age of Peace, a Camelot, is to reign once again in the heavens and begin to manifest on our precious planet Earth. Each of us has a part to play in creating it.

In the high Rila Mountains of Bulgaria the 21st and 22nd August are the main days that celebrate the sacred circle dance Paneurythmy. Each year thousands of people from around the globe travel there to celebrate and dance in many concentric circles. Paneurythmy means the dance of the angels. Its purpose is to bring peace and unity to the hearts and minds of those dancing. In 1996, I travelled to Bulgaria to learn this dance and was asked to share it globally at specific sacred sites. Danced with a love-filled unified group, the energy generated opened formerly closed sacred portals to higher dimensions.

After Mary Magdalen made herself known to me while studying evolutionary astrology, D.K. asked me to write a book with him. I agreed, with a reservation. Saying I could not do it the left-brain intellectual way, we made a deal. This is the book. The dance, the journey, and my starry experiences culminated in the resurrection of an ancient evolutionary astrology system.

The great cosmic changes influencing our small planet in the far reaches of our galaxy are occurring for a purpose – to awaken those still sleeping. A new Age has birthed. Managing the finer and lighter frequencies of this Aquarius Age requires self-awareness, and the development of higher consciousness. A solution to every problem is always available and Gaia will never cease to support us to live in peace.

***

The Southern Cross Constellation

7ᵗ October 2017: Snuggled in my bed at my son's home in Washington State on the eve of my departure to travel to Sedona to complete this book, a familiar character in my life's theatre knocked on the door of my mind. Chiron was urging me to travel on yet another adventure. Eagerly jumping on his back, he took me to a high mountain and asked me look around. Nothing. I turned 180 degrees. Nothing. Turning again to 240 degrees I observed a faint glimmering light way into the distance. We travelled to it through unfamiliar territory. The light had a soft glow. As we entered its field we were strongly sucked in by its magnetism. Landing in a seemingly luminous area I noticed groups of semi-etheric children happily playing. Their form was almost indistinguishable from their light and they appeared to glow from within. A little like I imagine fairies to be. Each group were singing and dancing while playing with three balls. The four groups of happy children formed a cross. Focusing on one group and one set of balls and puzzling over the symbolism, I noticed the group behind me had introduced two more balls. The other groups followed. As the five balls in each group were thrown high I realised they symbolised the five stars of the Southern Cross. The Children of Light were playing a cosmic game.

The Southern Cross constellation of stars was important to the ancient astronomers of the Andes, Maya and the First Australians. Ancient Andean wisdom has the Southern Cross as their most revered night light. A stone image of it was found at Machu Picchu. The Inca knew it as the Chakana, which means 'the stair'. The stairway to heaven and higher consciousness?

Why was I shown this as I was about to adventure once again to Sedona? Let's view this experience symbolically. A five-pointed star is a pentagram, formed when the mid-points of each side of a pentagon are joined together. It's a profound spiritual symbol representing a cosmic human, and the evolution of the human soul towards perfection. This sacred geometric shape is also associated with the divine feminine. A ten - pointed star is created by two intertwined pentagrams. This is the image revealed to me as I was completing this book and is depicted on the cover.

9 October 2017. Relaxing on the plane to Phoenix, Arizona, aware of the colour violet permeating my field, I invoke Chiron once again. As my teacher, space vehicle and healing guide for many decades, he quickly entered my expanded state and invited me to again jump on his back. Launching vertically into fathomless space for some time, he then formed a large circle. Above and below me were similar circles. I realised we were travelling a spiral. As we continued to travel up, I observed the spirals appearing to reduce in size until they formed a single point of light. We were catapulted into this light point, and propelled through it into an open, intensely bright white light channel. Flowing along this channel, I became aware it was infinite, seemingly without end. Chiron suggested we turn around to face the direction we had come. Doing so, and propelled by the former direction's light, as if a great force was pushing, we rushed through the light channel and, as we approached the exit, the bright light exploded into a multitude of colour rays, the colours of a rainbow. From that light burst we traversed the downward spiral to my 3D home. Chiron suggested I record the experience as soon as I came out of it.

As I did, I intuited the experience had shown me the birth-place of the Seven Rays of light that permeate creation. Some say this birth place was in the constellation of Lyra. These Seven Rays are received by Arcturus and then distributed to Sirius and the Pleiades, forming a triangle of force. Just like we download information onto our computers via the internet these coloured light beams, containing consciousness and information, are transmitted to the sacred planets in our solar system and the zodiac, via a series of starry triangles. We are the final recipients of the downloading programme. We have free-will choice to use the programme however we want.

10ᵗ October 2017. When I woke in my Sedona hotel room I looked out the window and saw a view of amazing beauty. A giant red rock mountain glowed with the bright light of the early morning sun. The magnificence and majesty of the view took my breath away. The vision of an earlier time flashed into my mind, of when I was shown an image of bright light bursting through the centre of a red rock mountain.

The ancient records, once stored under a red rock mountain in the Australian desert, have been shared at the Sedona red rock mountains.

And it came to pass that as greater light spread over planet Earth the beings upon her awakened from their deep slumber to see their world in a new light. The stars seemed to shine more brightly, the birds rejoiced and the earth herself shook off the shadows. A sigh of relief echoed throughout the galaxy as the tipping point of light overcame the dark. It was a time of rejoicing. The new Age began and 2017 will go down in history as the year the light presided.

It is not a time for global peace workers to relax their efforts. More is to be done. Unity requires constant maintenance. Where love is the dominating force unity will thrive.

A new Camelot is birthing. King Arthur is awakening and remembering the role he once played as guardian of the Great Bear. The Holy Grail has been found. The twelve knights of the zodiacal round table need no longer fight. Excalibur is held in safe keeping by the Lady of the Lake, and peace is her agenda.

The great red rock mountains of the southern and northern hemispheres, now joined by a sky bridge of light, share their stories. The stars foretell of continuing change. As more people awaken to truth of themselves and their creations, a wave of shame will engulf Gaia's etheric field. From that point, restoration quickly follows. The old ways no longer serve. Many adjustments need to be made.

Celestial and starry light beings took me on journeys to experience space, other dimensional realities and the birth place of the Seven Rays. They introduced me to the cosmic players involved in a new astrology system that underpins the further advancement of human consciousness evolution. The Arcturians symbolically demonstrated this system. It has been quite a journey! And, the journeys answered my persistent question – 'What cosmic system is available that continues to promote human consciousness evolution after we have worked through our Solar System's planetary challenges depicted in our birth charts?'

I now have another question. 'How can I make sense of this system and work with it so I can share it?' It seems there's another adventure story to write.

14th February 2018: *And it came to pass that a new breed of humans awakened from their deep sleep filled with the oneness of all life. These Rainbow Warriors had a task. To improve the lives of those still sleeping. There are many ways this can be done, one of which is to do whatever they can to raise their consciousness. Many of those still sleeping have been programmed to awaken. Others not so. Discernment is needed by those awakened. Eventually all lights will come on. Those awakened ones arousing those still sleeping will learn patience as well as discernment. Both are pathways to compassion. By the turn of next century most lights will be on and the planet filled with Rainbow Warriors. The prophesised Golden Age of Peace will be experienced.*

As an astrologer and messenger for the Age of Aquarius I offer my findings for your ingestion and digestion. I hope you find sustenance and nourishment from them. I have given you the essence, the amrit. May you allow *The Magdalen Codes* within guide your journey home to the Light.

Ashtara
April 2018

www.ingramcontent.com/pod-product-compliance
Lightning Source LLC
Chambersburg PA
CBHW020640300426
44112CB00007B/180